My Hilarious, Heroic, Human Dog

Chicken Soup for the Soul: My Hilarious, Heroic, Human Dog
101 Tales of Canine Companionship
Amy Newmark

Published by Chicken Soup for the Soul, LLC www.chickensoup.com

The publisher gratefully acknowledges the many publishers and individuals who granted Chicken Soup for the Soul permission to reprint the cited material.

Front cover and interior dog photos: dog jumping courtesy of istockphoto.com/K_Thalhofer (©K_Thalhofer), Weimaraner courtesy of istockphoto.com/vauvau (©vauvau), Chihuahua courtesy of istockphoto.com/Paffy69 (©Paffy69), Boxer courtesy of istockphoto.com/adogslifephoto (©adogslifephoto)
Back cover and interior photos: Pug puppies courtesy of istockphoto.com/Mordolff (©Mordolff), Greyhound courtesy of istockphoto.com/malexeum (©Mordolff), Dachshund courtesy of istockphoto.com/WilleeCole (©WilleeCole)

Photo of Amy Newmark courtesy of Susan Morrow at SwickPix

Cover and Interior by Daniel Zaccari

Distributed to the booktrade by Simon & Schuster. SAN: 200-2442

Publisher's Cataloging-In-Publication Data
(Prepared by The Donohue Group, Inc.)

Names: Newmark, Amy, compiler.
Title: Chicken soup for the soul : my hilarious, heroic, human dog : 101 tales of canine companionship / [compiled by] Amy Newmark.
Other Titles: My hilarious, heroic, human dog : 101 tales of canine companionship
Description: [Cos Cob, Connecticut] : Chicken Soup for the Soul, LLC, [2021]
Identifiers: ISBN 9781611590784 (paperback) | ISBN 9781611593181 (ebook)
Subjects: LCSH: Dogs--Literary collections. | Dogs--Anecdotes. | Human-animal relationships--Literary collections. | Human-animal relationships--Anecdotes. | Dog owners--Literary collections. | Dog owners--Anecdotes. | LCGFT: Anecdotes.
Classification: LCC SF426.2 .C456 2021 (print) | LCC SF426.2 (ebook) | DDC 636.7/088/7/02--dc23

Library of Congress Control Number: 2021937447

PRINTED IN THE UNITED STATES OF AMERICA
on acid∞free paper

25 24 23 22 21 01 02 03 04 05 06 07 08 09 10

My Hilarious, Heroic, Human Dog

101 Tales of Canine Companionship

Amy Newmark

Chicken Soup for the Soul, LLC
Cos Cob, CT

Changing the world one story at a time®

www.chickensoup.com

Table of Contents

❶

~Clever Canines~

❷

~Learning to Love the Dog~

3

~Our Protectors~

4

~Life Lessons from the Dog~

5

~My Very Good, Very Bad Dog~

6

~On the Road~

7

~Changed by the Dog~

8

~Four-Legged Friends~

9

~And Dog Makes Family~

10

~Grieving & Recovery~

Clever Canines

Pasta Penitence

Spaghetti can be eaten most successfully
if you inhale it like a vacuum cleaner.
~Sophia Loren

I arrived home to the loving, spastic antics of our beloved two-year-old Bloodhound. He ran around, brought me one of his plush toys, and leaned up against me to enjoy some ear rubs.

"Did you have a good day at Grandma and Grandpa's house today, Hunter?" I asked, as he grumbled lovingly and leaned his head into my hand as I continued scratching behind his ears.

"Hi, baby!" my husband called as he entered the living room. "Your mom said he played well with Lily all day, but he did get into a little bit of mischief just before I picked him up." He looked affectionately yet sternly at our oversized baby of a dog.

Lily was my parents' Rhodesian Ridgeback who happened to be the same age as Hunter. We were lucky my parents were retired and watched Hunter during the day while we were at work so the two pups could play and burn off their endless energy.

"Uh-oh, buddy. What did you do at Grandma's house today?" Hunter looked up at me with his sorrowful eyes, his wagging tail slowing down a little as he sat down in front of me.

"Your mom made spaghetti for dinner. While they were eating, Hunter ate the extra noodles out of the colander in the sink," my husband explained.

"Hunter, is this true? Did you eat Grandma's pasta?" He lowered his head, avoiding eye contact with me. "Bubba, you know you aren't supposed to do that." Poor Hunter slinked over to his living-room bed, lay down, and put one of his paws over his eyes, indicating he knew he had made a mistake.

"Aw, I think he really understands what we are talking about," my husband chuckled, as he went and sat over by Hunter and consoled the poor puppy. "It's okay, buddy. We all make mistakes. You just have to maintain some control and try not to do this again," he explained as he cuddled with our pup. Hunter rolled over and showed my husband his belly to be rubbed. We both laughed.

That weekend, a few days after the spaghetti incident, we planned to head over to my parents' house for a barbecue. I was gathering up the cheesy potatoes and fruit we had cut up to bring over as our contribution; my husband was playing with Hunter and getting him ready for the car ride.

"Are you ready to go to Grandma and Grandpa's house, Hunter? You'll get to play with Lily!" he told him, as he grabbed his leash. Hunter came bounding over to my husband, settled his bottom on the floor, but got up again immediately and bolted into the kitchen as if he had forgotten something.

"What do you need, buddy? Don't you want to go play?" my husband inquired, as he walked after Hunter to see where he had run off to. With potatoes and fruit piled in my arms, I followed as well, and we both watched as our beloved Bloodhound trotted over to the counter by our sink where we had some dry ingredients from the weekly meal kits that had been delivered to our house. One of the meals for the week included pasta — spaghetti, to be exact. Hunter poked his head onto the counter, retrieved the spaghetti, and trotted back to the front door, ready to leave for the barbecue. My husband and I giggled in disbelief as we followed our intelligent dog back to the front door.

"Are you returning Grandma's spaghetti, Hunter?" I asked him. He lifted one of his front paws, placed it on my arm and looked up at me with his loving eyes as if to tell me, "I am going to make this right, Mom." I could not believe what I had just witnessed, and I patted him on the head as I set my food platters on the couch for a moment.

Hunter held that package of spaghetti in his jowls the entire drive over to my parents' house. When he got out of the car, he was on a mission to get to the front door. When my mom opened the door, he dropped the package of spaghetti at her feet, looked up at her with his tongue hanging out, and put one of his front paws on her as if asking for forgiveness.

We laughed about the spaghetti the entire evening, but my mother couldn't help but hug the well-intentioned puppy and show him forgiveness for his mistake. Hunter reminded us all that day that while no one is perfect, it is always best to ask for forgiveness and try to make things right with those you love. It has become a running joke in our family: After any argument, we present a package of spaghetti to the other person. It always lightens the mood and makes us laugh as we remember one of the many adventures we have shared with Hunter the hound.

— Gwen Cooper —

The Dog That Wouldn't Bark

Dogs travel hundreds of miles during their lifetime responding to such commands as "come" and "fetch."
~Stephen Baker

One summer day, I went out my back door and found a medium-sized dog sitting in the grass. The dog stood up and wagged his tail when he spotted me. I petted his short brown-and-white coat and checked him for a collar or an ID tag. He had neither.

"Where did you come from?" I asked. I lived in a small, rural town in upstate New York. I knew all the dogs in the neighborhood, but I'd never seen this fellow before.

Halfheartedly, I told him to sit. To my surprise, he sat obediently. "Stay," I said, as I made my way into the garage where we kept the dry dog food for our Beagles. I really didn't expect the dog to stay because he seemed anxious to be with me.

When I returned, he was sitting in the exact spot where I had left him. "Wow! You sure are trained," I told him. I set out a bowl of water and a hearty helping of food, and the dog started eating.

I left him in the yard and went inside to read through the newspaper's "Lost and Found" column. Unfortunately, nobody had reported a missing brown-and-white dog.

An hour later, my brother came home and asked why there was a strange dog in the yard. "I don't know where he came from," I said. "But he belongs to someone. Maybe he's just lost and will find his way home."

Later that afternoon, my brother and I went outside and found the dog lounging by the back door. When he saw us, he jumped to his feet and started wagging his tail. My brother tossed a stick across the yard, and the dog raced after it.

"He looks like he wants some exercise. Why don't you play with him while I go to the store?" I suggested.

After I got back from the store, my brother called me out into the yard.

"Watch this," he said. "The dog knows tricks."

Sure enough, the dog would fetch, sit, stay, roll over, and lie down on command. He also loved jumping to catch a tennis ball in midair. I was impressed — and a little suspicious. This was no ordinary dog. Someone had trained him extremely well. So, I had to wonder: Why weren't his owners looking for him?

When my parents came home, we showed them the dog and all his tricks. The "mystery dog" obeyed every command. My parents were stunned by his skills as much as we were. None of us had ever seen a dog so well-trained before. The dog got along well with our Beagles, and we gave him a comfy place to sleep in the garage.

The next day, I checked the "Lost and Found" column again, to no avail. I called the newspaper and ran a "Found" ad describing our new friend. If his owner didn't claim him after a month, he'd become a member of the family.

A little while later, I went outside and watched my brother playing with the dog. Suddenly, it dawned on me that the dog was quiet — too quiet.

"You know what?" I said to my brother. "Despite all the tricks he knows, this dog has never barked."

"What do you mean?" he asked. "He must have barked. All dogs do."

"Not this one. He doesn't bark. Tell him to speak," I said.

My brother told the dog to "speak." The dog just looked up at him and remained silent. My brother made a few barking noises at the dog, hoping that would make him understand what we wanted. The dog never uttered so much as a "woof."

"Maybe he can't bark," I mused. This super-dog was becoming more of a mystery each day. He could walk on his hind legs, balance a ball on the end of his nose, and give a paw for a "handshake," but he couldn't bark. I had never known a dog like him before.

Three days later, we got a call from a woman who had seen our "Found" ad in the newspaper. She said the dog sounded like hers and gave us a perfect description of his markings. I asked her if the dog knew any tricks. She laughed and said that he loved to catch tennis balls. I gave her directions to our house, and she said she'd be there within the hour to get the dog.

I told my brother that the dog's owner was coming to get him, and we played with the dog for a while. Neither of us wanted to admit that we had secretly hoped we'd be able to keep him.

When the woman's pickup truck pulled into the driveway, the dog raced to greet her. He wagged his tail and licked her face—but he never barked.

The woman explained that she and her family had gone away on vacation for a few days, and the dog, Peanut, had gotten out when a neighbor came over to feed him. I told her that we had never seen such a well-trained dog or one who knew so many tricks.

She chuckled and said that Peanut used to be a clown dog. He'd worked in a circus for years, and she adopted him when he retired from circus performing. The clowns had trained Peanut to do a vast assortment of tricks as part of their act.

"But why can't he bark?" I asked.

"Oh, he can, but he was trained not to," she explained. "Clown dogs have to be silent. The clowns don't want their dogs barking and scaring children at the circus."

The woman was extremely relieved to get Peanut back because her children were heartbroken without him. Finally reunited with his owner, the ecstatic Peanut jumped into the truck and wagged his tail at us as he headed for home.

I had never encountered a clown dog before, but I'm sure Peanut could have told us interesting stories about his years in the circus—if he could talk.

—Kelli A. Wilkins—

Rascal's Vanishing Act

The dog lives for the day, the hour, even the moment.
~Robert Falcon Scott

Rascal jogged beside me, the clasp on the leash jangling and wiggling like a loose tooth. His momma was a scruffy white Bichon. His pops must have been a Terrier. Rascal had the energy of both breeds put together.

Rascal was named for his temperament, and although I loved his zest for life, he drove me batty at times. He wanted to do things his way, which meant altering my way. I had to pause in the middle of my jog so he could investigate the trail of a squirrel or consider six different places before settling on one to do his business.

That spring afternoon, Rascal pitter-pattered along, finding new ways to delay me as I tried to get my daily exercise. He pulled ahead, lagged behind, and stopped to sniff at every scent of another dog.

Rabbits were everywhere on the trails that wound through our suburban Seattle neighborhood. A brown flash of movement caught my eye as a baby bunny darted off the trail and scooted under the brush. Rascal jerked at the leash, and in an instant, snapped free of the broken collar clasp and sped after the rabbit.

"Rascal!" I scolded. "Where are you? Come on." I jogged ahead and called again. My mind was on other things: what to make for dinner, which lesson plans to teach, and what time the twins would arrive home from school. A couple minutes passed before I realized Rascal hadn't caught up. Now I was going to have to stop running and backtrack to wait for my little scoundrel.

"Come on, Rascal. Here, boy." *Typical Rascal behavior,* I thought.

But a few more minutes passed with no sign of his furry face, and I grew concerned. I called for him with my alpha voice. That didn't work. I offered treats in a high-pitched, happy voice. That didn't work either. After ten minutes of fruitless calling, I began to panic.

I ran along the trail, crossing the road and worrying that Rascal might have done the same. As cute as he was, Rascal was not the brightest bulb in the chandelier. He'd been known to chase a frog into a swamp and whine when he found himself stuck in the mud. What if he tried crossing a street and got hit by a car? We were already about two miles from home in unfamiliar territory. By now, he'd probably covered another mile... but in which direction? As I called for him, my hopes began to dwindle. I decided I needed help.

Many folks were strolling or jogging the trails that sunny spring afternoon. I stopped each person I passed. "Did you see a little white dog?" In turn, each one gave me a sad shake of the head. I gave out my cell number and asked them to text or call if they spotted him. I worried that Rascal was getting farther and farther away.

I dialed my husband Steve's cell number. I hoped he could bring the car and help me look. The phone rang and rang. Then I remembered that he planned to mow the lawn. He would never hear the phone over the racket of the mower.

A half-hour passed. Nobody had seen Rascal. Then forty-five minutes went by. I was near tears. I ran farther along the five-mile loop. I crossed streets, my legs straining, my lungs aching, calling Rascal's name and stopping to question each passerby. An older gentleman meandered in my direction. Red-faced and out of breath, I asked, "Have you seen a little white dog?"

"Oh, sure," he said. "Back by the farm stand. Had to be about twenty minutes ago."

"Thanks!" I called over my shoulder. I was off like a shot. The farm stand stood at the corner of a four-way stop — the intersection of heavily trafficked streets. It would take at least ten minutes to race there — if I pushed myself. I went for it at top speed and soon spotted the barn-red roof in the distance.

At the intersection, I looked around frantically, but my hopes crumbled. No Rascal. I waved down motorists, motioning for the drivers to roll down their windows. A few refused — I must have looked like a crazy, beet-red lady as I asked folks if they'd seen him. Those who did stop replied, "No. Sorry. Good luck."

By now, an hour had passed. I decided to try a new tactic: run home, get the car, and solicit my husband's help. My legs pumped up the steep hill homeward, not my usual trudge up that final half-mile. From the edge of the cul-de-sac, I heard the hum of the lawnmower in our back yard and sensed the imminent arrival of our twins on the school bus. I imagined breaking the news and the hearts of my children. I took the corner at a clip and rushed down the sidewalk toward our house.

Then I noticed movement on our driveway.

Rascal sat on the edge of the drive, his white fur dirtied, matted and peppered with burrs. He was wagging his tail feverishly and he looked scared, relieved and apologetic all at once. I shouted with relief, lay flat on the driveway and pulled him on top of me for a hug. He danced on my chest and licked the sweat off my face.

After our happy reunion, I grabbed my cell phone and took a snapshot of my naughty, clever boy. I texted, "Found his way home!" to the many kind neighbors who'd pledged to keep a lookout. Their replies came back to me all afternoon. "So glad to hear it." "Good news." "Happy he made it."

Rascal had found his own way home! He'd traveled two-and-a-half miles, crossed five streets, and navigated his way back all by himself. Rascal was pretty smart after all.

— Ilana Long —

Every Time a Bell Rings

Dogs got personality. Personality goes a long way.
~*Quentin Tarantino*

Nothing brings a home to life like a new puppy. The companionship. The laughter. The snuggles. And the incessant ringing of bells.

When we adopted Parker, she was eight weeks old and smaller than the cat. Today, she's a sixty-pound, life-sized cartoon—a big, floppy mass of fun who has an abundance of love to share. Her loyal companionship and silly personality bring more happiness into my world than I ever thought possible. But, like any kid, she tests my patience daily.

A few days after bringing her home, I came across a YouTube video of a dog ringing a bell to go outside. I was game for anything that would assist in housebreaking our new family member. So, I visited a pet-supply website and ordered a small silver bell. When it arrived, I hung it next to the back door at puppy level.

Following the video's instruction, I took Parker to the back door, lifted her paw, and touched her toes to the bell. "Jingle. Jingle." Then I led her outside. If she did her business, I gave her a treat. This process was repeated every hour throughout the afternoon. By nightfall, on the following day, she was ringing the bell on her own. *Wow!* I thought. *My dog is a genius!*

The next morning, after a bell-ring, I walked to the back door to let Parker outside. There was a puddle on the floor. "Oops," I told her. "You're supposed to do that outside." She caught on quickly, and within a couple of weeks, accidents were rare. But it didn't take long for my dog-genius to learn that ringing the bell brought me running. It became unclear who was training whom.

The bell is no longer a simple signal, telling me she needs to go potty. It is a form of communication, alerting and informing me of a variety of Parker concerns. I work from a home office and try to be mindful about distractions. I turn off my phone, mute notifications on my computer and don't look at e-mail before noon. But the chorus of rings, dings and jingles that beckons me from down the hall creates more distraction than any smartphone could.

On most days, she has rung the bell and been outside at least five times by 7 a.m. — twice to go to the bathroom, once to dig a hole in the snowbank, once to stand at the gate and bark at a bird, and then to play with a frozen poop she carried onto the back porch.

I try to start work by 7:30 each morning, but at that hour, Parker's antics have just begun. Approximately nine minutes into a project, I'm beckoned by the bell. I traipse down the hall, let her out, and then go back to my desk. Before my hands have touched the keyboard, I hear her barking at the door.

Because it's only four degrees outside, I make my way back down the hall to let her in. She races past me and across the living room, and then onto the couch, leaving a trail of muddy black paw prints. In the short three minutes she was outside, she found time to dig in a flowerpot and wet her feet in the snow before barking to come in. I carry Parker to the bathtub and spend fifteen minutes bathing her, and then another ten minutes wiping down the muddy tub. An additional half-hour is invested in spot-cleaning black paw prints from the carpet and furniture, and then sweeping the porch and removing the half-empty planter.

When I return to my desk at nine o'clock, I stare at the screen and try to get back into the zone. Just as words begin to dance across the page, I hear, "Ringy, dingy, ding." I stop typing and holler down the hall, "Give me a break, dog. You were just out. Go lie down."

"Ding, ding, ding. Woof!"

Obviously, she means business this time, I tell myself. When I open the door, she barrels off the porch and squats. "Good, Parker," I praise her for making a piddle outside, but what I want to say is, "Why couldn't you have done that the first time, you plant-digging, muddy-pawed, pain in the neck?"

When I turn to walk back down the hall, I hear a soft "jingle" from behind me. When I turn around, she is standing there with her tongue hanging out, smiling. In dog talk, she is saying, "Ha-ha. Just kidding."

The bell-ringing escapades have been going on for two years now, and I've become bilingual.

A loud, single ring followed by a groan means, "I really have to pee."

Two jingles and a bark: "There's a deer in the yard."

One ring: "Someone pulled into the driveway."

Three jingles and the sound of a bowl being flipped over: "Isn't it dinnertime?"

One jingle, a pause, and two more jingles: "The cat is playing with my tennis ball. Make him stop."

A series of soft ting-a-lings and a sigh: "I'm bored."

It's important not to get the signals confused. Without fail, she'll ring the bell just as I'm stepping out of the shower. Getting "I really have to pee" confused with "There's someone at the door" can be quite embarrassing.

Although the trips I make up and down the hall every day are a distraction, there is a bright side. Every time a bell rings, this pet parent gets her steps in. According to my Fitbit, I walk about four miles per day—sometimes, without ever leaving the house.

—Ann Morrow—

Baby on Board

Dogs do speak, but only to those who know how to listen.
~Orhan Pamuk

"What in the world, Bailey!" Eight months pregnant with our first child, I was standing outside our new home meeting our new neighbors when our five-year-old Cattle Dog/American Eskimo mix relieved himself on my leg.

Our first attempt at caring for a living, breathing creature had been successful until this point, not counting the time Bailey used our baseboards for teething. It had been five years without one potty-training accident. But now, only a few days after moving into our new home in the Ravenswood Manor neighborhood of Chicago, Bailey was treating me like a fire hydrant.

I removed my shoes and socks — no small feat at thirty-five weeks' pregnant — and headed inside to clean up. We went about our day, opening boxes, unpacking, and making plans for setting up the nursery. We decided to stay up late in our new back yard, taking advantage of our last few weeks of alone time, talking about everything and anything.

Around midnight, we headed up to our new bedroom, stepping around boxes along the way. After a couple of hours of sleep, I woke with the need to use the restroom. Just as I was about to head back for a few more hours of restless sleep, my water broke. I stood stunned, alone in the bathroom that we'd owned for only seventy-two hours.

I'm too early, I told myself. The doctor had said I was "locked up tight." *I'm not ready, the house isn't ready, and we don't even have a car seat yet to bring our son home.*

After convincing my husband that I did not wet myself, we headed to the hospital in the middle of the night. Lake Shore Drive never looked more deserted. It was a city of close to three million people, and no one was on the road. Fourteen hours later, we were the proud parents of a healthy but tiny baby boy.

Bailey adjusted well to the chaos of a household with a small child. The only toy he ever chewed on was a wooden name puzzle.

Eventually, I was expecting again. We were taking a walk on a beautiful spring day in Chicago, perfect for a long walk with Bailey and our son in his stroller. I was thirty-seven-weeks along and the doctor saw no reason why I would deliver early again.

But then, Bailey peed on my foot, something he hadn't done since that last day of my first pregnancy. We went home and I got in the shower, and then it dawned on me: *Could I possibly go into labor tonight?* There are dogs that predict seizures. Why not labor? I called my neighbor to arrange a plan for the care of my older child and made sure my hospital bag was packed.

As I lay resting on the couch that evening, my water broke. This time, I was ready, thanks to Bailey.

Bailey is still with us, now sixteen. He has slowed down and sleeps more. He is grayer around his muzzle and has lost his hearing. He has endured the noise and love of two little boys, now eleven and eight. And he has never again peed on me or anyone else.

—Jill Ann Robinson—

Caspar

When I look into the eyes of an animal, I do not see an animal.
I see a living being. I see a friend. I feel a soul.
~A.D. Williams

What do you give a person who has everything? I'd never been to Susan's house before, but I knew that she didn't need anything. I went over a mental checklist of my new friend's tastes. She had horses. She loved art. Her home was surrounded with flowers, and she wore stylish but understated clothes. She had two Corgis....

Ah-ha!

I'd get a dog toy for each of her Corgis! She spoke of them often, so I was sure that would be more appreciated than anything I could get for her. I stopped at a pet shop the next day and found two items that were identical except that one was red and one was blue.

On the day of my visit, I was greeted by Susan and her two Corgi dogs, Caspar and Lily. "Oh, how nice!" Susan smiled as Caspar and Lily took their toys. Lily, a quiet girl, took hers to another room to enjoy. Caspar followed Susan and me to a sitting area with his blue toy in his mouth. I saw a large basket overflowing with stuffed dog toys, dog ropes and pulls of different kinds, and what looked like a few high-quality chewies. *I should have known she'd have more than enough,* I thought with an inward grimace. Well, I supposed, it was the thought that counted. I pushed my disappointment to the side and watched Caspar, who stayed by our sides, as he nibbled in an almost thoughtful way at his blue gift.

"Caspar has something about him," I observed. "He's very Zen, isn't he?"

Susan smiled. "He's special. I bring him with me when I counsel some of my clients. He makes everyone feel so much more comfortable."

It was months before I visited Susan again. Caspar and Lily were there to greet me as they had the first time. And, like the first time, we moved to the windowed sitting area that overlooked a pasture. Again, Lily gently licked me hello and went to a quiet location, while Caspar looked up at me for a long time, taking me in with brown eyes that seemed knowing and perhaps wise. *He's an old soul*, I thought. After I spent some time patting Caspar while Susan and I caught up, that Zen dog rose and walked slowly to the basket. I didn't think much about it then, but I knew he was ever-so-slowly nosing through the items in it.

Susan and I talked about our work and a charitable project we had decided to take on together. My thoughts were interrupted when I felt a pressure on my leg. It was Caspar, and he was holding something in his mouth, pressing it lightly against me. When he had my full attention, he backed up and looked me full in the eyes with his own wise brown ones. He was showing me the stuffed blue toy.

"Oh, my. It's the toy I brought him the first time I came," I said.

"So it is!" Susan laughed. Caspar never looked away but held the toy toward me until I reached for it. He released it slowly, keeping his gaze fixed the entire time with what I can only describe as calm recognition. "He's letting you know he remembers who you are," Susan continued.

"Thank you, Caspar," I said. "I'm glad you remembered me."

I only saw Caspar a few more times before he passed on, way too young. But there was something about the way that old soul communicated with me that I will never forget.

— Tanya Sousa —

Unless

What's one thing we have in our lives
that we can depend on? A dog or cat
loving us unconditionally, every day.
~Jon Katz

I whipped my head around. "Jackie!" I shouted. "Jackie! Come!" I stared open-mouthed as my fourteen-year-old dog sprinted away down the forest trail in the direction of my car. Her leash flopped on the ground behind her, scattering leaves and twigs as she ran. I clapped my hands sharply—one of the few sounds my elderly Australian Shepherd could still hear. She skidded to a stop, looked over her shoulder, and barked once.

I motioned to the ground and softened my voice. "Jackie. Come." I crouched to meet her, and she nosed my knee and looked up guiltily. I cupped her face in my hands and stroked her copper eyebrows and silky black ears. I was mystified. This was the dog who rarely strayed more than a few feet away from me, who had been aptly nicknamed Shadow.

"What was that about, pup? Surely you're not scared of a banana slug?"

A far different creature had actually caused her to flee, but I didn't realize it at the time. The mottled yellow banana slug I had stopped to inspect, prompting me to drop her leash, was not what had alarmed her. Jackie had tried to warn me repeatedly with her slow gait, her manic sniffing of the air, and her intense gaze. But I had been committed to a vigorous hike before sundown and ignored all the warning signs.

Our hike had begun happily. At fourteen, Jackie was no longer able to run long distances, but a brisk walk in the hilly, forested area of Sea Ranch, on the Northern California coast, worked well. These walks pumped up our heart rates and transformed my gentle, old dog with her ailing hip into a pup again.

When I had parked at the trailhead, she bounded out of the car, her arthritis forgotten. She danced around me, eager to be off. A half-mile later, her behavior changed abruptly. She jerked to a sudden stop, tilted her nose up and spun in a circle. I glanced around but saw nothing awry and tugged gently on the leash. She braced her legs and stared at me imploringly.

I'd run this old logging road many times and knew the area was home to many creatures. But the resident bobcats, raccoons, and foxes keep to themselves. And while mountain lions are occasionally reported, it's rare to see one. As long as I stayed on the main trails, these solitary treks were uneventful. The deep quiet of the redwood forest was broken only by the soft thud of our footfalls and the occasional call of a Steller's Jay. It was sublimely peaceful.

But now, Jackie's forty-pound body was stiff with tension. She sniffed the air anxiously, her eyes large and round. My senses switched into high alert as I peered at the flora lining the trail and wondered what might be hidden behind it, watching us. But we were only a mile in, and I was determined to double that distance before turning around. I sized up the lengthening shadows and set off at a faster pace, intent on making up time. It can get dark quickly in the forest.

We hurried up and down the hilly trail until we arrived at my two-mile turnaround point, a broad clearing with clay soil. As we grew closer, I noticed a section of the ground that wasn't covered with forest debris. It was damp and shiny from the previous day's rain, making it a perfect spot to check for animal tracks, a favorite part of these excursions. And I could see, even from a distance, distinct imprints in the soil.

When I reached the area, I froze. I gaped at the oversized animal tracks pressed into the clay. I knew immediately they weren't made by raccoons, deer, or any other common forest creature. They didn't look feline, so at least they weren't from a mountain lion. But that didn't mean they weren't from a very large mammal.

I bent to examine the tracks, and my pulse thudded in my ears. The prints were huge, twice the size of my outstretched hand. The mud was still soft to the touch even though the area was in direct sunlight. These tracks were fresh.

Quickly, I took some photos with my phone. My fingers trembled as I sent a text to a naturalist friend.

"Dale, are these what I think they are?" The foot pad was about six inches across, with five distinct toes, two of which included visible imprints of long curved claws. Fortunately, my friend replied right away.

"They're definitely not feline. They're either from a really, really big dog or a bear. Probably a black bear."

I inhaled sharply and tapped my reply. "No dog I know has two-inch-long curved claws. And these prints are fresh."

His response was immediate. "Where are you? Are you alone?"

"I'm two miles up the old logging road. Near Timber Ridge." My eyes flitted around the clearing, and I blew out a breath to calm myself. "Just Jackie and me."

"Okay. Keep her on leash. You should be fine, as long as you don't corner the bear. He doesn't want to be seen." A pause. "Unless..."

"Unless what?"

"Unless he is a she and has cubs."

I stared at my phone. It was April. "Aren't black bear cubs born in the winter?" I tapped Send.

"In January. Just checked. You know what to do, right? Walk slowly, stay calm. You'll be fine. Black bears are usually pretty shy."

"Unless," I typed. "Thanks. Call you later." I clicked off.

I surveyed the clearing one last time. The wind had picked up, and the trees and underbrush were now in motion. In my hyperalert state, every shifting shadow in the scrub seemed to hide something. I walked backward and then forward, trying not to hurry and appear like a threat to a black bear's cubs.

My eyes swept my surroundings obsessively as I fought the urge to flee. I made my way carefully, moving as fast as I could without running. About a quarter-mile from my car, I paused for breath and stroked Jackie. She wriggled happily, the strain now gone from her eyes and body.

"How about a good run, pup? For old time's sake?" She nosed my hand.

That was all the permission I needed. My limbic system kicked in, and we took off. Jackie and I set a personal land speed record, leaping over fallen branches and dashing around muddy dips in the road until we arrived, panting but safe, at my car. I threw my arms against the hood and stretched until my breathing slowed. After Jackie noisily emptied her portable water bowl, I boosted her into the back seat.

When I slid the seat belt through a loop on her harness and snapped it shut, she gazed at me, unblinking. I had to wonder what she was thinking. *So, now you're worried about my safety?*

— Maureen Simons —

Uncle Homer's Dog

If there are no dogs in Heaven, then when I die
I want to go where they went.
~Will Rogers

Uncle Homer had a Collie named King, a very good dog who taught me how to walk when I was a baby. He would nudge me up, allow me to clutch his fur, and walk me around the house. Uncle Homer lived with my grandparents and we lived close by.

As my brothers and I grew, King became our guide, confidant, and even our partner in crime. We played with him for hours every day. I was the oldest child in my family, and I was excited to be starting at school until I realized how many hours I'd be away from King each day.

When summer came, Uncle Homer graduated from high school and announced he was joining the Marine Corps to fight in World War II. He gathered my little brothers and me and explained that he was going to California to learn to be a Marine. Would we take care of King for him until he came home?

Well, of course, we would. Poor King was very sad after Uncle Homer left but we kept him company. He played with us and showed us pretty places we'd never seen in the woods before. He even knew where blueberries grew. King didn't seem to like the berries much, but he knew we did.

A couple of weeks after Homer left, Grandma got a letter from him. He said that California was beautiful, and the Pacific Ocean was right there. Training was hard but that's what you had to do if you wanted to be a Marine. He wrote about King, too, and King thumped his tail up and down when she got to the part about him.

After Christmas, Uncle Homer wrote thanking everybody for the cookies, but he was really writing to say his unit was being deployed. He couldn't tell us where he was going.

Uncle Homer wrote just before school was out with some suggestions for things we could do with King that summer. He said he had seen some dogs recently and felt so bad for them. They looked hungry and alone wherever he was. King looked sad when he heard that. Uncle Homer went on to tell King to be a good boy and take care of us. He hoped maybe to get some furlough time before school started.

That was the last letter we got.

School was out, and we went to our grandparents' house nearly every day to play with King. One day, he wasn't there. We looked for him for two days.

On the third day, Grandpa found King under the house. He wouldn't come out even though he hadn't eaten for three days. Grandpa was sure King was sick. He questioned us about where we had been the past few days. Could King have eaten something that made him sick? We couldn't remember him eating anything.

Every day, we sat at the edge of the house and talked to King, but he wouldn't even look at us. It was almost the Fourth of July when a car pulled into the yard. Two men in Marine uniforms got out. They asked if our grandparents were there. I said yes. They went to the door and knocked.

Just then, King started howling. It sounded like he was crying. The one Marine said, "What is that?" I told him it was Uncle Homer's dog. The two Marines looked at each other sadly and shook their heads.

When my grandparents answered the door, the Marines asked if they could come in. Of course, they could. Inside, they revealed that Uncle Homer had been killed in the Battle of Saipan on June 18, 1944.

Once they were gone, Grandpa crawled under the house and hugged King a lot. He and King cried together and finally came out. Grandpa said he should have known about Uncle Homer. June 18th was the day King crawled under the house.

—Charlotte Lewis—

How Skyler Saved His Own Life

The bond with a dog is as lasting as the ties
of this earth can ever be.
~Konrad Lorenz

Skyler, a seventeen-year-old longhaired Dachshund, has been the only "child" of my son and daughter-in-law throughout his life. As such, he has been the sole recipient of all the adoration and attention that any pet/child could ask for. In return, he has, for the most part, been a great pet.

True, he has been known to bite someone now and then, but in his defense, he has never caused serious injury and has only bitten when a stranger reached out to pet him too quickly. And true, there was that one entanglement with a skunk, who sprayed his scent all over Skyler. It caused a frantic midnight run to an all-night pharmacy for skunk-repellent bath wash and a trip to the vet the next day to ensure that he didn't suffer any permanent damage. But despite these and a few other mishaps, Skyler has remained a king in his own castle his whole life (albeit a four-legged king, and a very short-legged one, at that).

His advancing age, however, has brought about numerous changes in Skyler's life. First, he has become increasingly hard-of-hearing, which is more of a problem for his owners since he no longer responds to their commands. Also, he has gradually become blind, often bumping into furniture and getting stuck in corners. As he is unable to get himself out, one of them has to stay nearby to help him. And, most upsetting, he is now incontinent. Even though he wears doggie "diapers," he often has accidents and requires almost daily bathing.

As troubling as all these realities are, what may be saddest, at least to the kids, is that they've lost their fellow adventurer. The three of them have always loved to explore the many hiking trails all around them and take road trips to nearby lakes to enjoy their canoe, with Skyler in tow outfitted in his own little blue life vest. But as Skyler's condition has weakened, these excursions have become impossible. Now, he spends most of his time sleeping.

This situation has led them to face the inevitable question all pet owners will face at some point: "Is it time to give my beloved pet a peaceful and painless death, when he or she has virtually little or no quality of life?" As hard as this dilemma is, what complicates it even more for them is that despite his limitations, Skyler doesn't seem to be in pain and is still eating and drinking. When he's held and cuddled, he responds with a sweet, wet kiss.

This has been the situation for several months, and though my kids live in another city, they have kept me updated almost daily. If they have been able to sleep uninterrupted for the whole night, without a distressing accident to greet them first thing in the morning, then they decide optimistically that they (and Skyler) can struggle along for a while. If they have a bad night, they are back to the turmoil of facing the inevitable.

One Sunday morning about a month ago, my son called me, obviously upset. "Mom," he said, "I just want to let you know. We've decided the time has come. We've called our vet, and she's coming over this afternoon to put Skyler down." That whole day, my heart sank every time my phone rang, as I didn't want to face the fact that my "grand-dog," whom I had loved for so many years, was gone.

Eventually, late that day, my son called again, and I answered reluctantly. "How did it go?" I asked, tears already streaming down my face as I braced myself for the dreaded report. He started laughing!

"You're not going to believe this, Mom, but we didn't go through with it!" He went on to describe what had to be an unbelievable turn of events. It seems that as soon as the vet entered the house, carrying her medical bag in one hand and a crate in the other, Skyler lifted his head from his bed in the corner and immediately became agitated. As they watched, he began pacing back and forth, howling "soulfully" every few steps.

My son, daughter-in-law and the vet sat in stunned silence, unable to believe what they were witnessing! How had this blind and deaf dog somehow sensed what was about to happen? Even more importantly, how had this dog, who hadn't barked in over a year, worked up enough energy to howl in protest, letting them know, in no uncertain terms, that it was not his time to go.

Yes, Skyler saved his own life that day, if only in the form of a reprieve. Though the end will come for him eventually, my kids now realize that Skyler will let them know when the time is right. In the meantime, without the pressure of having to make an arbitrary decision, they are enjoying Skyler in a whole new way and making his remaining days the very best they can be.

— Sandra Martin —

Pet Names

Animals can communicate quite well.
And they do.
~Alice Walker

"Honey, do you want anything from the kitchen?" I asked my husband, Eric. He shook his head, so I got off the couch and headed to the fridge. Our Pomeranian/Poodle mix, Piper, followed me into the kitchen. "I'm just getting some water, sweetie," I told her. "No snacks. Nothing for you."

I sat back down on the couch, and Piper curled up beside me. She laid her head down on my lap and closed her eyes.

"Honey, can I…" Eric started to say, and then he started laughing.

"What's so funny?" I asked.

"I was going to ask you for a sip of your water, but as soon as I started talking, Piper opened her eyes and looked at me as though I was talking to her."

I chuckled. "Of course. Who wouldn't want to talk to her?" I stroked her head. "She's fascinating."

Piper laid her head back down and closed her eyes again.

Moments later, Eric said, "Honey, I…" Immediately, Piper lifted her head and looked at him.

We both cracked up.

"Do it again," I said. He waited for her to lay her head back down, and then he said, "Babe, can I…"

It happened again. Immediately, she looked at Eric as though he'd said her name.

My kids heard us laughing and came into the room. "What's going on?" they asked.

"Watch this," Eric said. "Every time I talk to Mom, Piper thinks I'm talking to her."

"Sweetheart, I…" Immediately, Piper lifted her head and looked at Eric.

The kids laughed. "Let me try," said our youngest son, Nathan.

He waited for Piper to put her head back down, and then he said, "Mom, can I have a million dollars?"

Piper didn't move at all. She didn't even open her eyes.

"Oh, it didn't work when I did it," he said sadly.

"Baby, it's…" Piper looked up, and everyone laughed.

"She was talking to me, sweet girl," Nathan said, and Piper immediately turned her head to look at him.

"It's the pet names," I said. "That's why she thinks we're talking to her."

"A pet name? Like Piper?" Nathan said.

I laughed. "Piper is our pet, and that's her name, but a pet name means a sweet name that you use instead of someone's actual name to show them you love them."

"Like when you call me 'honey'?" Nathan asked as Piper turned to look at him.

We all laughed again. "Exactly," I said. "But let's make sure that's what it is."

I waited until Piper put down her head and closed her eyes again. Then I said, "Nathan, did you finish your homework?" Piper didn't open her eyes. "Jordan, do you have to work tomorrow?" Piper didn't move at all. "Julia, what do you want for dinner?" The dog was practically snoring.

Then I said, "Honey, do you…" Piper looked at me, alert instantly. Everyone cracked up.

"Let me try now," Nathan said. He talked to each person by name, and Piper didn't respond at all. "Mom, do you love me?" he said. "Dad, do you want to have a lightsaber battle?" he asked. He said something to each of his siblings. Piper snoozed away. But the minute he said, "Sweetie," she was awake and staring at him.

"I can't believe Piper knows all of our names," Nathan said, talking quickly. "She's so smart! She's a pet, and she knows what pet names are. She knows that when we use our real names, we aren't talking to her. But when we use pet names, we might be talking to her because we love her. So, we call her pet names and not just her real pet name that's Piper, but a sweet pet name. That's why she looks at us. She's like the smartest dog in the world."

I laughed at Nathan's very specific explanation. He was so excited and proud of Piper. It was adorable.

I rubbed Piper's silky fur. "You're such a good girl, honey," I said. She looked right at me and definitely knew I was talking to her.

— Diane Stark —

Learning to Love the Dog

My Dog Brother

It's just the most amazing thing to love a dog,
isn't it? It makes our relationships with people
seem as boring as a bowl of oatmeal.
~John Grogan

The second the phone rang, I knew we were going to talk about the dog. "I'm calling because it's your brother's birthday, and you didn't even call him," my dad said.

"Dad, Ernie isn't my brother," I retorted. "He's a dog."

Growing up, I was very attached to our family dog, Odie. Still, I've never considered myself a "dog person." I'm allergic to most hair; I don't like to clean up or spend money needlessly; and the thought of taking a pet outside several times a day (during Wisconsin winters) seems insane to me. Who would sign up for that?

My single dad, though, was a dog person. And although pets aren't my thing, I was in full support of him having a companion that made him happy.

The dog's birthday phone call became one of many family traditions—most of which revolved around Ernie, my dad's Standard Poodle, purchased soon after my youngest brother left for college.

At first, only my dad played these jokes. Since I was away at college and only home on the weekends, Dad said it was important that Ernie and I "bonded" as siblings. Dad would call so I could talk to Ernie. He'd bring the dog to visit me at college. And my birthday cards were always signed "Love, Dad and Ernie."

During one visit home, I discovered that the framed photos on Dad's wall had been rearranged, with Ernie's photo now above my brothers' and mine.

"Seriously, Dad!" I yelled. "I know some parents have a favorite child, but it's usually a HUMAN!" I said, rolling my eyes. Then, he giggled. I could tell he'd been planning the prank for a while and was pretty proud of himself. He never got around to fixing it—ever. On Dad's family photo wall, Ernie's 8x10 photo stayed at the top of the picture pyramid.

After a year of these pet-themed jokes directed solely at me, it seemed that even Ernie was in on it.

One Christmas, my brothers and I each received a wrapped box of cereal treats to take back to college. Ernie unwrapped my gift and then each of the forty-eight individually wrapped treats. Ernie didn't even eat the treats; he just made a mess. He left them all over the couch where I slept. There was even one under my pillow. The boxes with my brothers' names on them remained untouched. It was then that I knew: The dog was messing with me. If he wanted me to change my mind about being a "dog person," he was going about it the wrong way.

On my next visit home, I joked that I had to take my dad to a public place where dogs weren't welcome in order to get top billing. When we returned from our errand, Ernie had not only overturned my laundry basket in the kitchen, but he'd also unzipped my backpack and scattered my books and notebooks around the living room.

"Aww, your brother is happy you're home," laughed my dad. "He helped you unpack."

"You aren't the least bit shocked that a *dog* managed to unzip a backpack?" I asked.

"Family finds a way, Holly," he said with a smirk.

A few years later, I was pregnant and very sick. My husband was out of town working. We were living in a city where we had no family. Not wanting to be alone, I packed up the car and drove a few hours home to my dad's house for a prolonged visit. The next day, while out for a walk with my grandmother, Ernie managed to get sprayed by a skunk.

"He can't come in here!" I pleaded. "The whole house is going to smell for weeks!"

"But this is his home," Grandma insisted.

I cried as the two of us, one elderly and one pregnant, tried to hoist a traumatized dog into the bathtub. The smell of him turned my already distressed stomach. As we tried to scrub away the stink and calm Ernie, I started to feel protective towards… a dog! Ernie was gentle and intelligent, not one for getting into mischief (unless it involved me, of course). I knew the reason he got sprayed was likely because he'd been trying to protect my grandma.

Three dog baths later, I was exhausted. I curled up on the floor, nauseous from the skunk smell. Ernie snuggled up next to me. For the first time, I didn't move away. As smelly as he still was, I was glad to have the comfort. Bedtime came and went, and so did his normal bedtime routine and sleeping locations. He slept by my side until I couldn't stand the smell anymore and moved to another room.

A few months later, my husband and I brought our newborn daughter to my hometown for her first visit. Ernie didn't leave her side, either. During the day, he sat at attention next to her car seat. At night, he moved to a spot just outside the bedroom where she slept.

I'm convinced Ernie intentionally played jokes on me to get a rise out of me (a skill learned from my dad and brothers). Over time, this "non-dog person" warmed to the idea of Ernie as Dad's "favorite child" and even one of my "brothers." He was good to me, great to my baby and the perfect companion for my dad.

I'd put little effort into my relationship with Ernie, but he was determined to make me love him. As my dad said, family finds a way.

— Holly Rutchik —

The New Pack

I think dogs are the most amazing creatures.
They give unconditional love. For me they are
the role model for being alive.
~Gilda Radner

I must admit, I haven't always liked animals. In fact, I distrusted them greatly while growing up, and I still fear the ones I don't know personally. What set my beliefs in stone was being attacked—not once but many times, including the summer after second grade when I was bitten by a rabbit. Then, when I was nine and cruising my dirt bike down the road, a large dog charged me and tried to bite my ankle.

In another attack, my experience was shared by the whole high-school cross-country team. We trained by running through our small town, and one hot day we were chased by a stray Rottweiler. It must have looked like a scene from Mutual of Omaha's *Wild Kingdom*. I had safety in the mid-pack position, but I heard screams coming from behind as the lion tried to pick off stragglers in the back. I'm sure I achieved a PR (personal record) that day.

After all those negative experiences, there was one thing I knew for sure: All creatures, great and small, were no friends of mine.

After college in California, I returned to live the single life in Las Vegas. Unfortunately, every woman I dated had a pet or two or three. One had a bird who would hitch a ride on her dog. I got bitten, not by the girl or the dog—it was the bird that time. I figured it just wasn't in the cards for me to make peace with any beast.

Then I met Lisa. In no time at all, we fell in love, married, and moved into a new house. Despite my avoidance of animals, I became alpha dog of a new pack. Yes, Lisa had a cat and two dogs. The cat was a Ragdoll named Bandit. The canines were called Bailey and Daisy. Bailey was a massive, male chocolate-brown Labrador, and Daisy a thick, female black Labrador/Pit Bull mix. Bandit didn't like me, but he tolerated my existence once he realized I wasn't going anywhere.

During the first years of living under one roof, I began to accept the possibility of creature cohabitation. I was amazed at Bailey's gentleness. He grew up with Bandit and let many cat-claw attacks go without retaliation. He also pampered Daisy as if she were his wife by making sure to clean her face after every meal.

Things change, as they always do, and come spring we welcomed a new member to our family: our son, Evan. One evening while he happily tested the laws of physics in his playpen, Bailey lumbered by, and Evan grabbed hold of the dog's tail. The irritated dog paused and turned to look at his stuck tail but waited patiently until being released. Still, the stories I'd heard of animals attacking babies worried me.

At first chance, like an idiot, I said, "Uh, since Evan is now playing on the floor, I've been thinking that maybe it would be a good idea to find new homes for the dogs." A blowout of an argument ensued.

After we both cooled down, my wife explained that when Bailey was a few months old, she paid for an expensive-but-necessary hip surgery to provide him a chance at a longer life. My wife clarified that this "wild bunch" of a family wasn't breaking apart.

And then my worst fear occurred. I sat on the couch reading after a long day while my wife worked at the dining-room table paying the bills.

I saw Evan crawl across the family-room rug as he made his way behind the couch. I figured he was okay back there since there was nothing he could get into. One minute, all was quiet, and then Bailey entered the room and headed to where Evan had crawled. I nearly jumped out of my skin when I heard the dog start a fearful barking behind me.

Snapping the book closed, I rushed around the couch. The damn dog was barking directly at my toddler. I envisioned that soon his large white jaws would lock onto my son's head. Evan lay on his belly, his head held high. His little face frozen in fright as Bailey continued to bark at full volume mere inches away.

In that moment, I was sure I had been correct about animals all along. Lisa dropped everything and came rushing around the corner. "What the hell is going on?" I shouted.

Next, I saw myself arguing with Lisa; me calling animal control; rushing Evan to the hospital for surgery. As I moved to grab Bailey in a chokehold, my eye caught something on the floor directly below Evan's chin. A huge scorpion had its tail up and was prepared to strike. It blended in with the spotted brown carpet perfectly.

My fear shifted from barking dog to menacing insect. Without hesitation, I positioned my foot right under my son's head and stomped that scorpion flat. Evan's head came to rest on the toe of my boot. It was such a close call. Lisa scooped up our wailing child. Having witnessed our dog saving my son's life, I was speechless — and, I admit, near tears.

I gave that beefy brown dog some kisses — big, fat, sloppy ones like he gave Daisy. It was a wonderful moment I shall never forget. These animals I had learned to live with had learned to live with me, too.

As time passed, even more scorpions appeared inside the house. Within two months, we moved out. I didn't want to learn how to live with *them*.

Bailey protected our pack until the age of twelve, and then he passed away. I cried. We all cried. Shortly after, Daisy passed on, too. Of course, Bandit outlived them both. But before he moved on, we came to an unspoken agreement and got along fine.

Thinking back on my short time spent with those non-human beings, I'll never forget how Bailey was the one who first brought me into the fold. That "ol' hunk-a-junk," as we affectionately called him, showed me how both human and beast can live in harmony. I have a new belief now, not set in stone but in love. It is that some animals are the best people indeed.

— D.M. Woolston —

My Husband's Dog

Whoever said diamonds are a girl's best friend
never owned a dog.
~Author Unknown

"This is the one!" My husband Mark sounded triumphant, as if he had just scratched a winning million-dollar lottery ticket, something I would squeal over, too. But we weren't at a gas station buying scratch-offs. We were at a pet store on its monthly pet-adoption day. I had gone to the pet store under the assumption that we were just looking. Even though Mark wanted another dog to replace Toby, our previous dog who had been gone for a few years, I didn't.

I loved Toby, who was a wonderful dog, but since his passing I had come to love a clean, dog-free, bark-free house, too. We had four cats at that time, which was plenty for me. Mark was not convinced. On the contrary, he had become an avid proponent of adding a four-legged canine member to our family. It was driven, I suspected, by our younger son's abrupt and totally unexpected departure for his own apartment and life, leaving us with an empty nest we hadn't thought we'd experience quite so soon.

"I will walk him, take him to the vet and feed him," Mark promised the morning we drove past the pet store and learned it was pet-adoption day. His words made me feel more like a skeptical mom on a sitcom than a pragmatic wife, but I stuck to my guns. This was real life, not a rerun of *Leave It to Beaver*, and I wasn't interested in wiping up muddy paw prints any longer. "Besides, he'll keep you safe when I'm not home."

Having never felt unsafe when Mark wasn't home, I still wasn't sold, but softie that I am, I agreed to go to the pet store on adoption day as long as we were just looking.

The pickings were pretty slim that day, with only three dogs seeking their forever homes: a sweet-faced mutt named Oliver, a hyperactive ankle biter, and a big black dog going by the moniker Pluto. Mark focused on Pluto immediately.

"Him," he said, pointing at Pluto who was busily holding up an empty plastic water bottle to each person passing by while whipping his long black tail back and forth. "That's the one."

"He's too big," I protested. "How about this one?" I pointed at Oliver, who was sitting quietly next to the volunteer. If we had to get a dog, I didn't want one that used his tail like a machete.

"No," Mark said emphatically, "that one. Look at his feet! He has big feet, which means he's going to be a big dog. I want him. Remember, I'll walk him every day and take him to the vet and…"

"…feed him," I finished. "I know. You already told me." Mark and I have been married long enough for me to know when it's pointless to argue. This was one of those times. "Well, if you swear he's going to be your dog…"

"I swear," Mark said as he reached for Pluto's lead.

The first inkling that my skepticism was well-grounded occurred approximately one minute later as I sat with the self-appointed drill sergeant in charge of all adoptions. (Having conveniently forgotten his reader glasses and claiming blindness, Mark was busy bonding with Pluto.)

After quizzing me thoroughly on my character, raising one eyebrow judgmentally after each of my responses, and then making me fill out more paperwork than it takes to buy a house, I was sure I had failed. I wasn't the dream pet adopter all animal shelters hope to find. The sergeant, whose name was Cherry, asked many probing questions.

"Do you work?"

"I work part-time," I responded, unsure if that was a good or bad answer. "I work from home the other half of the time."

"Hmmm," Cherry replied. "You have other animals?"

"Cats."

"Hmmm." This was accompanied by a frown. "I'm not sure how Pluto will behave around cats."

This went on and on before Cherry finally agreed to accept our money and let us take Pluto home. "Buy him lots and lots of toys," she instructed as we headed for the pet store's exit. "He loves to chew things."

Wonderful...

The first order of business was changing Pluto's name to something we both liked. The animal shelter changed his name to protect him, so he hadn't grown accustomed to being Pluto. On his very first walk, we noticed that he bounced in much the same way that Sylvester Stallone bounced while he trained in *Rocky*.

"How about Rocky?" I suggested. Pluto/Rocky turned his head and cocked it toward me. At that moment, I felt a small piece of my icy heart begin to thaw. Not melt, mind you, but a minor thaw.

"I like that," Mark said.

Mark's vow to take care of Rocky's every need continued to unravel. One evening a few days after he joined the family, Rocky began doing the dreaded "doggy scoot" across the living-room carpet.

"Your dog has worms," I told Mark.

Flashing me the I-know-you'll-do-it smile that I receive yearly at tax-return time, Mark responded, "Would you mind taking him to the vet? I really can't miss work this week, and we should get the Rock Man in there as soon as possible."

Since, of course, he was right, and since, of course, there was no one else to take the Rock Man to the vet, the following day I found myself writing an enormous check to a veterinarian after learning that Rocky had packed anal glands—an occasional occurrence when a dog has been under stress.

"He was probably nervous moving to a new home. We rinsed out his anal glands," the vet told me, thankfully sparing me the details, "but I don't think he liked it. His pride seemed injured."

I looked at Rocky, and Rocky looked at me. In that moment, a connection between the two of us was born, a bond created over his injured pride and a joint dislike of examinations of any kind given by someone wearing a white coat and sporting a latex glove. At that moment, Rocky became my dog.

As expected, I took over the care and feeding — and walking — of Rocky. Since we now understood each other, I didn't mind. Actually, I became somewhat territorial when it came to the Rock Man, slipping tidbits off my plate when Rocky's less-attentive parent wasn't looking.

Our walks became my favorite time of day since that was when Rocky and I had our most frank conversations. True, Rocky has never held up his end verbally during our chats, but he's communicated in other ways: a tilt of his head, understanding in his big brown eyes, and resting his head against my legs to show he gets what I'm talking about.

I tend to talk a lot to Rocky since I know I can tell him anything without having to worry about loose lips or arguments. Rocky hears about my job, children, and an occasional grouse about my marriage. A wag of his tail and a look of pure ecstasy on his face as he lunges for a squirrel or eats a discarded crust of bread reminds me what is really important in life: Live in the moment because if you sweat the small stuff too much, you might end up with packed anal glands.

Although I'm trying very hard to adhere to the live-now-and-don't-worry-about-the-future philosophy, there are still moments when it pierces my heart to remember that dogs don't live as long as people. Barring an accident or illness, I'm most likely going to outlive Rocky by at least a few decades. I used to think pet bereavement cards were silly at best, pointless the rest of the time. "Really? You're that upset over losing your dog?" That was in my pre-Rocky days. Now I'm deeply aware of the fact that when the time comes to say goodbye, I'm going to be a wreck.

But I'm not going to think about that now. It is autumn, and the air outside is loaded with fresh scents for Rocky to sniff on our daily jaunts around our neighborhood. Today, we need to talk about some issues I've been having with an especially annoying co-worker, and I also want to touch base regarding a recent dog-park incident. Rocky will listen, wag his tail and, in his doggy way, assure me whatever

I'm sharing is not only the correct response, but most likely the only response.

While we're strolling, it's possible a friend might drive past and shout out the window, "I love your husband's dog!" — something I've heard more than once, as I had told everyone I knew about my husband's insistence on adopting a dog. If that happens on our walk today, I will make a mental note to correct that friend the next time I see her. Rocky is *my* dog. For now and forever.

— Nell Musolf —

A Gift Called Boomer

Dogs are not our whole life,
but they make our lives whole.
~Roger Caras

Grief. One small word. One short syllable. But there is nothing small or short about it. As anyone who has lost a family pet knows, grief can throw you into a tailspin. It hurts, and the hurt doesn't go away for a long time. Recently, we had our fifteen-year-old Chihuahua put to sleep. Boomer was not my dog. He belonged to my wife, Linda. Still, I found myself pretty choked-up the day my daughter, Emily, and I took him to the vet.

At times, Boomer was not easy to live with. He barked at strangers, turned up his nose at dry dog food, and relieved himself on the floor instead of going outside. A difficult dog, yes, but it's become even more difficult to live without him since his death.

Our family developed a love for Boomer the day Linda brought him home. He was a complex creature, capable of rich and deep emotion. He had a personality with strong and weak points. Boomer also had incredible patience with children. Our two-year-old son, Tyler, would sometimes yank on his ears, but he never snapped.

Boomer wasn't my dog, but he was an excellent running partner. At the time, I was a member of Six Rivers Running Club, training for marathons seven days a week. I did most of my running in the mountains behind our home in McKinleyville. Boomer always accompanied me. I'm not talking about a short jog in the forest. I mean ten, sometimes twenty miles. How could a small dog run that far? I'm not sure. He must have had a special running gene other Chihuahuas don't have. My friends called him the Olympic marathoner of small dogs. Together, we slogged through mud, wind, heat, and hailstorm. We scampered up mountains so steep they would make a Kenyan distance runner "cry uncle." The little guy didn't have an ounce of quit in him.

Boomer was treated like a king around our house, with lots of food, a warm bed, and oodles of affection. Linda and I pampered him more than a four-star hotel concierge. When he wasn't sneaking scraps from the table or snatching a cookie from the hand of an unsuspecting child, he was eating steak, ham, and turkey dinners. Begging for tasty tidbits was Boomer's favorite pastime.

When Linda died of cancer in 2004, it was a very difficult time for our family. Boomer mourned right along with us. He lay in his bed and (shockingly) refused to eat, no matter what kind of yummy morsel I placed in front of him.

Emily headed off to college a few years later, and the relationship between man and Chihuahua continued to grow (although I still refused to call him *my* dog). Boomer was always there for me through good times and bad. I took him for walks, gave him treats, talked to him and caressed him. In return, his love was unconditional.

Not long ago, he had a stroke. Boomer's health began to fade quickly. Walking became a problem, and his appetite began to diminish. Before long, he stopped eating completely. Emily and I decided it was time to put him down. It was a tough thing to do. Boomer had been with us for a long time. He was also our last living memory of Linda.

It was another heartbreaking hurdle for our family to overcome.

A storm blew in the morning we took Boomer to the vet's office. Rain was coming down in buckets. I was grumpy and out of sorts that day, and I foolishly snapped at the poor receptionist who asked me to fill out a few forms.

"Dad, you sound like a cranky old man," Emily whispered. I apologized and confessed that the thought of watching Boomer die was just too agonizing. I'd been through the death of a loved one before. I wasn't sure I could handle the grief again, that period leading up to the last exhale that is so excruciating and unbearable. Emily understood.

The vet came in to administer the anesthetic. I massaged Boomer's head one last time and stepped out of the room, leaving my daughter to shoulder the burden. I was glad she had the strength to be there with Boomer in those final moments, to ease his passage. I was proud of her.

On the ride home, I thought about how much happiness Boomer had brought to our family. I reflected on what a gift he had been. The tears came when I finally understood that Boomer had been my dog all along. I'd just failed to realize it.

— Timothy Martin —

The Other Female in Our Bed

Love — that which biologists, nervous about being misunderstood, call "attachment" — fuels the bond between dog and master or mistress.
~John Bradshaw

I would rather have come home from my spa weekend and discovered my husband in bed with another woman than with a two-month-old Labrador Retriever curled between his legs. The woman would have been gone within seconds. As for that puppy? She was here to stay.

"Don't you just love Ziva?" my daughter asked several days later as I sprayed yet another carpet deodorizer that promised to bring "pine freshness" onto our living-room carpet. "Isn't she adorable and fun?"

I didn't find anything adorable about chewing up every paper product in our house: coasters, napkins, books. Or anything fun about moving items with the slightest hint of wood pulp to a higher altitude.

"But you have to admit, Mom, a puppy is the best thing for Dad."

On that, I had to agree with my daughter.

The previous year had been tough for my husband. After being diagnosed with a rare brain tumor (ironically, a type more prevalent in dogs), he survived an eight-hour surgery followed by seven weeks of radiation.

During that period, his best friend and business partner of three decades died from liver cancer. After his friend's passing, my husband spent hours watching TV. He lost his passion for cooking. He quit playing his guitar. He hadn't seen a sunrise or sunset in almost a year.

Once Ziva entered his life, everything changed.

During those first weeks, he got up every few hours to let her outside. I'd often find him in the morning stretched on a lounge with Ziva cuddled on his chest. He began taking her for walks. He brought her to the pet store to pick out her collar and leash. He spared no expense on the finest puppy food. He took her to obedience school — where he learned to obey her commands.

The TV went unwatched. Our kitchen became filled with savory aromas. In the evenings, we watched Ziva run circles through the back yard.

As the months progressed, Ziva grew from twenty to fifty pounds. Her culinary tastes expanded to include plastic items such as gift cards, inhalers and pens. And, for dessert, she loved stuffing. And I don't mean the kind found inside a turkey.

There went our patio chairs, swing cushions and her heart-shaped bed.

And, little by little, there went my heart. How could I not love this precious puppy who brought my husband back to me?

These days, if you enter our home in the evening, you'll find all three of us in bed together — snuggling, loving and taking care of each other.

— Janie Emaus —

Over My Dead Body

Happiness is a warm puppy.
~Charles Schultz

"Our deal is, when I die, she can have a dog." My husband was sure this was "our deal."

After sizing up my husband's words, my neighbor — a crass, dry-humor kind of guy — looked me square in the eye. "We can arrange that."

A devoted dog owner, this neighbor was just one more person on my doggie bandwagon. On the other hand, my husband Mike didn't think we needed any furry, four-legged canines. He'd always loved dogs, but just never wanted a dog of his own — or so he preached whenever I or one of my doggie-loving cheerleaders listed all the reasons why adding a dog to our family was the best decision.

He thought his reasons were legitimate. Dogs cost too much. They shed too much. Eat too much. And make messes. You have to arrange care for them if you want to travel.

He was convinced all his points were justifiable grounds for saying no to life with a dog. But any time a neighbor strolled by with their sweet pooch in tow, Mike was the first to greet the dog. When visiting family members with doggies, he was just as excited to see the furry family member as the two-legged relative.

Over twenty years, my daughter and I had a total of three Labradors. Barney was our first, and Darby joined our clan a few years later. When Barney finished his long and happy life at thirteen, we decided Darby needed another buddy, and Sammy came into our lives. We adored all three of our Labs and each enjoyed thirteen years of being spoiled and loved. When Sammy passed on, life took a different turn, and I was without the unconditional love of a dog for the first time.

By then, my daughter was away at college. There, a young, emaciated and flea-ridden mutt found her one sunny day as she walked to her car. Emily didn't hesitate to make this cute runt her own and named him Seymour. Now I had a grand-dog, at least. But I missed having my own dog.

From day one of our relationship, Mike stood his ground about his no-dogs rule. I accepted this, knowing I'd soften his stance one day. In the fall of 2013, we made the decision to move to a small town by Lake Michigan. It was a fun adventure, and we enjoyed our time there together, celebrating with family and friends in our lake home where we married in 2017. We even hosted my daughter and son-in-law's beautiful wedding over an unforgettable weekend.

While there, our family and friends kept pressuring Mike about getting a dog. They knew how much I wanted one, and how I thought he would love one, too. I suggested we get a small dog. An easier option, I thought. To my amazement, this man who refused to allow any dog began using a different language that wasn't an absolute no, but now an if.

"*If* I got a dog, no small dogs for me! I'd get a Lab." It was progress.

Besides, I loved Labs. I had three Lab angels of my own watching over me.

In the spring of 2018, we made a decision to continue our adventure and move back closer to family. I took this opportunity to share with him the convenience of being close to family: built-in doggie-sitters. He was softening even more. One evening while we were out to dinner and discussing our upcoming move, he made a comment—a game-changer.

"When we move back home, you just might get a dog." His words were sweet and golden.

Well, I only heard, "I get a dog." There was no "might" about it. He had signed, sealed, and delivered the contract, and I started planning for our doggie. He couldn't change his mind now. He said it. I heard it and announced the news. I was ecstatic to welcome a furry family member once again. My grand-dogs, Seymour and Louie (yes, even Seymour had a buddy), would soon meet our new doggie.

We both agreed adoption was the perfect way to find our pooch. Once settled in our new home, we wasted no time. We called the local Lab rescue and started the process. It didn't take any time to get approved for adoption. We were getting excited. The rescue explained that older Labs were easier to place while puppies were in high demand. We didn't care about the age and looked at all potential candidates. Then we found them.

Jake and Porter were mixed black Lab puppies from the same litter. The moment I walked in the door of their foster home, I fell in love with both of them. We left knowing one of those little guys was going to be ours. But which one? Even my "no dog" husband was having a hard time choosing. Everyone we told said the same thing: "You can't separate them."

Mike, Mr. No Dogs, couldn't process choosing just one. Could this be a wonderful dream? For me, the answer was simple: both. I'd always had two at a time anyway. It was easy, I thought. But Mike had to think. We agreed to sleep on it. By morning, with no prompting at all, Mike said what I hoped and prayed he'd say: "We can't separate them. They're brothers and need to stay together."

Everyone thought we were crazy to take on two puppies, but I knew we could handle it. We made plans with their foster mom. We picked up our two adorable puppies and, aside from normal training woes, over two years later, life is wonderful with our two knuckleheads, as we call them with much affection and love. My husband loves his boys. I love seeing him smile and laugh. His joy with our doggies is priceless. And he's alive and well.

— Karen Zimmerman —

Home Together

It is amazing how much love and laughter they bring into our lives and even how much closer we become with each other because of them.
~John Grogan

A few days before Thanksgiving 2019, I saw a social-media post from my pastor's wife. She'd found a stray dog, scared and hungry with no collar or microchip. "She's a sweetie, but we can't keep her," the post said. "Please let us know if you'd be able to offer her a home."

I looked at the photo of the small black-and-white dog, and my heart melted. We went to meet her the next day. She was scared of us, particularly my husband Eric, but I was sure it was temporary.

We checked with the Humane Society and waited several days to give her previous owner the chance to claim her, but no one called about a dog matching her description. She was ours if we wanted her, and I really did.

We took her to the vet, who proclaimed her to be thin but healthy. She was approximately five years old, and a mix of Beagle, Terrier, Schnauzer, Dachshund, and Chihuahua. She was a mutt but cute.

We named her Peyton. (We live in Indiana, and we're Colts fans.) Just days in, I was completely smitten with her. My daughter and younger son adored her. She bonded quickly with our other dog, Piper. There was just one problem: Peyton was terrified of Eric and my college-aged son, Jordan.

During the day, when Eric and Jordan were at work and school, Peyton ran around the house, chasing Piper like a carefree puppy. But as soon as one of them came home, she'd cower under the kitchen table as though she was waiting for someone to hurt her.

It was clear that Peyton had a rough past with men.

Months went by, and the situation got no better. When Eric and Jordan were away, she'd play with Piper and cuddle close to me for treats and belly rubs. But the moment she heard the front door open, she morphed into a scared little creature who hid in corners and under tables. Both Eric and Jordan were kind and patient, but nothing they did seemed to help Peyton trust them.

It was so sad to watch, and I had no idea how to fix it.

And then a brand-new word entered America's vocabulary: coronavirus. Jordan's university moved to online classes for the remainder of the semester. Eric began working from home, too.

Gone were the eight hours a day when Peyton was free to play and relax without fear. With the guys home all the time, poor Peyton was relegated to her hiding place under the kitchen table. When she couldn't see them from that vantage point, she'd dash out to eat and go potty. If she was feeling especially brave, she'd curl up in my lap, hiding her face under my arm — the whole "if I can't see them, they can't see me" thing.

It was heartbreaking to see how fearful she was.

"Peyton, you're going to have to get used to them being here," I told her nearly every day. "No one knows how long we're all going to be home together. It's going to be better for everyone — especially for you — if you can learn to relax around them."

Daily, I promised Peyton that Eric and Jordan would never hurt her. They took over feeding her, hoping she would learn to associate them with good things. Both of them played with and snuggled Piper where Peyton could see them, thinking that would help build trust.

But Peyton continued to hide under the table.

One evening a few weeks into the quarantine, our family was playing a game at the kitchen table. Jordan took his turn and then said, "Piper is sitting on my feet, and it tickles."

I glanced into the living room where Piper was lying on the couch. I shook my head. "It must be Peyton on your feet. Don't look, though. You might scare her away."

For the next thirty minutes, Jordan sat as still as he could so he wouldn't frighten Peyton. When we finished the game, he peeked under the table. As soon as Peyton saw him, she dashed upstairs and stayed there until bedtime.

"She must have thought she was lying on your feet, Mom," Jordan said.

But the next night as we ate dinner, Peyton lay on Eric's feet. I looked under the table and saw that her eyes were closed. She seemed completely at ease. She remained that way until she saw that Eric was looking at her. Then she dashed upstairs like she had the previous night.

This became the new pattern. Every night, Peyton fell asleep on either Eric's or Jordan's feet under the kitchen table. She was only scared when they looked at her.

Now we had a strategy. Every morning, instead of rushing off to other parts of the house for school and work, both guys would take turns sitting on the floor to pet Piper. When Peyton's curiosity got the best of her and she came close, they would turn their heads away. Only then would she allow them to pet her.

But if they turned back to look at her, she was gone in an instant.

"We're getting there," I said one morning.

"Yeah, I can pet her, but I just can't look at her," Jordan joked.

"I know it's strange, but she's getting used to you and Dad on her terms. I know it's taking longer than any of us thought it would, but she's learning to trust you. Thanks for being patient with her."

Jordan nodded thoughtfully. "I wouldn't have had time for this before. When I had school and work, I didn't really care that Peyton was afraid of me. But when the quarantine started, I was home all the time and realized how hard her life must have been before we got her. It made me want to work harder to help her feel comfortable."

I smiled. "She appreciates it, and so do I. She's such a different dog when you and Dad aren't home. She's so cute and playful. I hope that, someday, she can overcome her fear and be that way all the time."

He smiled back. "We'll get there, Mom. It might take a while, but I've got the time now to work on it."

The coronavirus and the resulting shutdown brought change to every family in America. While so much of it was scary — even devastating — many people reported that they felt closer to their families than they did before.

I am one of those people. Our family used to spend each day running in all different directions to our own jobs and obligations. Often, we ate dinner in shifts and had to catch up with each other on the weekends. Our lives were just too busy.

Life at our house was much slower during the shutdown. We had time for puzzles and board games. And we had time for our new family project: helping a little black-and-white rescue dog acclimate to her new home with her new family… as long as certain people didn't look at her.

— Diane Stark —

My Priceless Present

Opening up your life to a dog who needs a home
is one of the most fulfilling things you can do.
~Emma Kenney

In 2006, it seemed like our economy came to its knees overnight, especially where we live in Florida. Just about everyone was going through some type of financial hardship, some even losing their homes. There were whole abandoned neighborhoods of new homes, halfway through construction.

We thought the crisis wouldn't end, but by 2009 we were cautiously optimistic about the future. Just the same, as Christmas approached that year, we decided that we would skip the presents. That meant getting back to the basics of family time, walks on the beach, board games, and baking cookies.

The day after Christmas, our older daughter and I decided to run a few errands before she headed back to college. On the last of our errands, I was waiting in line at our neighborhood mom-and-pop grocery store when I overheard a woman announcing that a breeder would be bringing in a litter of Pug puppies to give away. She went on to say that the breeder didn't get the puppies sold as Christmas presents, as she had hoped, blaming the poor economy. Sadly, the puppies' mother died, leaving the poor pups languishing, sickly and malnourished. They needed to find homes for them as soon as possible.

I only had a vague notion as to what a Pug was at this point. Nevertheless, I scribbled my phone number on the back of a receipt and handed it to the woman. I didn't really expect the call. But an hour later, my daughter and I returned to the store and stood among the other hopeful Pug parents, anxiously awaiting the arrival of the puppies. As I glanced around, I noticed a couple of older ladies and a young couple. I wasn't sure there would be enough pups to go around, but I was okay with that. I was more curious than anything, and I wanted to see what these Pug dogs were all about.

The puppies looked more like aliens than three-week-old dogs. Nestled in the bottom of a laundry basket lined with newspaper were two males and one female. The males were bigger and stronger and taken quickly by the two older women. The remaining Pug was a scrawny, sickly, and sleepy female. Without hesitation, I felt myself reach for her. She was skin and bones, with patchy bald spots on her thin black coat, and sad, pitiful eyes. It was obvious she was deathly ill.

I held her close to my chest and heard a faint whimper, as if she was asking me to take her. Using a hand towel I had grabbed from home, I wrapped up this tiny, alien being and handed her to my daughter. The car ride home was silent, neither of us believing that we had taken on this Christmas puppy project.

I shook my head in disbelief at what we had done. The last thing we needed was veterinarian bills. And training a new puppy is always a challenge. What was I thinking? *I cannot do this,* I told myself. *I must take her back right away.*

As I was talking myself out of keeping the Pug, my two daughters were choosing a name for her. I knew I was in trouble when I found the girls sitting on the floor by our Christmas tree, giving her a bottle of goat's milk.

That evening when my husband got home, we agreed that while we were in no position to adopt a three-week-old puppy with so many health issues, we should try to find a suitable home for her as soon as she got well enough.

A friend directed me to a veterinarian willing to treat Betsey right away. He scraped, poked and prodded the poor pup as I explained my predicament to him. This "free" puppy was hardly going to be free. I also asked him to help me find a nice home for her once she got well. Dr. J determined that Betsey was blind in one eye, and the other eye didn't look great, either. He diagnosed her with mange, probably brought on by malnutrition and poor care. He recommended weekly visits for at least two months due to the mange's severity and put her chances of survival at only 50/50. He sent me on my way with an arsenal of antibiotics and ointments, and a list of strict dietary recommendations. She needed to gain weight to boost her immune system.

As I left the vet that day, I felt annoyed that this strange little dog would require so much work, time and effort at such a tumultuous financial time. But I knew I had to follow through with my commitment.

I read up on mange and then made Betsey a little bed out of an old shoebox and baby blankets. I hoped for the best, but she looked so sick that it was hard to believe she could recover. My two girls promised they would help with Betsey's care and then left to hang out with friends. I could see the writing on the wall, and it had my name written all over it! This Pug needed a good home, and I needed to get her well fast so I could find her one.

So, my quest began. I asked everyone I knew if they wanted her. My neighbor said, "No way!" My daughter's orthodontist said, "Maybe." And my friend whose dog had drowned said, "I'm not ready." I put posters of her in pet stores, too: "FREE PUG." Maybe the picture of her deterred interest because she was a sight! Try as I may, no one seemed to want this little Pug. Yet, week after week, I dutifully went back to the vet's office, cringing as Betsey endured the visits and I confronted the bills.

The kind vet must have felt bad for my situation with this "free" puppy and decided to cut me a break on my weekly vet bill. I started to cry, of course, never expecting such generosity. Soon, I could tell that his treatments were working. Betsey started getting stronger. I could also tell that I was becoming more enchanted with her each week. Suddenly, I noticed that having her around was pretty nice. In fact, she was good company. She brought our family even closer as we rallied to get her healthy.

As Betsey started feeling better, I realized what a breeze she was to house-train, and she was so obedient that she rarely needed a leash.

She learned commands quickly, and before I knew it, she had made her way out of the shoebox bed and into my bed. Not even my husband minded the intrusion as she snuggled right between us. I kept reminding him that it was only temporary. He would just chuckle softly.

Even though she was weak, Betsey pranced around our house with confidence. Her sweet eyes started to clear up, her bald spots started to fill in, and her personality came through as a sweet, intelligent, spunky little dog. Our family delighted in her, and we simply could not understand why no one was stepping forward to give this little dog a good home.

How could they not see how wonderful she was? Sure, she wouldn't win any beauty pageants, but her attitude more than made up for that.

Betsey was small, which meant I could take her everywhere I went. Suddenly, I became one of those people pushing a dog stroller, and I didn't even mind the occasional snicker. Betsey was important to me, my husband and children. She made our family come together; we would sit on the floor playing with her for hours.

My college-aged daughter and I would FaceTime so she could see Betsey from her dorm room. My younger daughter would take Betsey on "play dates" with her friends' dogs… all in the name of "socializing her" for the new family that would adopt her.

After two months, Dr. J pronounced her fit enough for a new home. My heart sank a little as he said the words. Betsey would no longer need weekly visits but should come back in six months for a check-up. I reminded the vet that a new family would own her by then, but he just grinned at me with a twinkle in his eye. He could see that I loved that little dog. I think he liked her, too.

About a week later, on a Saturday morning, the doorbell rang. I answered the door with Betsey in my arms. Before me stood a man and his young daughter, who had come to get the "free" pug they had heard about from a friend of a friend. My heart raced as I held Betsey tightly and looked at my husband in disbelief. In an instant, I knew what I had to do. My husband gave me a wink because he knew, too.

I crouched down to the little girl and said in a soft, emotional voice, "Honey, I am so sorry, but the Pug already found a good home."

As I watched the dad and his little girl walk slowly back to his car, I knew that this unwanted, sickly Pug was the best Christmas present that I almost didn't get.

— Kim Johnson —

Ode to a Basset

Everything I know, I learned from dogs.
~Nora Roberts

What is a Basset?
How can I explain
Why we love them so much
Though they drive us insane?

Their statures are short
But personalities large.
They're sassy and brassy
And always in charge.

They leave hair everywhere,
Emit terribly loud howls,
Have dirty, long ears
And dripping wet jowls.

They steal spots on the couch,
In the bed, on your chair.
When you tell them they're naughty,
They really don't care.

They leave slobber on carpet,
Ceiling, and wall.
Take the food off your counter.
Don't come when you call.

If you give a command,
They're sure to obey,
But only if they want
To do what you say.

Yet for all of the challenge
And the hassles they bring,
All Basset owners know
We wouldn't change a thing.

Those deep, dark brown eyes
Show us love beyond measure.
Each white-tipped tail wag
Is a gift that we treasure.

What price could we place
On the snuggles they give?
They're the hearts of our homes
And the lives that we live.

So when they go flat Basset
When they're out on a walk,
Or ignore everything
That you say when you talk.

When they hog all your covers,
And snore when they sleep,
And walk through the pile
You're trying to sweep.

You're still going to love them
'Cause at the end of the day,
We know what they're like
And we love them that way.

—Andrea K. Farrier—

Canine Delicacies

My dog is worried about the economy
because Alpo is up to $3.00 a can.
That's almost $21.00 in dog money.
~Joe Weinstein

As responsible dog owners, my wife and I buy our dogs premium foods with esoteric ingredients such as venison that cost more than my lunch. In fact, one of the treats we give them for rare good behavior is a piece of a meat log, which I'll confess I've secretly dreamed of having with eggs and toast. One would expect our dogs to agree with our responsible choices for their nutrition. These expensive items, fit for the most royal of pets, are what every healthy canine should crave.

Well, one would think so; however, our dogs eat what is essentially garbage. Don't misunderstand me, they also eat the good stuff that we put in front of their snouts a couple of times per day in carefully measured amounts. But what do they do when we let them out to play in the yard? They eat branches, grass, weeds, dead (and live) bugs, pebbles, and any other organic or inorganic matter they can find. That is what they eat outside. Inside, they have a much "better" diet of paper towels, napkins, cardboard, lint, and their all-time-favorite: stuffing from the plush toys they disembowel within fifteen minutes of their arrival from the pet store.

There are other delicacies in their diets, too: blankets. Sometimes, we give a small blanket to each dog when it's particularly cold or we think they might like to rest their heads on a folded blanket. Blankets last longer than napkins, as they're a bit harder to digest, but they gobble them in pieces. There is more than one Swiss cheese blanket lying around our house.

Here's another all-time favorite: paper. This is not a universal offense since it depends on what the paper is. Apparently, the more valuable the better. One of them ate a thirty-dollar rebate check a few years ago.

Another delectable piece of food is the smoked bones we buy at the pet store. They don't splinter like their non-smoked counterparts. The dogs chew on these bones until the smoky part is gone and only a very bare piece of hollow bone remains. What puzzles me is that they continue to chew on these bones regardless of how worn, bare, cracked, jagged, or tasteless they may be after months of daily gnawing. In fact, they fight about these ghoulish items all the time. The good news is that these keep them distracted for long stretches at a time.

Will our dogs grow up to be healthy? Sure. Is it worth getting high-quality dog food after all? I've heard considerable debate on this topic; however, whatever we can do to prolong our canine kids' lives, we will do. Otherwise, why have pets? So, what's a dog owner to do? The very best he can, given the strange appetites these creatures exhibit. This translates into keeping dangerous items ("dangerous" could be anything from shipping materials to cellophane) and liquids away from them and watching what they eat while they play in the yard.

As one of them is having his morning napkin, I wonder why we just don't buy hay. Their fancy, premium, limited-ingredient diet foods are not getting any cheaper. The other one seems to be heading for the cats' litter box. Evil thoughts fly through my mind: If we were to allow this on a regular basis, we would only have to buy food for our cats. Then again, cat food is a primary target of their covert garbage-eating missions, especially for the taller dogs that can reach the kitchen counter by standing on their hind legs.

But back to reality. How do we stop such eating behaviors? We don't. We just keep on picking up old, dried-up bones, toy-animal stuffing, broken twigs, and leaves they bring in from the yard. It's just how dogs are. And we love them, even when they eat a sock or two — or a thirty-dollar check.

— Joe Sainz —

Our Protectors

The Four-Legged Nanny

No animal I know of can consistently be more of a friend and companion than a dog.
~Stanley Leinwoll

A four-legged nanny lived in our house when our daughter Karen was a toddler. Our oversized, male Golden Retriever watched over her like an angel sent by God.

Most Goldens run around seventy-five pounds, but Rusty weighed in at 104. He wasn't overweight, just big. Even so, he was gentle and loving. Rusty, named for the color of his coat, watched and followed Karen in the house. When she'd hold a graham cracker out to him, he'd take it gently. Conversely, if we grown-ups held out food for him, he inhaled it like a heavy-duty vacuum cleaner.

One day, I sensed that our little blond girl was not in the kitchen or family room. Neither was Rusty. I looked out the kitchen window and drew in my breath. Our fenced-in back yard was on two levels with natural stone steps leading from the lower level next to our screened-in porch to the larger open area above. At the highest point, there was about a five-foot drop. When I looked out the kitchen window, I saw Karen on the upper level heading to the edge.

I didn't want to shout and frighten her into losing her balance and toppling headfirst to the ground below. So I started to open the screen door slowly. But then I noticed Rusty beside her, slowly moving to get in front of her and block her from falling over the edge. Not to be deterred, our little miss started to walk to an open spot. Just as quickly, Rusty moved himself in front of her. Wherever she moved, he beat her to it, standing guard.

Finally, she got frustrated and moved to the center of the upper level. I opened the screen door fully and ran up the stone stairs to child and dog. "C'mon, Karen," I said. "Let's go inside and get a cookie." She clapped her hands and then grabbed my outstretched hand, and we made our way down to the house slowly and carefully. Rusty stayed right by her side, moving at her pace, feathered tail wagging.

When we got to the screen door, she let go of my hand and crawled through the doggy door. Rusty followed. Now, I knew how she'd gotten outside without the door banging shut, which would have alerted me long before she made it to the upper level.

By the time I got to the kitchen, Karen and her four-legged nanny were both waiting by the counter for the promised cookie, and I gave one to each of them. I never worried about Karen playing outside after that. Wherever she went, Rusty the nanny followed.

— Nancy Julien Kopp —

Clyde

He is your friend, your partner, your defender, your dog.
You are his life, his love, his leader. He will be yours,
faithful and true, to the last beat of his heart.
~Author Unknown

He was a Saint Bernard mix, an enormous canine weighing 180 pounds. He was the most beautiful dog we had ever seen, a gorgeous shade of reddish gold. He was our new dog, promptly dubbed Clydesdale by my older brother in reference to his size. But he quickly became just Clyde, and the name fit him. It was an easygoing name for a happy-go-lucky dog.

I was barely eleven years old when Clyde entered our lives. Previously, he had belonged to a friend of the family, but that person was moving to an apartment, and Clyde needed a home. Recently married to my stepfather, my mother thought Clyde would be a good dog for all of us — five sons in addition to her and the new husband.

We had a perfect home for Clyde, located in a somewhat rural area. The home boasted a large, fenced-in yard, a quarter of an acre in size, ideal for a big dog. Our neighbors were friendly but not too close, and a few horses grazed in the surrounding fields, sometimes coming to the fence to observe our family and the dog.

It was an idyllic time, a late-1970s picture of life in a large family where there was love, laughter, and the natural combination of rambunctious sons and playful dog... except for one small detail: I was terrified of our big, slobbery dog.

It wasn't that Clyde was rough; in fact, he had a wonderful temperament. He was happy to be part of whatever was going on, whether it was chasing a ball, watching the birds that helped themselves to the food from his dish, or sitting contentedly while someone brushed piles of shedding fur off him. Clyde got along easily with everyone, except me. My fear made me wary, and I spent far less time with him than my brothers did.

Clyde established a fast friendship with the neighbor's dog, a solid-white male German Shepherd mix named Blanco. Clyde and Blanco were inseparable, and it wasn't uncommon to find that one of them had dug under the fence in order to visit the other. We arranged for the dogs to spend time together, but their habit of tunneling under the fence left us befuddled. No matter how often we filled in the holes, they dug new ones… bigger ones.

My mother wondered aloud if the dogs had decided that this was a game that was as much fun for us as it was for them. Personally, I was a little jealous that Clyde and Blanco were such good friends. I really didn't have friends at the private school I attended with two of my brothers. As I turned twelve, I finally understood why I felt different from the other kids. I realized I was gay.

Unfortunately, my peers at school knew it too, or at least suspected it, with that harsh discernment so common in the school environment. Not only was I lacking a friend, but I was tormented at school. Not a day went by when I wasn't bullied, at least verbally, but often physically, too. Despite my growing size, I wasn't a fighter, and I couldn't defend myself. I was a convenient target.

At that time, there wasn't any awareness of bullying, and my rare instances of sharing with adults about what I was going through elicited not a single note of sympathy, but plenty of admonishment about what I was doing wrong…. and how I was the one who needed to change. I was told I should get active in sports and not act like a sissy. No teacher ever stepped in to stop the bullying, although a few joined in the laughter and jeering.

As for my family, this was beyond anything they were prepared for. Their advice wasn't too different from the advice others had given me—I needed to fight back. But I wasn't prepared to fight back against the entire school, including several of the teachers. It was a very different time, and I felt very alone.

I was alone in my bedroom the day I heard the neighbor come to our front door, shouting about Clyde and Blanco. She said she'd figured out why they were so close and dug those holes under the fence to see each other. Clyde and Blanco, she announced loudly, were having a *gay* relationship! Suddenly, I was up and out of my bedroom, bolting quick as a flash into the living room where the neighbor lady continued her loud, amused announcement.

Clearly, our neighbor had had a bit too much wine and was feeling its effects. No one else in my family took what she was saying seriously. But being so young and immature at the time, I took her completely at her word. I was too naive to understand that this revelation on her part was fueled by inebriation more than anything else.

It didn't matter that he was a dog; I finally had someone I could confide in, someone with whom I could share how hard it was to be different and cast out. Maybe Clyde knew what it was like to be gay, too.

He proved to be a good listener.

After that, I lost my fear of our big, majestic Saint Bernard. I spent many hours brushing his red-gold fur and telling him about the latest bullying. It helped to be able to talk about it, even though I never got a verbal reply. But Clyde was always available to listen. If I came out into the yard, even if he was busy digging yet another tunnel under the fence, he stopped and gave me his full attention… along with a side of slobber.

Growing up is never easy, and growing up outside of the mainstream has its own challenges. As I grew older, I found that I really wasn't so alone. I just didn't know that many others were going through the same thing. In fact, plenty of people suffered the same things I did without a friend or confidant. My four-legged friend with the shedding fur was always there, even when everyone else shied away from the kid who was different.

The old adage says a dog is man's best friend, and during a time when the different kid truly needed a friend, Clyde was certainly mine.

— Jack Byron —

Buck

A dog will teach you unconditional love. If you can have that in your life, things won't be too bad.
~Robert Wagner

Had I dreamt that noise? At 1:15 a.m., I couldn't be sure what I'd heard. I nuzzled my snoring five-year-old's ear and placed my feet on cold linoleum. There it was again, and this time there was no mistake. Someone was trying to break in through my back door!

I parted the blinds but saw nothing. Closing the bedroom door, I crept down the hallway. Approaching the kitchen, I heard a pounding noise. The sound was distinct now... clanking metal. I looked out the backdoor window and choked down my scream. It was my new neighbor's son, nineteen and a drug user. He was backlit by my security light, and I saw him wielding a crowbar with fury on his face.

Recently, I had reported his parents to our school district for their refusal to send their third- and fourth-grade sons to school. Instead, they had encouraged them to shoplift at our neighborhood grocery store. Now this kid was out for revenge.

My daughter was still sleeping. After he killed me, what would he do to her? I had only steak knives for defense. I bowed my head and sent up a tearful prayer. "God, send an angel. Watch over us and deliver us. Hold my hand, guide me, and give me strength." Dead silence followed. I had been biting my lip so hard that blood oozed down my neck, and salty tears stung the cuts on my lips. An eerie peacefulness ensued. As I stood in the shadows, I felt a shiver of sudden change. We were not alone. Quietly, I walked toward the window and froze.

The kid lay sprawled on his back, but what stood over him was a mystery. His words were garbled, and his legs flailed about. Whatever was pinning him down seemed in no hurry to release its catch. Then the thing shifted and was illuminated by the security light. It was a massive dog that was growling ferociously and had its jaws around the kid's throat. Suddenly, the dog let go, and the kid got to his feet, swearing, and took off. I never saw him again.

I had never seen this animal before, but he turned to me, staring and waiting. I was too stricken to move right away but gradually warmed up to him due to his patience. With caution, I cracked open the back door but kept tight the screen door. He never flinched. Then I opened the screen door by inches. Again, he did not flinch. Moving like molasses and gauging his body language, I opened the door wider. He seemed to read my trepidation and waited for my invitation. I took another step and quietly called to him. He slowly advanced, gingerly, and then stopped short of my feet on the top step, laid his head on them and let out a huge sigh.

Gooey, milk-chocolate eyes locked with mine and held my stare. I should have been wary of this big, fierce warrior, but I felt no reservations when I clutched him in a bear hug. From where he came, I cannot say, but I knew where his future lay.

My little one slept peacefully through the night and awoke to find this massive dog licking her face. She laughed uproariously and begged to keep him, and I told her that had "already been decided." She asked if Santa came in May, and I said, "He sure did last night." She said he needed a name and christened him "Buck."

By 8 a.m. we were at the vet's office. We learned that Buck was between seven and nine years old, and that this 112-pound gentle giant was a Doberman/Hound mix. We headed to the pet store for Buck's introduction to shopping and left there loaded down and penniless. Buck was worth every cent!

That evening, we three strolled the yard. My neighbor, Gary, had just cut our grass, and I noticed a faint path worn around my house's perimeter. Buck fell in line with the path and began to walk it slowly. I sensed his familiarity with the outline when he did not sniff for traces of other animals; his actions were deliberate, as though on guard.

Shortly, Gary waved to us and crossed into our yard. Introductions were made, and Gary said, "I've seen him before. Sometimes, when I take a late-night stroll, I see him circling your house. He does it for hours." Stunned, I had no words. How could I have missed this? Buck knew us already and had literally placed a protective boundary around our home. That night, we put an extra steak on the grill.

Buck's days became routine: love, gourmet cuisine, belly rubs, naps, and more love. He wanted for nothing. We held an elaborate birthday party for him monthly, sometimes mailing invitations to my daughter's friends. Buck held her in high esteem, and he was her gentle protector. His handsome face graced our Christmas cards, and the ice-cream-truck lady always had a SpongeBob Popsicle ready for him. Sometimes, his inner hound dog came out, and he would coo us to sleep by the light of the moon. Life was unimaginable without him—until one night in January.

The vet said his heart's blockage was the worst she'd ever seen. With his breathing raspy and labored, I knew I had to let go of my selfishness. I held him tightly and kissed him as he left our lives, the same way I had when he entered five years earlier. Gary dug his grave under our crab-apple tree, and another neighbor, Andy, fashioned a roughhewn wooden cross. My blessed angel had gone home.

—Nancy Gail Collins—

Holding on for Dear Life

The poor dog, in life the firmest friend.
The first to welcome, foremost to defend.
~Lord Byron

The horrific noise stopped me dead in my tracks. Fear shot through me for I knew that sound well.

I hadn't seen the rattlesnake that passed behind my feet. When I left the dog kennel, he'd slithered in and now sat coiled, in striking position, next to our Huskies' water bucket. With no time to spare, I squeezed through the door and prayed he wouldn't bite me. Rattlesnakes can stretch one-third to one-half their length, and this guy was fairly long and within striking range.

I'm no football player, but I dove through the air, tackling Eska in the nick of time as she lunged for the snake. I locked my hands around her neck, fingers clasped, and held on for dear life, but it took all my strength.

Eska is a bubbly and friendly Husky, but I hardly recognized her. She curled her lips, growling and snarling as if possessed.

Both of our Huskies were lovable goofballs who had always snubbed every command we'd ever tried to teach them. Therefore, it came as no surprise when Eska ignored my pleas to sit and stay.

"Help!" I screamed as loud as I could. "Rattlesnake!" I had high hopes that my sons, who were inside the house, would hear me and come to the rescue.

The beautiful but dangerous snake rattled away in striking position, but now he stretched his upper body higher. Still fighting to keep hold of Eska, I caught a glimpse of Igome behind us.

Igome and Eska were great friends but also competitors. Whatever one dog did, the other had to follow. Their competitive nature had gotten them in a lot of trouble over the years. At that moment, I couldn't believe Igome had remained in a far corner, burying the bone I'd given him only minutes ago when I'd left their kennel.

As if reading my thoughts, Igome approached from behind. I could feel my heart thumping in my chest as I tried to figure out what to do. It took everything I had to hang on to Eska, so I couldn't grab Igome. How could I choose which dog to save? I'd often heard that the bigger the person or animal, the better the chance of surviving a snakebite. Igome was larger, so he would have to take the fall.

Horrible thoughts filled my head. Our neighbors had gone on vacation. My husband was at work and had taken our only car. The pet hospital was an hour away. If he were bitten, Igome might die before we could get help.

I had to try to stop him. "No, Igome! Sit! Stay, boy! Please..." But he refused to listen. By this time, tears were streaming down my face. When he brushed my side, I couldn't bear to watch. I closed my eyes, waiting for the sickening scream that would soon follow.

And then I felt a glorious sensation — Igome's tongue as he licked away my tears. He nestled his head into the crook of my neck as if trying to tell me all was well. It astounded me when he sat and then stayed, continuing to lick my face while I wrestled with Eska.

It felt like forever before my sons arrived and removed the snake. Eska went wild, sniffing the dirt where the snake had been and racing around like a crazy dog. But Igome remained by my side, comforting me until I calmed down.

That day, Igome was forgiven for all the times he'd ignored my commands. When I needed him most, our goofy, lovable Husky came through like a hero.

— Jill Burns —

Morning Walk

My little dog — a heartbeat at my feet.
~Edith Wharton

I awoke early one Sunday morning, as I often did. The house was quiet. Only my faithful Airedale Terrier, Willie, was awake. He and I were both three years old. Large even by Airedale standards, Willie weighed at least four times as much as I did.

"I bet you're hungry," I said to him, tired of sitting on the floor stroking his side. I was going to be a grown-up and take care of the dog. So, I gave him his morning dog biscuit. "Good boy," I said. Willie wagged his tail.

Sitting back on the floor with him, I felt pretty proud of myself. I might have been the youngest in the family, but I could still do things… like feed the dog. I smiled. My brothers had to let me do other things, too, like play blocks and cards with them, and read books.

Suddenly, it hit me.

"Uh-oh," I said, standing up. Dad always took Willie for a walk around the block after his breakfast. Sometimes, I went with him, running nearly the entire way on my little legs. My greatest triumph was about to become the worst thing I'd ever done. What if Willie had an accident in the house? It would be my fault.

There was only one thing to do. It never occurred to me to wake anyone. I'd created this problem; I was going to solve it. I felt even bigger. Unfortunately, all those feelings didn't make me tall enough to reach the leash. Well, I could reach it all right. But I couldn't get it off the hook that taunted me several feet above my head.

After yanking and swinging the leash so many times I lost count, it finally fell free, clinking to the floor. It truly was a wonder that all the noise didn't wake someone.

Willie held perfectly still while I put on his leash. If Dad was his master, Willie was my faithful companion. I was sure he understood the momentous occasion; he would behave for me as I proved myself worthy.

Our house was on the corner at the top of a hill. A walk always began downhill and ended uphill. Going out the front door, I turned right, immediately rounding the first corner. We passed our garage and then walked on to the neighbor's house. Willie kept pace with me. It was pretty brisk, but for Willie it must have felt slow.

"This is fun," I said. "Good boy." He stayed right by my side. We turned the second corner and continued our journey down to the far corner of the block. As my house got farther away, I got nervous. We were almost there—the farthest point from home. My feet slowed. What was I thinking?

"Maybe we should turn around," I whispered. The corner drew closer. It was just as far to keep going as it was to turn around. "Come on, boy, let's get this over with." I ran the last few steps to the corner and then kept running, now up the sidewalk.

Halfway up the street, I stopped dead in my tracks.

A big, nasty part-Doberman stood on alert on the other side of the street. He was as mean as his owner, only this morning he was on his own. Nothing stood between him and Willie. Nothing but me. How could I protect my dog?

I wasn't just thinking about how to keep that mongrel away from Willie. I knew that Willie could decide to charge after the dog. I'd seen him tear after rabbits and squirrels behind our house. And it dawned on me that if Willie decided to cross the street, there wasn't much I'd be able to do about it.

As all these thoughts formed in my young brain, Willie put himself between me and the other dog. Growling a deep, low warning, Willie didn't take his eyes off the dog as he nudged me home, his loyalty for me stronger than anything else he might have felt. We shuffled forward slowly as if any sudden movement might cause the dog to attack us.

When we were even with the dog, Willie and I began to speed up simultaneously. Finally, we were around the last corner, the other dog out of sight.

"Good boy, Willie. Almost home. Look, right up there," I said to comfort myself. I knew it was there, just out of sight.

The yard came into view first, and my pace quickened. And then I saw them; my family appeared on the sidewalk looking for us. I ran full out, letting go of the leash as I dove into my mother's comforting arms. I had done it. We were safe.

"Good boy, Willie," Dad praised him. "You did a good job taking care of her, didn't you?"

I smiled, glad to be home and safe in Mom's arms. I didn't even mind that Willie seemed to be the center of attention. It took me years to learn what they already knew: I hadn't taken Willie out that day; he'd taken me.

—D. B. Zane—

A Family of Four

Our pets are our family.
~Ana Monnar

"Squirrels!" He whined at the back door, waiting for me to let him loose. He was desperate to go after those squirrels at the bird feeder. "Go get 'em!" I said, swinging the door open, knowing there was no chance he would ever catch one. With all his pent-up energy, my three-year-old mutt Bucky was faster than me, his speed and agility no match for my sprint to the big bay window to watch him running and jumping in circles at the base of the bird-feeder pole.

I wondered if the squirrels egged him on through the window each day when I was at work. I had never seen such determination for such a fruitless endeavor day after day.

My dogs loved it when I was home. We spent as much time outdoors as we could, going for walks and exploring the woods and fields around our house. We lived on a dead-end dirt road at the edge of the airport and visitors were almost nonexistent.

The dogs were well-trained. They came when called, sat when asked, and lay down when told. They knew they couldn't go in the kitchen; they didn't bother the cats; they never ran away. The past few months had been challenging for them. There was a new baby in the house, and they didn't have as much time with me as they once had. They were curious about the baby, and when he fussed, they walked with me to the crib to investigate what all the noise was about.

It was my off day in early fall. I brought the playpen outside so my three-month-old son and I could enjoy the fresh air, and my two buddies could explore and stretch their legs. We hadn't been as active as we had before the baby.

I sat in my lounge chair by the playpen and stretched my legs. The summer heat was fading, yet the midday sunlight lifted our spirits. I was a young, single mother, exhausted from parenting and working, and wondering how I was going to manage. While my son slept, my two dogs poked their noses around the yard, sniffing at this or that while I read a book. We were all appreciating the weather, peace and sunshine, and being together.

From time to time, I would look up, watching all my boys. Sparky, a black Labrador Retriever, and Bucky, a Dalmatian look-alike, loved to patrol the flower beds looking for bees and squirrels. Sparky would sit at attention for hours next to the purple rhododendron bush and wait. I'd watch his head tip left or right as he listened keenly. Then, he would dive into the bush, capture the unsuspecting fat bumblebee and shake his head furiously trying to spit out the offender. He would repeat this all day long if I let him. After he got one, he would go back to being on guard, waiting for his next opportunity.

Not wanting him to get stung or any bees to die, I called over to him, and he came happily. Scratching his back, I spoke conspiratorially with him. "Did you get that mean old bee? Are you okay? Let me see your mouth." He sat patiently as I looked, glad of my attention. Assuring myself that he was okay, I let him go, and he sauntered back to his stakeout, waiting for the next victim. There was no stopping him.

Never wanting to feel left out, Bucky came to see what all the excitement was about. He loved his belly rubs, so I spent a few minutes making him happy. Finally having enough and noticing a treat was not part of the offering, he went back on his walkabout, eventually settling in the shade of the maple tree.

The phone rang, and I went inside to take the call. I stood at the back hallway's window that looked over the yard and the playpen. After a minute, I saw Bucky stand and look toward the back wooden fence. I watched, intrigued. Sparky left his rhododendron-bush duty and went to stand next to Bucky. He looked at the fence and then back toward the house. I believe he saw me standing in the window. He turned as if to say to Bucky, "I'll be back," and then walked to the playpen and sat, still watching the wooden fence.

Then Bucky barked and stood at full attention. Sparky stood purposefully and echoed the bark. Again, he looked back at me. I hung up the phone, wondering what was going on. Opening the door, I stood on the top step, looking around. I suspected an animal had them riled. I could hear a low warning growl from Bucky and noticed the fur at the top of his shoulders stood on end, much like an angry cat. The growl turned to a menacing, warning bark. It was a sound I had never heard from him before. Suddenly, I felt scared.

Sparky wasn't sure if he should stay next to the baby or go help his buddy.

"What is it, boy? What do you see?"

He looked from me to the fence.

"Go get 'em!" I whispered.

He was off like a shot. Not to miss out on the action, Bucky ran with him.

They both charged the fence, and I heard a man scream. I saw two heads pop up, and then fall away. By then, I had picked up the baby.

"I would suggest you leave because you do not want them jumping over the fence and taking you down," I yelled.

"We're leaving! We're leaving! Call them off!" a man yelled.

"I'm calling the cops now," I responded loudly.

I could see their heads backing away.

"We meant no harm. We were just going to cut through."

"This is private property — no cut-throughs allowed. I am calling the cops, so I would suggest you leave now!" I yelled again. The dogs barked loudly as if they were chasing the men.

I went into the house and called 911, leaving the dogs by the fence. Police officers arrived a few minutes later. My dogs sat in the yard, unleashed and not moving. The officers couldn't find the men after searching but did let me know that two men had escaped the nearby halfway house. The men were considered unstable and had mental-health issues.

My bumblebee and squirrel chasers had chased away some potentially dangerous men and protected their family. They had stood on guard for the baby. I knew then that they accepted little Matthew as one of their own. We had become a family of four.

— Kristine Benevento —

Couper

The one absolutely unselfish friend that man can have
in this selfish world, the one that never deserts him,
the one that never proves ungrateful
or treacherous, is his dog.
~George Graham

My family has always been a big fan of the Boxer breed. I've had several of them over the years, and they are incredibly sweet, affectionate, eager-to-please and energetic dogs. The way they swing their whole backside into a U shape with excitement, how they lean against people for pats, make it hard to remember that Boxers were originally bred to be guard dogs.

When I was a teenager, our family had a dog named Couper, a particularly affectionate Boxer. He loved people and attention, and he was convinced that he was a lap dog. It made things a little difficult at times since he was over seventy pounds, but he was just so happy to be cuddling with someone that we powered through the numb legs.

We were fortunate to live near a huge park in those days, and Couper and I often walked there several times a day. He needed an outlet for all that energy.

One August night, we went out for our last walk a bit late. The path through the park was well-lit and in a very safe suburb, so I wasn't concerned.

There was a stretch of the path that was parallel to the roadway, separated only by a few feet of grass. While we were walking down that particular stretch, I realized a car was following us. It slowed down to our walking speed and stayed even with us for more than a block. I started to get nervous.

I was alone. I didn't have a cell phone in those days. There was no one in the park or on the street other than me, the car's occupants, and Couper.

He was a great dog, but we'd chosen him partially because of how friendly and easygoing he was. For all intents and purposes, he was a dog-shaped sponge, just waiting to soak up love and affection. He wouldn't be of any use in a confrontation.

Or, at least, that's what I thought.

The car continued to follow us. I couldn't see who was inside, just that there was more than one person. I didn't know if turning around would do any good. I'd still have to walk all the way back to my house. To get help from any of the nearby houses, I'd have to cross the street.

Couper had been trotting along by my side quite happily. Walk time was his favourite, second only to mealtime, and he enjoyed having a good sniff of the boulevard.

I don't know if my body language, a tension in the leash, or a combination of the two tipped him off, but he started turning his head to look at me. Just a glance every few steps, just checking in. When I didn't relax, he started looking around.

I was debating whether to head deeper into the park to get away from the road when my sweet, even-tempered dog decided he'd had enough.

He turned toward the car on the road, planted his front paws, bulldogged out his chest, and peeled his lips back from his teeth.

And snarled.

I froze. I didn't know what to do.

All the hair on Couper's spine stood on end. He barked and continued to snarl. Then he put his body between me and that car and faced them down.

The car drove away.

Couper waited until the taillights vanished around a corner, gave a little triumphant sneeze, and started trotting along again. As far as he was concerned, it was settled.

I think I was more shocked at his Cujo impression than I was by anything else, but I followed his lead.

I don't know who was in the car or what might have happened that night, but I do know a dog who got far too many treats and biscuits before his bedtime.

—A.L. Tompkins—

Gypsy

Gratitude; my cup overfloweth.
~Author Unknown

A few years ago, we adopted an adorable Rat Terrier whom we named Gypsy. She was a rescue, so we didn't know her age, background, or how she ended up wandering the streets of a large southern city with no collar or tags. But we felt sure she'd had a difficult life, as she cringed whenever we approached her with a hand out. She seemed particularly afraid of strange men.

Gradually, Gypsy adapted to her new home with us, and she followed me around like a little shadow... a silent one. Nothing seemed to prompt her to bark or growl, but we assumed she was just a quiet dog as she seemed happy with us otherwise.

Not long after we brought her home, I had hip-replacement surgery. Gypsy seemed to resent the coming and going of physical therapists, occupational therapists, and visiting nurses—especially the males. She was still silent, but she snapped at the ones she liked least. This led us to believe it must have been a male who had mistreated her previously.

One day about a year after my surgery, I was in the bathroom giving Gypsy a bath. I finished and lifted her out of the tub, and then turned back to gather up the towels. Suddenly, something snapped in my hip, and I crashed to the floor. Luckily, I fell between the tub and sink. Had I hit one of them, I feel certain that would have been the end of me.

Unfortunately, I had no way to summon help. The door was closed, and I didn't have my phone with me. My husband wouldn't be home from work for hours, so I did the only thing I could think of: I started screaming for help as loudly as I could.

Gypsy was clearly confused by my screams, shivering and shaking, but after a few minutes, she did the only thing she knew to do — she lay down with her (wet) back pressed against mine. It comforted us both. She licked me now and then, as if trying to reassure me all would be well.

After an hour had passed, and my throat was hoarse and rough from shouting, I heard a voice outside that sounded like an angel. "Do you need help?" It was my next-door neighbor, who had just come home and heard my shouts.

"Yes! I've fallen, and I think I dislocated my hip!" I called. "I'm in the bathroom upstairs."

Soon, my neighbor was in the house. Luckily, she was an EMT, so she knew just who to call and what to do. I was so thankful for help but worried about Gypsy. She didn't like strangers, and the ambulance crew was mainly male. "What about my dog?" I asked my neighbor. She assured me she'd take care of her after the ambulance took me away.

I expected Gypsy to freak out with all the strange men in the house, but she seemed to realize they were there to help me. I said goodbye to her, and she tried to follow me, but my neighbor shut her in a bedroom as the EMTs carried me on the stretcher down the steep staircase and into the waiting ambulance.

In the ER, they ran all the necessary tests and knocked me out so they could force my hip back into the socket. With pain pills, I was able to go home later that day. No sooner did I get into the house than Gypsy came running. She was beside herself with glee to see me at home, jumping and bouncing, and I was delighted to see her as well.

Since then, she has appointed herself my guardian and companion. I can't even use the bathroom without her following me. Oh, and her silence? That's gone; she barks now with great gusto whenever she hears someone enter, and then looks at me for praise. And given what she went through with me, how could I withhold it? She's my bright-eyed, black-and-white heroine. We rescued her, but she in turn rescued me. Who could ask for more?

— Elizabeth Delisi —

Lifesaver

You see, sometimes in life, the best thing
for all that ails you has fur and four legs.
~Mark J. Asher, All That Ails You

On April 30, 2018, I was nervous and alone with a new dog in a hotel room in Concord, California. I had made the decision to get a diabetic alert dog after living with diabetes since 1974. I was assigned a petite, black Labrador/Golden Retriever mix named Laurene. She was to sleep at the side of my bed, and then we would return in the morning to Early Alert Canines for training.

I went to bed at 11 p.m. At 2 a.m., the dog jumped onto my bed, waking me by licking and pawing me. It dawned on me that I should look at my insulin pump, since I had not heard any alarms. When I looked, it said PUMP FAILED at 11:08 p.m. I had no insulin delivery, and there were no blood-sugar readings on the pump. I did a fingerstick test, and it said "High." It took four hours with insulin injections to get a 388 reading, meaning that my level had been dangerously high! Without Laurene, I could have lapsed into a coma or even died. Laurene had just been introduced to me, but she had already saved my life!

Laurene has loving, concerned, caring eyes that stare at me as if to say, "Check your sugar," just prior to giving me a gentle paw, as if to say, "I detect the chemical change. Do something before you can't function." If I am sleeping and cannot get this message, she will jump on the bed and lick my face to wake me and make sure I take care of the situation. I used to set the alarm to wake up every two hours to check my sugar, but with the confidence I have in Laurene, I can now sleep through the night.

Laurene is relentless, yet gentle and loving. She does not have an "off button" and will continue to alert me until the sugar is under control. Even if Laurene is in the middle of playing with a toy, she will drop it and be at my side.

She has changed my life with her kind, silent way of nudging me. It's different from having a nagging husband or doctor saying I must check my blood sugar. She is a sweet friend doing her job with eyes that melt my heart at the same time she is improving my life. My dog makes me smile and laugh every day while doing something magical — saving my life.

— Marcia Lee Harris —

On This Night

It is astonishing how little one feels alone
when one loves.
~John Bulwer

Lincoln was about six months old when he was taken home from a local animal shelter by a well-intentioned married couple. But shortly thereafter, the pup's new life fell apart. His adoptive humans quit their marriage, and Lincoln was relegated to an outdoor kennel. He was fed and watered daily, and the kennel was kept clean. But as Lincoln's newly single parent was distracted by life, there was little human interaction.

On my occasional trips to this small farm, I always looked forward to visiting the kennel for a rendezvous with Linc. He was a handsome, buff-colored Husky/Shepherd mix. His dreary existence seemed forgotten during our visits; his joyful exuberance could not, or would not, be contained. Frequently, I thought about taking him home with me. But I was young, busy, had a kitty named Trina, and was living in an urban apartment.

After much consideration and some months of visits, I finally popped the question. Lincoln's owner was relieved by my request to take the dog off his hands.

Within an hour or two of returning to our small apartment, it was clear that the honeymoon was over. I had always lived with dogs while growing up, and I understood there was work to do. If Lincoln had ever been housebroken, he had forgotten about it during his kennel tenure.

These were our first lessons, and I was grateful for his willingness and ability to learn. Obedience classes gave us more skills to develop, and life with Lincoln became tolerably civilized within several months. Over time, he became a well-behaved and loyal companion, and he and Trina adored each other.

They were both with me almost constantly. My job at the time allowed me to take Lincoln along most days. Trina came with us on many outings, as she was almost doglike. She trotted along on hikes, and loved car rides, new places to explore, and new people to meet.

Lincoln, Trina, and I had been a threesome for a year or two when a friend made an interesting offer. If I were to help her plant five thousand blueberry bushes on her rural property in the spring, she would allow me to camp there for the summer. Open for adventure, I accepted.

The blueberries were planted as soon as the ground thawed. My job was to ride an antique trenching/planting machine—which was pulled along behind an equally antique tractor—and rhythmically place each little twig of a plant into the parting earth. The cool of the season and the vista of verdant hillsides made the work a joy.

As far as Lincoln was concerned, life could not have been brighter. Sometimes pacing along beside the tractor, sometimes scaring up a ring-necked pheasant or grouse, sometimes chasing rabbits, he always made sure to stay within sight. These were rich days.

With the arrival of warm weather, I set up camp. I got a job in town and didn't get home each evening until after dark. My parking spot was nestled amid a small stand of trees and thick brush. It was close to the county road, but out of sight of the few cars that traveled by after sunset. I always looked forward to the half-mile hike up to the secluded spot that was our summer home.

This area was sparsely populated in the 1970s. Any predators that might threaten dogs and cats had long ago been hunted out. Trina and Lincoln stayed at camp while I was gone. They had access to the inside of the tent, food, and water. And they had each other.

Upon arrival at the property after work one summer night, I turned off the headlights, only to find that it was pitch black. My hand was barely visible right in front of me. Usually, I carried a lantern in the car, but I had not done so on this night. Ordinarily, the sky provided enough light, illuminating at least the open areas of the walk to the tent. I hesitated before heading up to camp, pondering the uncertainties of the walk ahead of me.

The first stage was easier than anticipated. Warm air comforted me, and a well-worn footpath through waist-high grasses provided a channel to follow across the lower meadow.

The next stage was marked by my arrival at a thick hedgerow of saplings and brush that bordered the fields of blueberry plants. I was greeted by the rich, familiar smell of recently cultivated earth. I began my trek up the hill, knowing that as long as I stayed within reach of firm saplings, not straying into the fields, I would stay on course.

When the hedgerow ended at a broad band of older growth trees, I stopped. I had reached the final stage: a heavily wooded swath that sheathed a thirty-foot-deep ravine. The sides of the ravine held rocks, trees, and thick brush. At the bottom splashed a brook—the source of our water. The air had turned chilly and damp. On other nights, I followed a narrow, winding path that skirted the top edge of the ravine, the point at which I usually turned on a lantern.

I had not been in the habit of calling Lincoln from the bottom of the hill, wanting to reinforce his habit of staying home when I wasn't there. But on this night—confronting what seemed a daunting final stage—I called for him. He was at my side in a flash. We expressed our mutual delight over being back in each other's company, with my fingers reveling in the warmth of his silky coat. Our enthusiastic hugs and kisses lasted several minutes. With greetings over, I explained my problem. Then, firmly wrapping my hand around his collar and covering my face with my free arm, I said, "Lincoln, take me home."

I felt the power and confidence of his seventy-pound frame as he gently led me forward. His stride was slow, deliberate, and steady. He hesitated patiently each time I needed to navigate branches, brush, and rocks. Any sense of time and space was blurred. I'm not sure how long we wove our way through trees and woody brush before he stopped. I said again, "Lincoln, take me home." He stood firm.

Stepping forward cautiously, something caught my leg. I uncovered my face and reached out to search the darkness, while still clinging to Lincoln's collar with my other hand. Within inches of where I stood, I touched a familiar wall of cool nylon, tethered by the taut rope that was pressed against my calf. Trina said hello. We were home.

— Barbara Woods —

Chapter 4

Life Lessons from the Dog

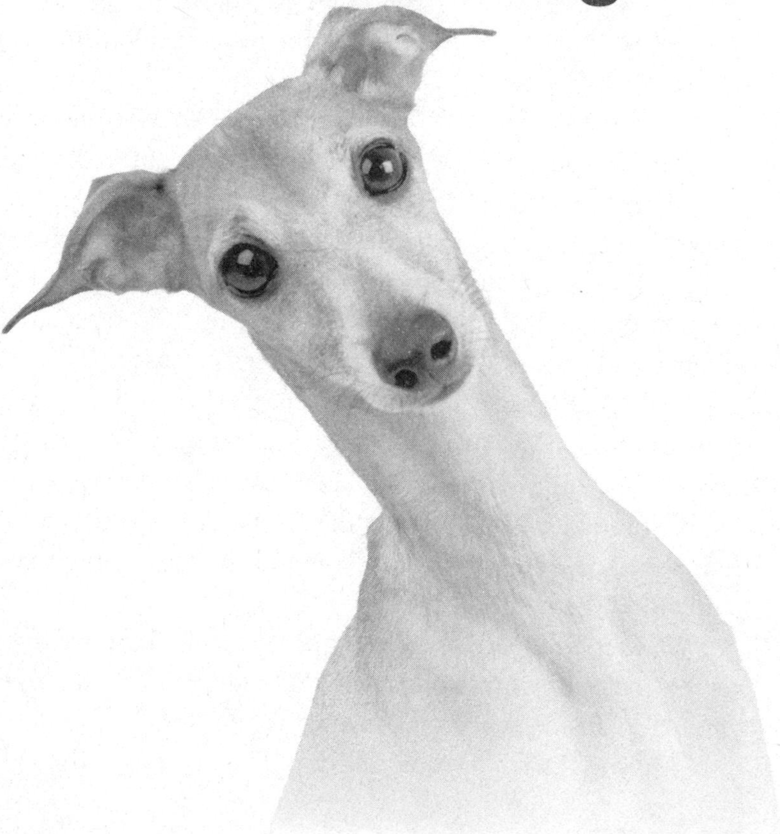

Interpretive Agility

When a dog show is over, whether you've won or lost doesn't matter. As long as you've gone home with the best dog, everything's fine.
~Pat Tetrault

"Why don't you enter Kedzie in the agility trial that is coming up?" my instructor asked me one week during class.

"Oh," I said, surprised. "I'm not sure we're ready."

"I think you could both handle a beginner course," Cindy said.

My mind conjured up images of Kedzie, my rescue Shih Tzu, and me performing course after flawless course like perfectly choreographed dancers. I knew I would be extremely nervous putting myself in the spotlight, but on the other hand, I had a strong desire to have Kedzie compete and earn titles like the other dogs in class.

I brought the entry form to class the next week to ask my instructor what we should sign up for. Together, we picked out one beginner class to start with, which was all I felt I could handle. Even just filling out the information and writing the check for the entry fee made my heart speed up and my hands sweat and shake so badly that I could hardly hold the pen.

We were prepped, primped, and overpacked for our big debut. I was very nervous when we arrived, but I found a friend there attending with her husband, who competes with their dog.

"Are you ready?" Donna asked.

"I don't know if I can do this." I confided a long list of my worries about tripping, forgetting where to go, or calling out the wrong commands.

"Don't worry," Donna said. "Remember, everyone out there has been in your shoes before. They've all been beginners, too. Just have fun." She helped me interpret the course map and reviewed it with me until I heard the steward call Kedzie's name to come to the in-gate.

I walked to the start line as if being carried helplessly by a fast current, knowing the rapids were just around the bend.

"Run fast, run clean!" Donna called after us.

I looked at her one more time, hoping she'd throw me a lifeline. I positioned Kedzie in front of the first jump. I tried to take deep, calming breaths. The sweet odor of the polymer floor mats filled my lungs and made me slightly dizzy. The fluorescent lighting seemed to glow brighter by the millisecond. As I waited for the signal to start, I knew my parents would be proud that their money spent on my twelve years of Catholic education was being put to good use, as I mentally recited every prayer I could remember. The electronic voice startled me out of my incantations. "Go!" it commanded.

My frantic fingers fumbled as I bent down to remove Kedzie's collar. "Sit," I pleaded with him. I heard the Heavenly Chorus sing as Kedzie sat! He locked his shiny brown eyes on mine with the focus of a chess player contemplating his winning move. He perched ever so lightly on his haunches, like a lion waiting to spring on his dinner. We licked our lips simultaneously. I could tell he was thinking, *Let's do this, Mom.* The weight of a thousand Greyhounds was lifted off my shoulders. *I got this,* I thought. I felt a moment of peace and was able to breathe as I stood up to begin our course. At that same moment, Kedzie was gone.

Kedzie cleared the first jump like a Grand Prix thoroughbred, which started the timer, and he left me at the start line. My leaden feet were melted to the ground; we didn't cover this in class! I began to sprint after him and realized Kedzie was running me through the course, instead of me running him. Clearly, he was enjoying himself, galloping lap after joyous lap, his furry little legs digging into the ground. I followed behind in some bizarre game of chase that reminded me of old-fashioned slapstick comedy. Kedzie even managed to jump a few jumps and go through a couple of tunnels along the way with no coaching from me. After several rounds, he buzzed over to the exit gate, obviously satisfied with his turn. Donna caught him and handed him to me.

"Well," she said, "at least he got the run fast part right."

I realized I had fretted needlessly about tripping over a shoelace or forgetting what came next. Never once did I consider what Kedzie might do. He looked up at me as if to ask, "How did I do, Mom?"

I gave him a big hug. "You did a good job, buddy."

Even though that first show didn't go the way I imagined, it gave me the confidence to keep trying. The worst-case scenario came true, in a way that never occurred to me, but I survived! We have gotten better, but every so often Kedzie still performs what I call his "interpretive agility." Now, instead of freezing up, I laugh at the sheer enjoyment he expresses in the moment. He puts smiles on the faces of all who watch him, and he has quite the reputation. The more people who watch him, the more creative he gets, as he appreciates an audience. I am blessed to learn from my dog, both in and out of the agility ring. He has taught me to enjoy the present, not take myself too seriously, make smiles whenever I can, and run, jump, and play whenever the mood strikes.

—Amy Rovtar Payne—

A Place to Call Her Own

Home is where we should feel secure and comfortable.
~Catherine Pulsifer

One of the positive aspects of staying home during the pandemic was having the time to deep-clean our house. Spring cleaning hadn't been this intense in years. One day, after my son, Johnny, had finished cleaning his room, he decided to tackle the Chihuahua "home": a long, thin box that once housed a Christmas tree. Johnny had insisted that the Chihuahuas needed a safe place to call their own.

At the time, I grumbled, as I saw it as a rather large box with ugly holes cut in it, sitting beneath a table in the living room. When I suggested he paint it, he shrugged his shoulders. He didn't want it to be too "girly." Instead, he went about cleaning out the debris our two Chihuahuas had carried into their box.

I went back to my task, working nearby just in case he finished his self-appointed job and decided to sneak out the door before I could give him anything else to do. I was appalled by the amount of trash and junk he found hidden in the box.

Wrappers, fruit peelings (stolen from the compost bin), a blanket, and various toys that had disappeared were all hidden in there. It was impressive that our two Chihuahuas could fit in there, too. I became so engrossed in watching my son pull out item after item that it became a game of "How did she get that in there?" or "When did she do that?" I forgot about anything else.

When my son pulled out Dibble's favorite toy, a squeaky frog, she jumped off the back of the couch where she had been watching. She started whining at his elbow. My interest shifted from the horrors hidden in the box to Dibble's reaction to her daddy cleaning out her space. The tiny blond Chihuahua whined as she paced from one side of Johnny to the other. Being on the autism spectrum, Johnny was absorbed in his task and didn't notice.

As Johnny began throwing away the handfuls of trash, Dibble became frantic, complaining and scratching at Johnny's leg. When he didn't respond, she took her favorite frog, ran to Johnny's room and sat on his bed, whimpering while wrapping herself around her treasured toy. It hit me that the little puppy was attached to the way things were. Dibble and her sister Belle had worked hard on this collection and now Daddy was throwing it all away!

The emptier the box became, the more desperate she was. Finally, feeling bad for her, I pointed out that maybe Dibble needed a compromise. Johnny acquiesced. Replacing the blanket, toys, and a few (clean) wrappers, Johnny put the box back in its spot beneath the table. Lastly, he tucked Dibble's frog under the blanket and invited Dibble to go inside. Dibble didn't need to be told twice! She slipped through the small opening and disappeared into the dark box. A moment later, I saw a flash of butterscotch-colored fur slip through the opening. Belle, who had been silently watching the drama, joined her sister.

After helping my son dispose of the remaining contraband and Chihuahua-proof the compost bin, I finally had time to sit down. Looking across at the "eyesore" Chihuahua home, I was surprised to see Belle's sweet little face in the opening. At a closer look, Dibble sat behind her sister, watchful of the activity in the room. I had to laugh despite myself. I had planned on getting rid of the box because I didn't see a need for it. After all, Belle and Dibble are tiny dogs that take great pleasure in curling up with my son and me. I had never seen them stay inside the box for more than a half-hour at a time. What was the sense in keeping an old box that took up space?

Now I realize that even if the girls only used the box for thirty minutes a day, it was still their place — a sacred place just for them.

Being forced into close proximity with family can be difficult, and sometimes it feels nearly impossible to get along. But with the help of our Chihuahuas, I realized the secret to remaining calm, loving, and loyal in the face of the unknown is a space of our own. With an area (be it as big as a room or as small as a corner) and a dedicated time to separate ourselves, our home has become more peaceful and filled with laughter. Who knew a tiny dog could teach us such a magnificent lesson?

— Kitty Larousse —

My Mom's Last Gift

When an eighty-five-pound mammal licks your tears away, then tries to sit on your lap, it's hard to feel sad.
~Kristan Higgins

I wasn't ready to lose my mom. Even though she'd been sick for a year, it was inconceivable. "Of course, she'll get better," I'd comforted myself after the second diagnosis. She'd already done it once.

She was my favorite person in the world. Sure, we butted heads occasionally as mothers and daughters do, but hardly a day went by without exchanging a call or text. I ran nearly all decisions — career moves, clothing purchases, and dinner choices — past her. She was the first person I craved when I needed comfort. She was always telling me how much she loved me. I even had it tattooed on my arm in her handwriting.

My world was knocked off its axis when she died. And so much was left undone. We hadn't gone wedding-dress shopping. She hadn't taught me how to take care of a newborn.

In the months following my mom's death, I gave up on happiness. But there was a way out, a final gift from my mom: her dog Cooper. She picked him out at the Humane Society just two years before her passing. Could she have known how much I would need him?

Caring for Cooper became my responsibility. Keeping a dog alive at a time when I can barely take care of myself hasn't been easy, but it's made my life full. Who would have thought a creature who can't talk would have so much to tell me?

Each morning, Cooper wakes me with the reliability of an alarm clock. When I resist his efforts to stir me by retreating under the covers, he becomes more insistent, whining and slapping my bed with his tail. Even when I'd rather not, he makes me get out of bed and see the world.

I watch him live in the moment, greeting each passing dog like a long-lost friend. What looks to me like a basic one-way street and crumbling sidewalk is an exotic safari for Cooper. Cooper sees each new day as full of possibility. Despite having no control over his daily routine, he finds joy in each activity. He lives in the moment, free of worries and regrets. He revels in each action as if experiencing it for the first time, even though we've walked this route dozens of times or this is the 517th time he's eaten this kibble.

I realize that I never knew how to be truly happy. For me, happiness had always been the next promotion or international vacation, shared on social media through dozens of carefully selected photos. The time between these highlights was just a drudgery to get through. I'd been moving through the world on autopilot.

Through Cooper's example, a chilly morning walk is a meditation on the beauty of nature. A subway delay becomes a great time to jot an entry into my gratitude journal. A long line at the grocery-store checkout offers an opportunity to hear a favorite song on the radio.

Cooper doesn't let past failures inhibit him. While fear of yet another rejection holds me back from applying for jobs, he's unplagued by self-doubt. He didn't catch the squirrel yesterday, but that doesn't matter. Today could be the day! He keeps looking, hunting, and trying. His message is clear: Never give up.

Today is the only special occasion he needs. He adores squeaky toys, but doesn't hesitate to rip them to shreds, his favorite activity. I once hung on to a special perfume for years, waiting for the perfect moment to wear it. When I finally opened the frosted pink glass decanter, it had dried up. I didn't get to use it at all. Cooper doesn't decide some toys are more precious than others, so he gets full enjoyment from each one.

My furry guru isn't afraid to go after his desires. One day, I stopped to get breakfast at a local bakery. I set the brown paper bag on the sidewalk out of his reach, or so I thought, as I untied him from the bike rack. While I was preoccupied with his leash and the lock, Cooper seized the day, sticking his snout in the sack and taking a large bite of my blueberry muffin's perfect top.

Rather than being annoyed, I burst out laughing. He was so pleased with himself! He smelled muffin, wanted it, and ate it. I finished off the rest, sans giant doggy bite, and shared the crumbs with him. No matter how out of reach a desire may seem, go for it. We may not get the whole muffin, but at least we'll get a mouthful of the best part.

Cooper's never afraid to ask for attention when he craves it. His favorite place to sleep is in bed with me, and he loves to lie on my side so I'm "forced" to curl around him like he's a little spoon, safe and snuggly. He isn't shy about getting close when he needs love, and he doesn't worry about rejection when he puts himself out there.

He's taught me so many lessons, especially that grief and healing of this magnitude can't be rushed, only experienced and accepted.

— Kathryn Santichen —

Emily

Dogs come into our lives to teach us about love;
they depart to teach us about loss. A new dog never
replaces an old dog. It merely expands the heart.
~Author Unknown

After losing my precious Gypsy, I swore I'd never have another dog and experience that pain again. But after being nagged by my friends, I finally agreed to go to the local shelter. There, I dismissed every dog available and headed for the exit. Being on crutches, I nearly fell trying to open the door. My friends had lingered, petting the dogs. At the exit, I waited stubbornly for help.

I ignored the dogs whining frantically at the fencing, each striving to capture my attention—all but one. A little tri-colored dog in the back pressed tightly against the wall, and I saw a mix of desperation and fear in her wide eyes. Focused on her, I moved a little closer to the cage.

An attendant approached eagerly, but I shook my head.

I can't do it! I thought. If I adopted another dog, I was simply setting myself up for more heartbreak. I turned to leave, but glancing back one last time, the inevitable happened. I couldn't look away.

With a sigh, I asked to see the black-and-tan dog with the white blaze on her chest. Pointing, I saw the attendant blanch when her gaze fell upon the little dog.

"Oh, no, she's not available… She's not even supposed to be in the kennel at all. Oh, no!"

She rushed away, returning with another employee and two catch poles. Entering, they snared her and pulled her to the gate where they tried to muzzle her. Her desperate attempts to free herself broke my heart. Upon my insistence, they towed the exhausted dog to an observation room where I pushed my way in. Sitting down quietly in a corner, I watched as she paced frantically until she was exhausted. Then she crouched in the corner as far from me as she could get. Turning out the lights to give her some calming darkness and time to recover, I left the room and asked the employees why the dog was not to be adopted.

They told me that it had taken weeks to catch her. She had exhibited feral behaviors and was highly aggressive. After the mandatory three-day waiting period to see if someone claimed her, she would be euthanized.

Although she acted wild, I was willing to bet that somewhere within her was a dog who yearned to be loved. She probably had no memories of man at his best, just negative interactions. She only saw humans as a threat.

Ignoring the warnings, I returned to the room. The dog sat up as I entered. I sat in the corner again, waiting to see what she would do. Emily (God help me, I had already named her) eyed me warily. I remained very still for the next hour and then I reached out to her, making coaxing, kissing noises. Despite her fear, she cocked her head curiously as I clicked my tongue and made every stupid, wheedling noise I could think of. It took some time, but eventually her curiosity led her to come and sniff my open hand.

Not daring to move, I allowed her to have a long sniffing examination, remaining very still as she carefully and tentatively sniffed my arms, legs and face. A dog "sees" through its nose, and as I sat quietly, she finished her appraisal, raised her head and finally looked into my eyes. At that moment, she decided to give me a chance. In my heart, I knew that I needed her as much as she needed me.

I talked the employees into letting me adopt her and then I rushed to the car, leading that terrified little dog wearing a collar for the first time. Emily allowed me to touch her lightly. She shrank away but never showed any aggression. Perhaps, she too dared to hope.

It would be heartwarming but unrealistic to say that she overcame her feral background overnight. It took several weeks to win her over, and it was two or three months before she began to tolerate people from outside the household. But over time she became my shadow, never far from my side.

Initially, she wasn't beautiful; she was an unkempt mess. Her fur was patchy, thin and full of burdocks, and her bones jutted out from a combination of malnutrition and rickets. She wouldn't have won any awards for beauty, but I saw her beautiful heart reflected in those gorgeous eyes, and her flaws fell away.

Now, thirteen years later, she has slowed down but is still my constant companion. She showed me that you can dare to love again, and that you can learn to trust as well, no matter how painful your past. She's also a reminder that love never dies; it simply expands to include another.

— Laurel L. Shannon —

Good Dog Goes Bad

A well-balanced person is one who
finds both sides of an issue laughable.
~Herbert Procknow

I met a friend for a hike through the woods with our dogs a few weeks ago. We trekked out into some state land in Michigan, off-trail near Lake Dubonnet, and let the dogs off-leash. Cookie, my Golden Retriever, was just ten months old and looked tiny next to my friend's dog, a sleek gray Weimaraner. It was early spring with snow still on the ground, and we let them run.

Back at home, an hour later, Cookie came over and laid her head on my lap. Oddly. Lolling about. I chalked it up to her big hike.

Then I got up. And she didn't.

She tried but stumbled. Then she fell and sprawled out on the kitchen floor. Panic.

I tried to talk to her, but her eyes looked at me and then rolled away. I picked her up and put her on her feet. She peed all over, and then she fell down.

I made the kids leave the room. She was dying!

I called the emergency vet. (It was a Sunday, of course.) They had me bring her right in, and they flushed her system with charcoal, ran tests and hydrated her. They called us on the phone a few hours later to say that every test came back normal, and Cookie seemed to be coming out of it. But they had no answers about what had happened.

"We'll keep her overnight and make sure she's okay," the vet told me. She was kind but firm, all business.

First thing the next morning, I was down at the vet's office to collect my baby.

But they didn't just hand her back to me.

Instead, I was taken back to a bare room. With a single light. With two chairs. And made to wait.

Cookie's tail drummed the cage bars in the next room, and I could hear her telltale whine that she'd heard me. But still, I sat alone and waited.

What's the deal?

I started to sweat. I took off my winter layers and set my purse on the floor. More thumping, more waiting.

Finally, the vet appeared. Without the dog.

I didn't think twice, though. Instead, I jumped on her in worry. "What made her so sick?" I was not ready to give up the hunt for an answer.

Unfortunately, neither was she.

The vet pulled up her chair. Quite close to me, face-to-face.

"Are you sure there's nothing Cookie got into?" she asked, quiet and still.

"Nothing that I can think of," I said, the guilt consuming me.

"Are you positive?" she pressed.

"Yes."

"Certain?"

"Yes...?" I was starting to doubt myself.

Long pause. Things were getting heated, and I hadn't even seen the bill yet.

"*Think,* Kandace!" She was exasperated, awaiting my confession.

"Okay, okay..." I was buying time, up against the wall. "Wait, I know!" For some reason, I felt like I was lying even as I said the whole truth and nothing but the truth. "We painted. Did she lick the wall?"

"No." The vet was unmoved.

I was down to my T-shirt by then, dripping with sweat.

What was happening?

Then, I finally remembered that we'd passed the remnants of a bonfire with leftover beer cans and wine bottles.

"Wait! We walked by a party spot in the woods!" I nearly shouted. "It must have been beer!" That was it. My dog was drunk.

The vet held up one finger to silence me.

"Well, it wasn't beer," she said, "but we do finally have our answer."

I waited, terrified.

"It was pot."

I couldn't speak, and when I did, I'd never felt so goody-two-shoes in my life.

"Did you say pot?"

"Pot, a pot brownie probably," the vet said with confidence. "I knew it was pot by the way she came stumbling in."

We shared a good, expensive laugh then.

So, it appears that the vet had been waiting for me to confess to having illegal drugs. She would have called the police on me then, I suppose. I imagined her staff on the far side of the door, along with Cookie, waiting to hear what kind of story I was going to feed her.

But I had no story. The real story was that my dog was now more experienced than me.

***

The $600 vet bill was a great opener for a "Say No to Drugs" talk with my sons.

When I finished explaining what Cookie did and what a pot brownie was, I asked the boys if they had any questions.

"So, if someone offers me drugs, I should walk away?" asked my eleven-year-old son.

"Actually, *run* away," I said.

My nine-year-old had bigger concerns, though.

He pulled me aside and asked straight-faced, "But, Mom, what if someone offers me a *brownie*?"

Oh, the lessons learned by having a dog around the house!

— Kandace Chapple —

A Puppy's Power

In family life, love is the oil that eases friction,
the cement that binds closer together,
and the music that brings harmony.
~Friedrich Nietzsche

The twelve bits of paper had been stuck to the kitchen wall for months. There was one letter left to spell out LET'S GET A PUPP –. Four little girls had been working hard on their behavior, earning those letters as rewards. With only the Y missing, they knew we were getting a puppy.

The girls — eight-year-old twins, a nine-year-old and a ten-year-old — had been living with us for almost a year. Their lives had been turned upside down when they were removed from their family and placed in a foster home — our home.

We were pretty new to fostering but experienced in parenting. We thought we had everything under control. How difficult could fostering be? Really, just more parenting, I thought.

Looking back, I can't believe how wrong I was. The girls were sisters. We had planned to foster two children at a time, but we couldn't stand the thought of these sisters being separated.

In no time, we realized we were outnumbered. The difference between parenting and parenting through fostering is the child's perception that the foster parents are the ones who have taken them from their parents. In other words, we became the enemies.

The girls grieved their family and yearned to go home. In addition to missing family, they missed the animals they had left behind: horses, cats, dogs and rabbits. Although our last dog had died not long before the girls came—and we had agreed it would be our last dog—I became fixated on getting them a puppy. It would encourage better behaviour, and also lessen their pain by giving them someone new to love. If they ended up going back to their home, the puppy would go with them. Or we would arrange ample visitation, depending on what worked best for the girls.

Finally, the girls earned the letter Y. We placed it on the wall, and the time came for the puppy to arrive. We had allergies to consider, so I had chosen a Goldendoodle. She arrived, a soft golden bundle of puppy fur. We named her Maycee, and the girls and I settled in to enjoy our new puppy.

For a time, I wondered if I had made the right decision. Had I forgotten how much work a puppy could be? House-training? Chewing? For Christmas, we had bought the girls each a pair of fuzzy animal slippers, and the puppy constantly chased and nipped at their slippers. She jumped on them and tore their clothes. The girls excited the puppy, and the puppy excited the girls. The chaos and noise in the house increased, and I wondered what I had been thinking.

It became apparent that obedience training would be necessary for all of us. I enrolled Maycee in classes and always brought one or two of the girls with me so they could learn the right way to deal with an energetic puppy.

Progress came slowly. The girls began to understand that for Maycee to be calm, they had to be calm. Running around the house yelling would result in a puppy jumping and tearing at their clothing. The slippers had to be put away for a time, replaced by socks.

Looking back to those early days, I am amazed at how much Maycee taught the girls. At times, exuberant in their love for Maycee, they would hug her too tight. Maycee would tolerate most of this extreme affection, but when it became too much or too tight, she would give a low growl in the back of her throat. Never more than that. I explained to the girls that Maycee's growl was her way of communicating with them, and they needed to respect and listen to her. Maycee taught them about boundaries.

The girls were expected to help care for Maycee. Lessons learned at obedience training were reinforced at home. The girls handfed Maycee and taught her to sit and stay. They learned that dogs are pack animals, and we were all part of her pack. The way they handled Maycee would establish a relationship whereby Maycee could understand that the girls were the top dogs, not her. Feeding her, taking her for daily walks and picking up her mess on people's lawns became part of their daily routines. Maycee taught them responsibility and an understanding of animal behaviour.

Anger continued to flare up in the house, but we established a rule that Maycee was off limits if someone's anger was out of control. We explained that Maycee deserved to be treated in a calm, loving way and did not deserve to be exposed to anger. Maycee taught the girls about the power of controlling their anger and how anger can hurt the ones they love, including their dog.

Maycee became their confidante. When they were sad, she always listened. If they yearned for their family, they could wrap their arms around her and cling to her soft fur. Maycee gave them unconditional love. They could trust her.

After three and a half years, two of the girls went home to live with their mom and two chose to stay with us. All four have grown into amazing young women who have fond memories of Maycee.

Maycee grew into a beautiful dog with a gentle spirit. She gave so much to all of us, but her real magic was her ability to teach these little girls lessons they didn't trust me to teach them.

We lost Maycee two years ago. We all miss her. The little puppy who started out chasing and biting the girls' animal slippers had done something amazing: She helped heal the hearts of four little girls.

— Catherine V. Moise —

Five-Card Draw

Ever wonder where you'd end up if you took your dog for a walk and never once pulled back on the leash?
~Robert Brault

I'm walking Shasta, the wonder dog. Light snow has fallen overnight; an appetizer for the banquet yet to come. We can see our breath in the crisp air. Snow crunches under my boots.

Shasta wears Muttluks, an urban version of an Iditarod sled-dog's booties. With the boots, she is happy spending the day in the cold and snow. Otherwise, she would be focused on the smallest lumps of snow between her toes within minutes.

A nine-year-old Bearded Collie, Shasta has never stopped acting like a puppy. She lives life from a personal fountain of youth — playful and impish, treating each experience as new and fresh, even for the 100th time.

Her nose plunges into each tiny mound of snow. Snuffling from one hidden fragrance to the next, her course is marked by the furrow her nose makes in the fluffy layer. My wife says Shasta is reading "pee-mail." Some receives cursory attention, the equivalent of human junk mail. Others are carefully considered, sometimes from more than one vantage point. The odd one rises to the level of demanding a reply, though there are fewer of these important missives than for her male fur friends.

Shasta runs with exuberance, flinging herself headlong into a drift. Rolling on her back, she wiggles and waggles, feet waving in the air to make "snow puppies." With a shake that moves from stem to stern, she makes her own blizzard, eyes bright with excitement.

I watch the antics of the innocent and cannot help but feel a lightness. It sets me to thinking....

It is now early spring, and we have survived short days and frigid walks. The snow is gone, but the nights remain cool. Frost sits heavy on the trees. Rime-laden branches glitter like diamond necklaces in the morning light.

Shasta pursues the chatter of a squirrel, sniffs intently at the ground, her attention moving to low branches that tell the story of a passing animal. Her nose inhales a wilderness bouquet that eludes me. She cocks her head, lifts an ear and explodes into motion, wheeling in the direction of a snapped twig, leaping fallen trees in an effortless flow of energy.

Once again I feel that sense of lightness draw closer to my spirit. Again, I wonder, what really sets Shasta and me apart?

We are both living beings with wants and desires. We are capable of love and loyalty. We have times when we are busy; times we relax. There are times we are excited, others when we are bored. We have the same senses—touch, taste, smell, sound, sight—that feed us information about the world.

But Shasta is a sensory creature who absorbs what her senses convey. I am less apt to do that.

How much of the data gathered through my own senses makes it to a level of consciousness? My guess? Not much. How much gets taken for granted? My guess? Most of it.

For Shasta, a scent needs to be explored. Movement demands to be chased. Noises must be investigated. Everything makes an impression.

Picture life without the explosion of color in a fiery sunset; without hearing, "I love you." Imagine not feeling your lover's fingers caress your cheek; not knowing the smell of a rose, the flavor of chocolate melting in your mouth. Our experience of life would be forever changed.

Shasta taught me that things don't need to be immense to be significant. I've learned not to discard small things because they don't make an impression. I was caught up in the idea that, whatever we do, it has to be bigger than life. Actions need to be noticed. Otherwise, what's the point?

To get in touch with my senses and back in touch with myself, I play a game of five-card draw. Cards numbered 1 through 5 are labelled with one of the five senses. The game is played in multiples of five with two dice.

Each day, I roll a die and pick the card that corresponds to the number. If the card is labelled Sound, I devote five minutes or five one-minute periods to listening — *really* listening.

I close my eyes and focus. I go beneath the big sounds: someone talking, a car alarm, the slam of a door. I find the breath of wind gently moving through leaves, the whir of a bird's wings, a raindrop hitting the ground, the settling of a snowdrift, the groan of winter ice.

The next day, I roll the die and draw another card. I close my eyes and connect with the sense of Touch. I feel the movement of air from the heating system, the texture of my clothes, my lungs expanding as I breathe.

If I roll a 6, I take the day off. No need to pay attention to anything. On the following day, I roll both dice, pull two cards and spend that day paying attention to both senses.

Suppose I roll numbers corresponding to Touch and Sight? On a warm spring day, a breeze gently caresses my skin with a soft brush of promise. The grass sways, individual blades moving not quite in unison. The grass is young, supple with new life.

A squirrel scampers up a tree, smooth muscle bunching and relaxing under a tawny coat, tail flicking back and forth, eyes darting to and fro. My fingers trace splits in the bark and come away sticky with sap. Bits of sawdust from a bird pecking at the rough skin are caught in a spider's web.

An ant carrying a seed pod that dwarfs him in size walks onto my finger. I feel the tickle of tiny feet, the movement brushing through the hair on my arm.

Shasta and I have become more alike. She has taught me that life is so much more than waiting for the next big incident. When we start to find the little bits and pieces we so often take for granted, life bursts at the seams; the whole becomes much more than the sum of its parts. We explode into full radiance, like a flower bursting into bloom. We can become our own showpiece.

If we pay attention, we can learn a lot from walking a dog.

— Phil Taylor —

Right to the End

Old dogs, like old shoes, are comfortable.
They might be a little out of shape and a little
worn around the edges, but they fit well.
~Bennie Wilcox

"Her name is Emmy," I said.

"I'm not taking another dog," Mom said to me over the phone, her tone adamant. "It was hard losing Benji. We had him for a long time. I can't go through that again. It's only been two months...."

When my mom was fifty-seven, she brought home Benji, a Bichon Frise puppy. She claimed a dog would be fun for my daughter to play with on visits to Grandma's house. But that was just an excuse. Mom loved animals and had a huge heart. One time she'd returned from work with a cat found in the pouring rain and on its last legs. She and my stepdad nurtured the stray back to life and had him for many years.

Which was why her refusal to take this older dog didn't sit right.

"I know losing a pet is hard." I thought about my own dogs. "But when my friend at work told me about Emmy's owner dying, it felt like a sign. Like you were meant to have her. I mean, she's a Bichon Frise, just like Benji. And..."

"I can't do it." Mom's voice quivered. "Not now. Maybe a year from now."

I hung up, struggling to let go of idea that these two could be brought together. My heart told me fate sent this dog my way to help my mother heal from her loss. But I respected her wishes and didn't ask again.

So, imagine my surprise when Mom called me later that night.

"I'll take Emmy." Excitement rang in her voice. "I was thinking, I'll be turning seventy next year and have no business getting a puppy at that age. Taking in an older dog feels like the right thing to do."

Arrangements were made. Mom and Emmy met. It was a match made in heaven, with both dog and owner bonding quickly. When Emmy died, it was painful for Mom. They'd grown close, perhaps the sweet pup becoming my mother's most beloved pet ever. An urn with Emmy's ashes was placed on Mom's nightstand. She once told me, "When I go to sleep, I always say good night to her."

Only after this loss, my mother had found a mission.

"I'm calling the SPCA," she said a short while after Emmy passed. "I'm sure there's another older dog who needs a home."

Thus started a lineup of senior dogs that found a home in my mother's heart. Each one that entered her life gave her a purpose that took the edge off losing another pet. She'd pour her grief into love for the newcomers, who through no fault of their own ended up homeless.

They never lived with her and my stepfather for long. Maybe a few years. Sometimes one or two more. Yet as she welcomed each one, I knew they'd found the best place in the world to spend their final years. If they weren't treated like royalty in their first family, they were in their last. She made sure of it.

With each one she took in, she became more vocal about the importance of rehoming mature animals. If you knew Joyce, you knew she cared about animals. Especially older ones. She even started to volunteer at the local SPCA, where she not only helped forgotten animals in other ways but made new friends who shared her passion for giving to animals.

I never asked, but often wondered, if her passion for senior animals was because she was getting older, too. My mother's personality was as vibrant in her eighties as when she'd raised me. She was beautiful, younger looking than her years. But no matter how hard anyone fights it, signs of age creep in.

A person notices those signs on someone as special as their mom. When I'd observe one, it would remind me that nobody is immune from the passing of time. A sobering thought.

The world looks at aging people differently, leaving them to feel invisible in our youth and beauty-obsessed culture; the way an adorable puppy always catches a person's eye over a graying, immobile older dog. Maybe her passion grew with the idea that our need for love and attention doesn't disappear with gray hair or slower steps.

Though I'd love to talk with my mom about this, I can't. She passed away last summer. She became very ill and we took her to the emergency room. The next day, they admitted her to the ICU.

As her condition declined, I'd waited in the hallway with my family while the staff induced a coma in one last attempt to save her. All we could do was pray.

Minutes later, one of the very kind ICU nurses came up to me. "Okay, she's calm now. Maybe the meds can do their work. Oh, right before we put her under, your mom insisted I tell you something." She frowned. "I hope I got this right. She asked that you make sure your stepfather knows to warm Lexi's food before giving it to her."

I smiled. "Thank you. Sounds like a message she'd give. She worries about her dog."

"Well, it sounds like Lexi is well-loved."

Those feeding instructions were my mother's last words. She never woke from the coma and died peacefully with all of us gathered at her bedside.

But those last words are a testament to the type of person she was. Even as she was dying, she wasn't thinking about herself. Whether it was with her pets, family, or friends, my mother spread her unconditional love where it was needed… the best gift a person can give to the world.

There are many ways to leave your mark during your short time on earth. I'm proud of Mom for doing more than just talking about a cause but listening to her heart and acting upon those feelings.

And it all started with the magic that brought her Emmy.

Emmy's ashes are now with Mom in her final resting place. Doing so seemed right. That shy Bichon who entered our lives through a series of fate-filled events taught all of us why older shouldn't mean forgotten. A message my mother dedicated her days to sharing.

— Sharon Struth —

Buddy the Miracle Dog

Miracles come in moments. Be ready and willing.
~Dr. Wayne Dyer

We met Rita, a semi-retired teacher, amid the holly wreaths, chocolate logs and colourful Christmas ornaments. We were at the local high-school Christmas extravaganza, and the place was abuzz with the elevated energy of the holidays. Rita had a radiant smile that, as it turned out, belied the true story.

She said, "I know you have an Australian Shepherd and was wondering if you could take my dog. I was diagnosed with cancer and don't think I can look after my Aussie."

We looked at her, feeling an enormous wave of regret and sadness for her situation, but we knew we could not take her dog at that time. We had Mookie, aka Mr. Curmudgeon, at home. Introducing a new dog would have been unfair, as Mookie's health was failing and he would probably not live out the year. Mookie's joy was found in hanging out in the kitchen, being with us, and strolling around the yard, luxuriating in the variety of smells that lay in wait for his twitching nose. Another dog would upset his universe, and we would never be forgiven.

We expressed our regrets, explained the situation and said our goodbyes. Three months later, Mookie passed away, and a month later I found myself driving past Rita's house. I felt compelled to pay her a visit. I wanted to see how she was doing and ask if she still had the dog.

When I entered Rita's home, I walked upstairs to the sunroom and looked into a pair of amber eyes. A black, white and tan Aussie was lying on the couch. He looked at me with an air of great expectation. I had the distinct impression he was saying to me, "What took you so long?" Then he leapt off the couch and greeted me with great exuberance. Rita and I laughed at this warm reception. I asked how she was doing, and she said with a smile, "The cancer is gone." I was so happy to hear the news and realized that Buddy would be staying with Rita… or so I thought.

Rita and I spoke about her health journey, and she said eventually, "How would you like to share Buddy?"

I thought that Buddy might be confused by going from one home to another, but I said, "Well, I'll introduce him to my husband Bruce and see how he does."

Without hesitation, Buddy jumped into my car, and we drove the short distance to my house. He and Bruce became immediate friends, and Buddy settled himself happily on the kitchen floor. Buddy proved to be the most loving dog I had ever met. He was calm, affectionate, quiet, well-behaved and very Zen-like for a two-year-old dog. And so, after that initial meeting, our lives started to include Buddy. He graduated to overnight stays with no problem, always happy to be with us.

One day, which we'll remember forever, we took Buddy for a walk along an old, defunct railway line, now a recreational trail. Buddy was free to roam, and he ran up the small embankment whenever there was an enticing important smell. He ran out of sight for a moment, though, and then we heard a scream! It was Buddy. We ran up the embankment thinking he had run into a porcupine, but Buddy had been ensnared by a conibear trap.

This deplorable instrument of death clamps down and breaks the neck of the animal. Luckily, Bruce knew how this trap worked. We grabbed the two bars around Buddy's neck and tried to pry them apart in order to relieve the pressure around his neck. The force with which the bars were clamped was unbelievable. With herculean strength, Bruce was able to pull the bars apart just enough to provide some breathing space and prevent this spring-loaded vice from closing in on Buddy's throat for good.

"Go find help," said Bruce as we seemed to be losing the battle. "I will try to keep the trap from closing on his neck, but hurry!"

I took off, but my pace was slowed by wet, mud-sucking fields. Panic and tears drove me on to the nearest house. I pounded on the door. A woman appeared, and I said, "Please, my dog is in a trap, and he is going to die. Can you help?"

This dear soul was in her boots in seconds. Her thirteen-year-old son was right behind her. They ran around and grabbed a few tools (none of us knew what we needed, but metal objects seemed a good idea), and we jumped into her truck, skirting the hedgerows and avoiding the muddy fields. We jumped out of the vehicle, and I called to Bruce, "How is he doing?"

Bruce shouted, "His eyes are fluttering. Quick!"

As we hurried to their location, I felt sick with dread. After all, we loved Buddy dearly, but more importantly, he really wasn't our dog.

Bruce asked the young boy, Jeremy, "Are you strong?"

He replied honestly, "Not really, but I'll try."

Jeremy and I grabbed onto the metal bars and managed to pry open the trap far enough so that Buddy could squeeze his head out. We were beyond relief at the sight of Buddy freed from this lethal prison. Buddy shook himself, gave us a slightly stunned yet grateful look, and recommenced sniffing as if nothing had happened.

After what could have been a horrific disaster, I can only say that the way the events lined up had to have been divine intervention. The vet was beyond incredulous that he survived, let alone that there was no injury to his throat. The story found its way into social media, and Buddy became famous across the country. People in Canada and the U.S. shared sad stories with us of how their dogs had succumbed to such a trap.

Today, Buddy is a therapy dog, giving love to all he meets. I often wonder if his calm nature saved him. He did not fight us as we tried to set him free. He just stayed still. Is this a message to us all? When disaster strikes, stay calm, have faith, and the seen and unseen forces will come into play.

— Rosalind Forster —

Nikki the Insightful Pup

The gift which I am sending you is called a dog
and is in fact the most precious and
valuable possession of mankind.
~Theodorus Gaza

Nikki was a spunky Bichon Frise with a mind of her own. She came to us as a Christmas gift from Teri, the school nurse whose Bichons had puppies. Although she could have sold Nikki as she did her other puppies, Teri thought the little white fur ball would make a nice surprise for my kids on Christmas morning. Just three months earlier, their dad, my husband, had died in the 9/11 attacks. Nikki did exactly what Teri had hoped—she brought some excitement and joy to an otherwise difficult time in our lives.

As Nikki grew and began to develop her personality, some days we would question her intelligence, while other days she seemed cleverer than her family of four humans. Typical of her breed, she was a jumper. Even though she was all of twelve inches tall from the floor to the top of her back, she could jump like a kid on a pogo stick. If there was something on the edge of the counter, she would jump… and jump… and jump until her mouth grasped whatever treat she was after. Off she'd run with her treasure to hide under the coffee table, hoping no one would notice. One day, I came home to find Nikki had jumped her way into the garbage can — after she managed to pull open the sliding cupboard where it's kept — but she couldn't figure out how to get out, so she just sat in the can, looking guilty.

She was also a runner... rather, a sprinter. She not only ran through the house in circles, but as soon as anyone opened the front door, she'd be gone. She'd dart through our legs, around our legs, whatever it took to be outside, running, sniffing and exploring the neighborhood. She either forgot all she learned at puppy-behavior school or chose to blatantly ignore it for a few minutes of unattended frolicking in the great outdoors. When we called her, she took it as permission to run faster and farther. One snowy night, she ran out after the deer that were in our front yard. Despite more than a foot of new snow on the ground, she bounded across it after the fleeing deer. We were not so nimble running after her in our pajamas and slippers, with the deep snow and darkness hindering our speed.

After chasing her too many times, we decided to keep a leash on her inside the house until she learned to "stay" when commanded. Whoever opened the door had to ensure they had hold of the leash, and if she did get out, it was at least a little easier to catch her by grabbing the end of the leash and stopping her in her tracks. One day, I called Nikki to come into the foyer where we kept her when no one was home. She was housetrained, but still had a little trouble and sometimes piddled on the rug, so we put her in the rug-free foyer area with toys, her bed and water. This particular time, when I tried to get her to go in the foyer, she began her crazy run through the house, with the leash attached to her collar and the handle end trailing behind her. Then she showed me how quick and witty she could be. She saw that I was about to reach for the leash, so she stopped, took the end of it in her mouth, and gave me a look that said, "I outsmarted you." Then she continued with her run. I could almost hear her laughing at me. I was stunned, impressed and highly amused at the same time, and I gained a whole new respect for what the crafty pup was capable of.

Eventually, she stopped running away when someone opened the door, and we no longer had to keep the leash on her indoors. Like most dogs, she would get excited when she saw the leash because it signified a walk. Nikki went to doggie heaven in 2016, but we still laugh about her antics and appreciate her for the joy, companionship and laughter she brought us when we needed it most.

— Christie Schmitt Coombs —

Chapter
5

My Very Good, Very Bad Dog

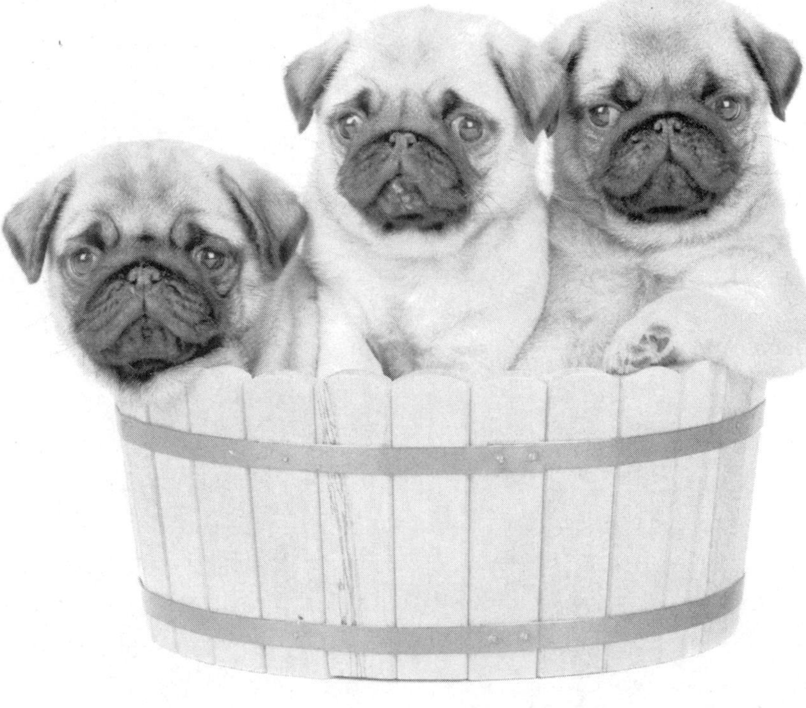

Showtime

Humor is merely tragedy standing on its head with its pants torn.
~Irvin S. Cobb

The judge looked at me with an encouraging smile. "Are you ready?" she asked. I looked down at Paisley the Wonder Dog, who was poised in anticipation. My stomach was filled with butterflies the size of pterodactyls, but this was our moment. This was what we had trained for.

"Ready!" I answered. "Paisley, heel!" And so began our very first obedience trial.

I didn't want anyone to know it was our first go. My little black Cocker Spaniel and I were going to look like seasoned pros. Before entering the ring, I remembered what my instructor had told me.

"If you look at your dog while you're doing the heeling exercise, it looks like you don't trust your pup. Look straight ahead."

Heeding this sage advice, I threw back my shoulders and stood tall, marching across the grass with precision, breaking into a confident trot when the judge called "fast." *Look at us,* I thought. *We're doing it! Paisley is a show dog!*

The whole exercise went brilliantly. I knew we were impressive. In training class, heads would turn, and people would stop what they were doing to watch my dog work. I was used to hearing their awed whispers. But what was that sound I heard now? A giggle?

"About turn!" the judge called, the command to change direction.

I turned crisply on my heel, making sure not to look at Paisley. I needed to show that I fully trusted her. Soft laughter spread through the crowd. What in the world? I stood taller still, throwing out my chest and tossing my head. I was a kid, sure. At fifteen, I was the youngest at the trial. But I knew what I was doing, and Paisley and I were an unbeatable team. I had no time for jealous people.

The judge called a few more moves in the heeling pattern and then said the phrase that indicated our task was complete. "Exercise finished."

I reached down to give my dog a well-deserved scratch behind the ear. She wasn't there.

"Would you like to get your dog?" the judge asked, swallowing laughter. I turned to look at her, and there was Paisley, sitting politely on the judge's shoes. The rotten pup had watched me do the entire heeling exercise entirely by myself.

My face burned with embarrassment. I shot Paisley the stink-eye and went to collect her, taking her by the collar and giving her a gentle reminder of who was in charge.

"It's time for the recall," the judge said. I nodded and took my dog to one end of the ring.

"Sit your dog and leave when ready," the judge ordered. At least we were going to finish on a good note. Paisley's best exercise was the recall. When we practiced in training class, she came running toward me with the focus of a laser and the speed of a cheetah, long ears flapping, mouth open in a gleeful grin. She would skid to a sitting position in front of me with such momentum that she wrinkled the rubber mats. She was nothing short of beautiful. I prepared to change this crowd's perception of my canine companion. We were going to knock their socks off.

"Sit!" I commanded. Paisley sat obediently. "Wait!" I said firmly, showing her the palm of my hand. I strutted to the other end of the large ring and then turned back to face my dog. She sat staring at me, alert and waiting for the word.

"Paisley, COME!" I shouted. She threw herself toward me with the force of a bullet. I couldn't help but smile. She was my pride and joy. Many dogs slowed up several yards before reaching their owners, losing precious points in the process. Not Paisley. She barreled toward me at top speed. Here she was! And there she went...

Paisley bolted past me and out of the ring with the steward and some volunteers in hot pursuit. She didn't go far before she stopped and came back to the ring to watch me work.

"Paisley, come!" I repeated through gritted teeth, unsure whether to cry, faint, or sell her to the circus. She trotted toward me with alacrity. I snapped her leash onto her collar, and we left the ring. I stalked past the laughing crowd and went to a quiet place to think.

We had already failed. Was it worth going back into the ring with the other dogs for the sit-and-down stays, or should we cut our losses and just go home? In the end, I knew I had to see the whole thing through. When I heard our number called, we presented ourselves and filed into the ring with the rest of the dogs.

"Sit your dogs," the judge ordered. As one voice, we said, "Sit."

"Leave your dogs," the judge said.

"Stay," I told Paisley firmly. I wasn't worried, though. She was unshakable when it came to staying where I put her. I walked with the other owners to the other side of the ring and turned back to face my dog. Her eyebrows wiggled, and she shifted her gaze to one side. What was she doing? She never got up until I told her to. Ever! Her whole body shifted uneasily. Suddenly, I knew what was about to happen, and there was absolutely nothing I could do about it.

Slowly, Paisley's bottom rose off the ground until she was hunkered into a squat. There was no laughter this time, only horrified gasps from the audience as my dog finished her business in the show ring. The elegant Golden Retriever next to her gave her a look that said clearly, "Heathen," and a ring steward scrambled to do a hasty clean-up.

I returned to Paisley as soon as the judge would let me. I put the leash on my dog, and we took our walk of shame out of the ring and slunk home. I didn't have the courage to stick around for more.

I never did show Paisley again, and I'll never forget what I realized that day. Some dogs are put into our lives to give us love and companionship. Others are given to us to keep us humble.

— Heather Debord —

Mail Confetti

At the height of laughter, the universe is flung into
a kaleidoscope of new possibilities.
~Jean Houston

It was a sunny Saturday morning and we'd slept in. As we stretched contentedly in bed, we heard the newest member of our family stir from the couch he had claimed as his own. His nails clicked on the wood floor and his wagging tail thumped against the walls as he made his way down the hallway toward our bedroom. By the time he got to our bedroom door, he was running full speed. Then he leaped onto our bed to join his people on this idyllic morning.

Hunter was a one-and-a-half-year-old Bloodhound we had rescued three months earlier. He bonded with us quickly and was very routine-oriented, knowing when it was the weekend. He would sleep in with us, only getting up once he heard us wake. But he always came to greet us in the morning the instant he heard us stir.

We began our morning routine of making coffee and tea and preparing a delicious breakfast of kibble and canned wet food for Hunter. We eased into the morning slowly, sitting on the back porch and enjoying the peace and quiet before the rest of the neighborhood flooded the morning with activity.

Fully awake and ready to begin our weekend errands, we compiled a grocery list and readied ourselves for our weekly trip. Hunter walked dutifully into his crate as I grabbed my purse, recognizing our behaviors that indicated we would be leaving. Hunter was quite the rambunctious Bloodhound and had been crate-trained before we rescued him. Ultimately, we wanted to get to a point when he did not need to be crated, but we knew it would take time. He had gotten into so much mischief when we first rescued him that we stuck with the routine.

"You know, he has been an awfully good boy lately. Should we try leaving him free in the house while we go shopping today?" my husband asked.

"Well, it has been about a month now since he has destroyed something that wasn't his," I pondered a bit apprehensively. "But I agree. I think he deserves a chance to prove himself." So, rather than close his crate door that day, we closed all doors in the house, so he only had access to the living room, kitchen, and hallways.

We did our usual grocery shopping and stopped at the pet store on our way home. We got some marrow bones and a new plush toy for Hunter as a surprise. We were gone for about an hour, and we took a deep breath as we entered the front door, not quite sure what to expect.

Our jaws dropped as we assessed the scene that unfolded in front of our eyes. The mail on our coffee table had been shredded into confetti that was scattered all over the living room. The boxes from an online purchase had also been shredded, including the autographed poster of Bas Rutten that had been in one of them.

"Hunter..." We said his name firmly and simultaneously, drawn out with a bit of disappointment. Hunter slinked over to us, his head bowed and tail low.

"Buddy, what is this?" I pointed to the mess, and Hunter continued to hang his head in remorse. We had a few words about what happened, and we set to cleaning up the mess.

Just as we began our clean-up, Hunter regained his pep. His tail began wagging happily, and he trotted over to the side of his crate where our Roomba was sitting in its charging base. He gave a quick bay to get our attention and stomped his paw down on top of the Roomba. It roared to life and began vacuuming up shreds of paper as it maneuvered around the living room. Proudly, Hunter trotted over to us and sat rather happily with his tongue lolling out of one side of his mouth. His tail wagged furiously, sweeping miniscule pieces of mail from side to side with the movement.

My husband and I burst out in laughter and didn't stop for a good five minutes. "Oh, Hunter!" I exclaimed. "How boring our lives would be without you!"

— Gwen Cooper —

*For Pete's Sake

I feel sorry for people who don't have dogs. I hear they have to pick up food they drop on the floor.
~Author Unknown

The sparkle of the holidays took on a whole new meaning for me one year, all because of our Golden Retriever, Petey. We've always lived with older dogs. Quiet, sedate dogs. It's nice, but maybe a bit predictable. Two-year-old Petey is younger and full of energy. And mischief.

One afternoon, I sat at the dining room table with my four-year-old granddaughter, Grace, making Christmas decorations. Our Golden Retrievers trotted over in case what we were doing involved food, a loose term for anything that could possibly be gulped, chomped, swallowed, or slurped. "Be good," I said as they edged up to the table. The older dog, Ernest, lay at my feet. He was usually sweet and obedient, just wanting to be near his humans. But Petey bounded over with an enthusiastic bounce, jumped up, and stuck his nose right into our work. "No, Petey!" Grace cried, as colored construction paper flew everywhere.

The playful pup pounced on the floor and shot up with a sheet of green paper hanging from his lips. "It's ruined!" Grace said.

"Oh, for Pete's sake," I said.

Petey didn't mean to be naughty. Being a Retriever, he always had to be carrying something in his slobbery grip. He couldn't greet us at the door without at least two toys and a shoe in his mouth. We were careful about keeping food out of his reach. We once had a dog who pulled a corncob out of the trash and needed surgery for an obstruction. No way was that going to happen again.

Still, Petey kept me on my toes due to the things he'd ingested or attempted to ingest. I pulled the green paper out of his mouth. Grace pouted. "He didn't mean to," I said, handing her one of the fat tubes of sparkly glitter glue.

She squeezed some onto a clean sheet of paper. "Remember when Petey ate the butter?" she asked.

Earlier that week, I was baking Christmas cookies and put three sticks of butter way on the back of the counter to soften. Later, I heard a strange noise and rushed into the kitchen. "Oh, for Pete's sake!" There he was, already having eaten two sticks of butter, wrappers and all, and working on the third. I reached into his mouth and retrieved half a stick. What a mess! Grace giggled thinking about her grandma catching Petey with the butter.

"But Petey was okay, right?" she asked. I nodded. He'd suffered the consequences. So had my living-room rug. But he was okay.

"Now, tell me again about Oma's cake," Grace begged. This story, a classic, always seemed to surface when Petey was naughty. It was a particular favorite.

"Again? Well, okay. One day, your Oma baked a beautiful chocolate cake, all frosted and decorated. And she temporarily stored it inside the oven, cleverly out of her black Lab's reach — or so she thought."

"But the dog got it, right?"

"Right. He pawed open the oven door, ate the entire cake, and somehow managed to close the door again. When Oma returned and looked inside the oven, there was nothing there but an empty cake pan."

Grace burst into giggles again, and then said thoughtfully, "Chocolate's bad for dogs. But he was okay?"

"You're right. And Petey's okay. But that's why we have to keep things he shouldn't eat away from him. Now let's finish our pictures."

"Okay. Where's the red glitter glue? I need red," Grace said.

I dug through the craft supplies on the table, but a sinking feeling told me what I already suspected. Petey! I turned, held his collar firmly and pried open his mouth. Sure enough, a long, slender plastic tube was tucked between his teeth. Worse, the open end was toward the back, pointing down his throat. I pulled out the empty tube. His tongue and cheeks were covered with red glitter. "Oh, for Pete's sake!"

The animal poison-control hotline and the manufacturer of the glitter glue put my mind at ease. I was told that some glues could harden in the digestive tract and cause a blockage, but since it was a non-toxic, kid-safe glue, he should be fine.

I hugged Petey tight. "Why did you eat that?" I asked. "Don't you know it's not good for you?" He just looked up at me and cocked his head innocently. His sweet, soft golden ears drooped. I gave him some easier-to-digest canned food as instructed and let him rest. He did leave us some glittery surprises in the back yard over the next few days, but otherwise suffered no ill effects.

The story of Petey's glitter-glue snack has now taken its place among the hallowed tales of cookie butter and Oma's chocolate cake. Supervising an active, spunky dog takes a little extra caution. But he rewards us in so many ways. He brings laughter and levity into our homes. He goes to obedience school, learns tricks, and tries so hard to be good. He barks at squirrels, is afraid of leaves blowing down the sidewalk, and charms us with his silly outlook on life. Maybe someday Petey will outgrow his mischievous tendencies.

But I love him either way.

— Peggy Frezon —

Mullins and the Dogcatcher

Dogs act exactly the way we would act
if we had no shame.
~Cynthia Heimel

Mullins, the German Shepherd mixed-breed dog I grew up with, could not stand being confined or tied. He would dig and pull stakes from the ground, chew through ropes, wriggle free of collars, leap over fences and even jump through car windows. Finally, even though we lived in a metropolis with leash laws, my parents gave up on confining him.

Without being fenced in, Mullins knew the boundary of our yard and usually left it only when following my two sisters and me. He was our constant companion and guardian. On school days, he would walk us to the end of our driveway, where the school bus picked us up, and be there waiting when we got home. Mom reported he knew the sounds of the different buses going by and would walk to the end of the driveway only when our school bus approached.

Mullins also came to recognize the sound of the dogcatcher's vehicle. The dogcatcher caught him once and caged him in the animal shelter. When we came to claim Mullins, he howled with uncontained joy.

The dogcatcher warned my parents. "You need to tie up that dog or cage him. If I catch him running free again, the fine will be even steeper."

"We can't cage him," my mother said. "He breaks free from everything. And he doesn't harm anyone. He stays with our girls."

"The law is he needs to be leashed or confined," the dogcatcher repeated. "I'm going to be on the lookout for him now."

Later, Mom told us girls, "You will have to put Mullins in the basement if the dogcatcher comes around."

We did this once or twice but were in school most of the time.

One day while we were away, Mom looked out the kitchen window and saw Mullins making a beeline for the basement. With his muzzle, Mullins grabbed the edge of the door, which never closed fully, and backed up until the door was wide open. He released the door and darted in.

Meanwhile, the dogcatcher had parked beside our yard and left his vehicle to catch Mullins. He saw Mullins escape to our basement but, legally, could not enter our house to capture the dog. He left empty-handed.

After that, Mom witnessed the dogcatcher try a few more times to catch Mullins. Mullins' ears would perk up at the sound of the dogcatcher's vehicle, and as the vehicle approached, he would run to the basement door, open it and run downstairs.

Mom was hanging wash on the clothesline one day when the dogcatcher pulled up. Mullins left her for the safety of the basement.

The dogcatcher strolled over to Mom. "I see you still haven't tied up that dog."

"Like I've told you, we can't," she said. "He won't stay tied."

"Well, I can't catch him," the dogcatcher said. "He's too smart. I've seen him open the door to your house by himself. So, I'm going to let him go, but if I ever get any complaints from the neighbors about him, I'll be back to lock him up."

No one ever complained, and my dad left the basement door hanging slightly ajar for the rest of Mullins' life.

—Ronica Stromberg—

The Dog Who Came Through Walls

Dogs are great. Bad dogs, if you can really call them that, are perhaps the greatest of them all.
~John Grogan

Conan-the-Barbarian was a twenty-five-pound, black-and-brown Dachshund mix. He was long, low, and muscular, with silky smooth fur, brown dots for eyebrows, and a barrel chest with a white star at its center.

He was barely two months old when I adopted him in 1982. *Just what a single mom with an art business needs,* I thought, *something more to take care of.* But the tiny pup was so adorable that I cast reason aside.

My son Doug, who was fifteen, said, "He's cool. Let's keep him." He named him after the hit film that year. Little did we know that his personality would fit his name.

He was innocent enough at first—a playful ball of energy and affection, who kept us laughing as we watched him explore his new surroundings. Since I worked mostly from home and had recently ended a romance, Conan and I spent lots of time together, taking walks, cuddling on the couch, and sleeping curled up in my bed at night.

Our first clue about his nature came when the doorbell rang one day. Little Conan let out a bark big enough for a Rottweiler and stood in guarding stance at the door. No one would mess with his family on his watch!

Then, it was one thing after another. Although he'd been easily house-trained and understood commands, he chose to ignore them. He delighted in chasing neighborhood cats. When the grumpy little Terrier three houses away got in his face and growled at him, Conan bit him on the ear and wouldn't let go until I pried his jaws apart with my hands.

When I began dating my current husband, Conan wasn't pleased about sharing my affections. The first time Lee was over for a romantic evening, Conan was fine with it—as long as we weren't touching. But after dinner, the instant my man's arm went around me, my dog jumped protectively between us. He didn't bark, snarl, or snap, but got his point across. Lee grinned. "I think your dog's jealous."

"Down," I ordered, but Conan persisted. Thinking there'd be no romance happening with Conan in the room, I put him in the spare bedroom—the one with the broken heating register I'd been meaning to get fixed and had left propped against the opening between the two rooms. "Now, where were we?" I asked, rejoining Lee on the couch.

Romance resumed. One kiss led to another. Soon, we were locked in a passionate embrace. Senses reeling, I sighed with pleasure, but should have stayed silent. The next thing we knew, the heating register crashed to the floor, and Conan-the-Barbarian burst into the room. Barking and snarling this time, he leaped to my defense.

"He came through the wall," Lee said, bewildered. Needless to say, the evening fizzled.

Happily, Lee prevailed, and by the time I moved in with him the following year, he and Conan were best friends. But life with this feisty dog kept us on our toes. He was a chaser of cats, skunks and raccoons, and dislocated his shoulder chasing one from his yard, sending us off to the animal ER.

Next, he cut his paw while walking in the woods. It bled profusely. Terrified, I stemmed the bleeding with my scarf and rushed him to our vet. "Lucky dog," she said. "That cut just missed an artery." Our vet knew us well, since Conan became known in her office as the foxtail king—with three up his nose and two in his ear—all on Sundays or holiday weekends.

Conan trained us to keep the backyard gate locked. Leaving it open meant he'd be gone for the afternoon. "Yi, yi, yi, yi!" he'd yelp joyfully as he raced toward adventure. On one occasion, he must have raided someone's garbage because he returned home belching pepperoni!

Still, we never realized the extent of his wanderings until the morning the backyard gate blew open, and Conan, seizing his opportunity, sprinted down the street.

"I'll get him," Lee said, driving off in pursuit. He returned a half-hour later, flushed and annoyed, with an unrepentant Conan beside him in the car. "I got to watch him cross Highway 1 in rush-hour traffic, dodging cars. I followed, calling his name, but he was busy exploring and refused to come. The only reason I got him," Lee said, pausing to shoot Conan a dirty look, "was because I reached out and grabbed him when he stopped to poop. He was still pooping when I hauled him into the car!"

Conan was a hothead. He never bit a human but had his share of scrapes with other dogs—his last at age thirteen, over a fish head on the beach.

But willful nature aside, he was more than a tough guy. Unfailingly, he sensed my distress during tough times in life and offered comfort. One day, I watched a film depicting animal cruelty. The heart-wrenching images made me sob. Without hesitation, Conan climbed into my lap, snuggling close and easing my pain with his loving presence.

Conan-the-Barbarian was the canine love of my life. During his final year, he could barely walk, but loved his daily outings, so we wheeled him around in a baby stroller. He died in my arms at age seventeen. He was a frail, old man—although Lee still refers to him as the dog who came through walls.

—Lynn Sunday—

A Thief Among Us

You can trust your dog to guard your house but never trust your dog to guard your sandwich.
~Author Unknown

We were not rich growing up, but we never went without. Sometimes though, I saw Mom and Dad sacrifice what they wanted for things we girls needed. As I got older, I noticed when Mom gave up a new pair of jeans because one of us needed a new coat or Dad said he wasn't hungry and didn't take a piece of chicken at the dinner table so there would be more for us.

One day, after dinner, Mom said to us kids, "This is my 5th Avenue candy bar. Don't anyone eat it." She walked into her bedroom and put the candy bar on her nightstand.

Since Mom rarely claimed anything for herself, I knew she must really want that candy bar. Perhaps she was having a bad day.

We cleared the dinner table and then went upstairs to our room to do our homework before we got ready for TV-watching time, snacks and bed. We were up there for a while when Mom, in a stern voice, called us downstairs to the kitchen. We could tell she was angry, but why?

She looked like she had tears in her eyes. She said, "I just told you kids that I saved a candy bar for me, and now it's gone! Who took it?" We all looked at each other, shaking our heads.

This made her even angrier. "I never take anything for myself, and all I wanted was this one candy bar…" she continued for a few minutes. We could tell she was angry, but we could also tell she was more hurt. Then she said, "Okay, if no one is going to 'fess up to this, you all have to sit in the living room with no TV, no radio, and no talking until someone confesses."

We marched into the living room, each taking a chair and a corner of the sofa. We had done this before, and we knew we weren't even permitted to sit near each other. Then Mom went into her room and slammed the door behind her. As the oldest, I knew I did not take the candy, and I spoke up in my oldest-sister voice. "Okay, which one of you brats took Mummy's candy?" They all shook their heads. We all blamed each other and began to argue. No one was coming forward. This was unusual. Normally, under the pressure of no TV or snack, someone would have cracked by now.

After what seemed like hours, Mom came out of her room, asked us one more time, got the same answer and sent us back up to our rooms to finish homework. No TV or snack and early to bed. I was being punished unjustly for something one of my brat sisters did, and no one was taking responsibility!

Well, everyone survived that ordeal, and the weekend arrived. Still a bit hurt that her children, whom she had taught better than to steal or lie, did not take responsibility for their actions, she must have felt like a failure as a mom.

Saturday morning after cartoons was usually cleaning day. We girls were upstairs making our beds while Mom was downstairs. This day, she decided to move the sofa and clean behind it. She did this occasionally because our dog Nicky used the space to get away from the cats and hide his squeaky toys and bones.

Mom called up to us to come down. We noticed that she used her nice-mom voice, and we came running down the steps. My mom said, "I was just cleaning behind the sofa, and look what I found!" She was holding a chewed and empty 5th Avenue candy-bar wrapper.

Mom looked at us… we looked at her… and we all started laughing! The culprit had been found. We all started talking at once. "I told you it wasn't me." "We tried to tell you, Mom." "You knew we would never take your candy, Mom." Mom kept hugging us and apologizing.

Mom called for Nicky, who came in wagging his tail. Mom held out the empty wrapper. She said in her stern-mom voice, "Nicky, did you do this?" He stopped wagging his tail and tucked it between his legs. He dropped his head, showing his sad puppy-dog eyes. We girls stood still, trying not to giggle. Mom got down lower to the floor and asked, "Well, did you?" He dropped down even lower.

Then Mom couldn't help but laugh. Her voice perked up, and she said to Nicky, "Come here." He got back up, ran into Mom's arms, and licked her face. We all started laughing and petting him.

That day, when we went out to play, my sisters and I took our pennies, went to the corner candy store and bought Mom another 5th Avenue candy bar. Order was once again restored to our household.

In the years to follow, every time something went missing or someone did something they shouldn't have, we jokingly blamed it on Nicky. We blamed him even long after he was gone.

— L. M. Bruno —

I Took My Dog to Work

All of life is the exercise of risk.
~William Sloane Coffin

It was the end of the school year. I didn't have any students with me that day, so as I completed paperwork, my German Shepherd, Baxter, kept me company. Suddenly, I was called away. "Don't worry, boy," I said to Baxter. "I'll be right back, and then we can go outside for a walk."

When I returned, he was gone. I ran up the long hallway looking for him, turned the corner, and came face-to-face with my principal. "Hello," I said. "How are you today?" Tucked behind my back was the leash.

I wasn't supposed to bring my dog to work, and at that moment, I was willing to disavow him if he suddenly appeared. I tried not to look guilty, but I got nervous when my principal asked how things were going for me at the end of the school year. She seemed to be trying to gauge my expression. I forced myself to smile even though I could see Baxter running back and forth behind her in the academic area of our school building. I hoped he wouldn't notice me and come racing over.

I reminded myself to breathe as my heart raced and sweat trickled down the back of my neck. I continued to be pleasant to my principal while answering all her questions. Then my principal glanced suddenly behind her; thankfully, my dog had just disappeared around the corner. "Well, I will talk to you soon," I said, hoping she'd take the hint, which she did. As soon as the principal left, I ran to where I had seen Baxter.

My fellow teachers were working in their classrooms. I ran from door to door, casually saying hello to each of them while looking for Baxter. This routine continued down several long hallways until I finally came upon a teacher who simply pointed and said, "He went that way!"

I made an abrupt turn and found Baxter in the middle of the same hallway. I said, "Baxter, what are you doing?" He wagged his tail, and with his tongue hanging out, he looked completely content. I watched his bum shake back and forth, wiggling at me.

If he could have talked, he would have said, "That's what you get for leaving me all alone in your classroom. Did you really think a German Shepherd would not be able to open that door?" Some days I felt like I got my master's degree just so I could outsmart the dog.

At this point, I needed to get my rambunctious dog back to my classroom on the other side of the building, which meant passing the principal's office. Praise is always good for reinforcement, so I said, "Baxter, come with me. Come on now, let's go on a little adventure. That's a good boy, follow me!" By the grace of God, that worked, and I was able to get him from one side of the building to the other and back into my classroom without the principal seeing us.

Once back in my classroom, Baxter went right over to the doorknob to show me how he used his nose to lift the door handle and his paw to open the door. He got an "A" in problem solving, but I was the one who learned a valuable lesson that day. As I sat down again at my desk, I thought back to that morning before I left the house when I said to myself, "I'll take Baxter to work with me today. What could possibly go wrong?"

— Tamra Anne Bolles —

Best Mistake Ever

We could have bought a small yacht with what we spent on our dog and all the things he destroyed. Then again, how many yachts wait by the door all day for your return?
~John Grogan

"Mom, what's the biggest mistake you made this year?" my daughter asked one night.

"Wow, that's a good question. My biggest mistake this year... Let me think about that." The wheels began to turn.

When we audit our life for mistakes, typically we think of financial gaffes, regrettable relationships, maybe a brush with the law or the consequences of a bad decision. As I began to visually rewind through the year, I was relieved that none of those types of mistakes came to mind and felt quite proud of myself. Maybe, after all these years, I was finally living a responsible life.

There was, however, Hank, our seven-month-old Vizsla. Even as a puppy, he was kind of a mistake. Normally, the word "puppy" conjures thoughts of a cuddly ball of fur romping about. For Hank, however, "puppy" was merely a technical term due to his age. He was a forty-pound cyclone with razor-sharp teeth, the energy of a nuclear reactor, and zero concept of the words "no," "ouch," or "animal control officer." Not only was he high maintenance as an overly energetic family member, but he was expensive. My big mistake involved grossly underestimating the psychic and monetary toll this dog would take on us.

"This is the last of the major expenditures for Hank, right?" I asked my husband as we exited the pet store with an eighty-dollar pet gate for the back of the car. (Hank had outgrown the $120 car crate.)

So far, we'd purchased (insert the *ka-ching* sound of a cash register after each item): an indoor crate, a car crate, three crate pads (he shredded the first two), a pet gate, a special-order collar with I.D. tag, a prong collar, an e-collar, a food bowl, an indoor water bowl, an outdoor water bowl, a dog house (since taken over by stray-cat squatters), how-to books we skimmed (sort of), T-bone-steak-shaped training treats, blaze orange cold-weather jacket, food, shots, squeaky toys, chew toys, a tennis-ball thrower, tennis balls, rawhide chews, a pet bed he ignores, a regular-length leash, an extra-long leash, a basket to hold it all, and a private consultation with a dog trainer to see if he needs therapy.

I won't even mention how much we paid to buy him from the breeder—okay, I will—$1,200. Is this ever going to stop? I can't decide if I should update my resume or borrow against my 401(k).

Then there were the vet bills, like the one for an emergency visit for an eye abrasion. When all was said and done, we paid over $200 for a cone, eye drops, ointment, and a "your dog is a hound from hell" lecture from the vet tech when he nipped at her. Ever tried to put eye drops in a puppy's eye? How about when he's wearing a cone?

When I called to make the appointment to have Hank neutered, I asked for an estimate. Around $130, I was told, which was pleasantly surprising. However, they didn't tell me about the long list of services the vet was happy to provide while Hank was sedated, such as ear check/cleaning, nail trim, blood tests, fluoride treatment, Botox injections—okay, I made up the Botox part—but by the time I was finished checking the appropriate boxes on the admission form at the vet's (who wouldn't pay twenty-five dollars for someone else to express a dog's anal glands?), the total was nearing $250. Ever tried to fill out a form with a manic dog leashed to your arm? How about a hound from hell?

As I left the vet's office, I was relieved to know Hank would be spending the night. After the waiting-room fracas minutes earlier, I would have paid $800 cash to have a twenty-four-hour Hank vacation. I was happy for the break, and surely this would be the last big expense, right?

Wrong. Turns out Hank needed training and lots of it. Even though he could manage to sit, stay, lie down, and shake, he struggled to perform them with distractions, i.e., other dogs, new people, loud noises, a bag of chips, the ironing board, peanut butter… Did I say he struggled? What I meant to say was he couldn't do them at all. Put another way, Hank's energy level made the Tasmanian Devil look chill. So, add to the tab six months of obedience training for $250 (*ka-ching*!).

Although I may have grossly underestimated the time, energy, and money Hank would cost, what my family underestimated was how determined I was to mold him into a great dog. I expected that by the time we'd finished with training classes, he'd be able to sit and stay as a marching band covered in peanut butter, carrying ironing boards, eating chips, and playing "Seventy-Six Trombones" passed by.

Now, back to my bedtime conversation with my daughter. "Nothing comes to mind, honey. Sleep well. I'll see you in the morning." No need to burden my daughter with these thoughts. Hank was not really a mistake, just a mistake in my own expectations.

Hank continues to be expensive eight years later. Yet when I take an inventory of Hank's life, I realize that my greatest underestimation of all was how much I would grow to love him. I can't imagine life without his exuberant happiness, fondness for cuddling, and the way he gazes at me lovingly with his smoldering eyes, now clouded with age. Though he had a rough start, Hank turned out to not only be a great dog, but a beloved and completely spoiled member of our family who was, is and will continue to be worth every penny.

Did I mention how adorable Hank looks in his new argyle sweater? It goes perfectly with his winter booties!

— Tonya Ranum —

Pepito's Tale

Everyone thinks they have the best dog,
and none of them are wrong!
~W.R. Purche

My guests will soon be coming.
I am busy sprucing up.
Getting the house all ready
means no time for my pup.

The candles are a-flicker,
the dessert and coffee made.
Pepito's underneath the bed
just wishing we had played.

Friends arrive, the party starts
and just when things are humming,
I quickly glance down the hall
and see Pepito coming.

What's in his mouth? Oh, no!
Not my black lace underwear.
That little runt is chewing
on my very finest pair.

Everyone is laughing
and playing tug-of-war
with that four-legged devil
and my lacy underdrawers.

He looks at me so innocent
with that adorable face.
Remorse or guilty conscience?
Not a glimmer or a trace!

He will not give them up
No matter how we try.
I hide my face, embarrassed,
and swallow up my pride.

This story, oh, too true!
I'll remember with regret—
such chaos brought about
by my spoiled, neglected pet.

This Chihuahua's days are numbered,
and when he's laid to rest,
his tiny coffin will be lined—
with my black lace Sunday best!

—Yvonne Evie Green—

The Gingerbread Massacre

The smells of Christmas are the smells of childhood.
~Richard Paul Evans

"Be sure to hang the delicate ornaments high," said Polly, my stepmom. "Jake might mistake the colorful glass balls for his toys and try to bite them." Jake was new to our family that Christmas. He was a beautiful brown-and-white puppy, with giant puppy feet and a supremely expressive face. And, of course, he was loaded with the puppy curiosity that makes everything a toy.

Two weeks before Christmas, we brought out the boxes of ornaments, many of which had been in Polly's family for ages. Among them were some handmade treasures, including a special box that held an entire gingerbread family. They were real cookies, hung with red ribbons, made with love by one of Polly's relatives many years earlier, and lovingly preserved.

Every now and then, I or one of my little sisters—Ruth and Sue—would pretend we were going to nibble one, knowing that Polly would say, "You'll break a tooth! They're so old that they're rock hard and tasteless." We didn't really want to eat them, but we enjoyed teasing Polly.

Since we didn't know how Jake would react to the ornaments

or the tree, we were careful to put delicate or potentially dangerous ornaments up high. No glass balls or ornaments, nothing small enough to choke him, no tinsel or lights were within his reach. Jake sniffed the tree a lot, probably puzzled and delighted that the outside was inside. Those first couple of days, Polly caught him starting to lift a leg on the tree twice. But he learned quickly and settled for sniffing from a distance.

The weekend before Christmas, Dad and Polly had a great idea. "That new holiday movie is playing. Let's all bundle up and go see it at the drive-in." Excited, we jumped into the car with our blankets, pillows and bags of homemade popcorn, and off we went for a great evening.

A few hours later, we returned home and opened the front door to find… a terrible mess. No, it wasn't the Christmas tree. In fact, we weren't sure what it was. We stood just inside the door staring at big brown chunks of… something. We all looked at each other sideways, fearing the worst, and wondering who would be brave enough to see what it was. As it turned out, the mess was Jake's bed, which he'd destroyed. Left alone for the first time, he must've gotten bored, attacked it and left it for dead. We didn't know then that the bed was not the only casualty.

The next morning was Saturday, so we girls were in the living room. I waited for *American Bandstand* to come on, while Ruth and Sue watched cartoons. I noticed that they weren't sitting in their usual TV-watching spots. Instead, they were very close to the Christmas tree. We weren't allowed to touch any of the presents, but we could look. So Ruth and Sue "took inventory" frequently, checking carefully to see if more packages with their names on them had magically appeared.

"Nothing new for me," said Sue. "Just a new one for Dad." Ruth continued to look, leaning in every direction as far as she could, without touching. Then something caught her eye.

"Hey, who broke Gingerbread Baby?" she asked, accusingly.

That brought Polly out of the kitchen and into the living room fast. "Where? Show me!" Ruth pointed out the former baby cookie, which was now just a head, still tied to the tree by its red ribbon.

"Here's another broken one," said Sue. "It's Gingerbread Grandpa. Or it was. Now it's just his head, hat and part of his bowtie."

That caused a flurry of inspection, and soon it was clear that four members of the gingerbread clan — Baby, Grandpa, Aunt and Uncle — were now just gingerbread heads.

"I didn't do it," I said, just in case anybody thought I'd had a midnight snack of rock-hard ornaments. Quickly, my sisters echoed me with denials of their own. In unison, we girls and Polly all looked at Dad. If anyone was famous for midnight-snack raids, it was him.

"Not me," he said. "I'm holding out for fresh gingerbread."

Polly stared intently at the gingerbread catastrophe. "Wait just a minute," she said as she realized that only the low-hanging cookies were affected.

As if in slow motion, she turned and said, "Jacob!" Until that moment, Jake had been sitting by Dad, looking happy as ever. Suddenly, his posture changed. Guilt spread over his face as surely as if he'd been caught with Gingerbread Grandpa's bowtie in his mouth. With his head bowed a little, he tried not to meet Polly's gaze, but it was clear what had happened. It was as if he were wearing a sign that said, "I killed three generations of an innocent family. Not sorry!"

We learned a lesson that year. To Jake, rock-hard, decades-old gingerbread cookies were just a different flavor of dog bone. Every Christmas from then on, when the ornaments came out, the first thing we did was hang the survivors of the Gingerbread Massacre, as well as the four gingerbread heads, high up on the tree, out of Jake's reach. And every year, he'd stare up longingly, as if remembering those tasty "dog treats" he enjoyed during his first Christmas season.

— Teresa Ambord —

Grab and Dash

Every snack you make, every meal you bake,
every bite you take… I'll be watching you.
~Author Unknown

It was the end of a typical busy workday, and I was preparing for the next day by showering and blow-drying my hair. My husband Thad was finding comfort in his favorite snack: a prune Danish with a glass of milk. He settled himself in bed to watch an evening show on TV and enjoy his well-deserved dessert. But our German Shepherd/Collie mix, Roxie, saw this as an invitation to play ball.

Nuzzling him with the ball in her mouth, Thad realized that ignoring her was futile. So, he got out of bed, set the pastry and milk on his bedside table, and began throwing the ball down our long hallway. Roxie would retrieve it and bound into our bedroom, only to find that Thad had disappeared. As she came farther into the room, Thad would rise from his crouched position at the foot of the bed and roar like a bear ready to attack! He would wrestle the ball from Roxie's mouth and throw it back down the hall again.

I watched this game in the reflection of the mirror for a good five minutes as I continued to blow-dry my hair. Each time, Thad would hide at the foot of the bed, and Roxie would retrieve the ball and come looking for him.

On a final throw, Roxie once again went bounding down the hall to retrieve the ball, and Thad assumed his crouched position again at the foot of the bed. Except this time, when Roxie came in, she didn't go to find Thad. Instead, she put her two paws on top of the nightstand and made a mad grab for Thad's pastry.

Thad heard her toenails clicking on the nightstand and rose up just in time to see that she had the pastry in her mouth. He roared like an angry bear that had just lost his honeypot. Roxie looked up, her eyes wide with fear as she and the Danish tore down the hallway. She lost traction on the tile floor and skidded as my half-angry, half-laughing husband chased her.

At this point, I was laughing so hard I had to sit down. While Thad was none too happy (it was the last pastry), he admitted readily that leaving the snack unattended on his nightstand was way too much temptation for a dog like Roxie who had spent the first two years of her life as a junkyard dog.

Thad joined me in laughter and said, "You can take the dog out of the junkyard, but you can't take the junkyard out of the dog."

— Loretta D. Schoen —

Rufus's Unwrapped Gift

In order to really enjoy a dog, one doesn't merely try to train him to be semi-human. The point of it is to open oneself to the possibility of becoming partly a dog.
~Edward Hoagland

The sun was barely up that Christmas morning, so most of the light in the living room came from the twinkling strands on the tree. I'd gotten up early to plug it in and bring a little extra magic into the house before my daughter walked down the stairs to open her gifts.

Gifts had been tucked around the base of the tree, under the bottom row of branches, for about a month. Rufus, our senior Boxer mix we'd adopted twelve years prior hadn't so much as sniffed at them.

That morning was different, though, because he watched as my onesie-clad daughter ripped the paper off her presents, tossed it aside, and marveled at what she found.

Next, it was my husband's turn. He unwrapped his gifts (more carefully than our daughter had). Then my turn. Then it was time for Rufus's gift. We were thrilled to give it to him.

It was a brand new, luxurious, extra-large bed where he could lounge and rest his old, aching joints. He'd been such a wonderful boy for all these years, eager to please, loyal, protective but friendly… He deserved a nice bed upgrade.

We'd taken our time picking that bed out as a family. The colors needed to match the living room décor because that was the room it'd be in. Plaid was nice and masculine while also classy and sophisticated, and Rufus was quite the dapper gentleman. From the first week we had him, he'd trotted through the house with a Nylabone hanging from the side of his mouth like a pipe. If he'd been a human, he'd have spent most of his time in his study, surrounded by leather, books, and gleaming mahogany.

So we bought the bed that was the perfect match for the living room, his age, and his personality. We didn't wrap it up in Christmas paper like the other gifts; we just brought it downstairs and lay it in front of him, expecting him to check it out for a few seconds and then curl up, settle in, and almost immediately start snoring.

Rufus had other plans. He was one of the family and everyone else had ripped the outside layers of their gifts away to reveal the true prizes underneath. He started to check it out the way we expected him to, but the lying on it part never happened.

All of us humans ended up distracted in one way or another—either by making breakfast or opening a toy—and within minutes, Rufus had torn the "wrapping paper" off his gift while no one was watching. Stuffing was strewn all over the carpet and puffed up from the middle of the bed. None of us were sure how it had happened so fast, but there was Rufus, looking undeniably confused and surprised, as if he just knew he'd followed the rules and done what everyone else did, but things didn't turn out just the way they were supposed to. We all saw the "Oh, no, I messed up…" realization wash over him. He was ashamed of himself and probably more than a little sad about not having a chance to fall asleep on something so cozy.

In hindsight, it would've made perfect sense for us to wrap the bed in shimmering Christmas paper just like all the other gifts. Rufus was smart and a part of the family. He'd finally figured out the art of unwrapping presents on Christmas morning, and we hadn't given him paper to tear through. Oops.

(And yes, we bought him another bed.)

—Crystal Schwanke—

Chapter 6

On the Road

Travel Wizard

The bond with a true dog is as lasting
as the ties of this earth will ever be.
~Konrad Lorenz

I grabbed Merlin's leash as he hopped out of my car in the busy airport parking lot. "Promise me you'll be a good dog," I said, uttering a silent prayer.

Almost two years earlier, Merlin had moved into my home and heart as a three-pound Toy Australian Shepherd ball of energy. Now he'd reached his full weight of seventeen pounds.

I've discovered that Australian Shepherds have unlimited energy. Merlin loves to run, play and bark—especially bark. He's not a watchdog, but he barks whenever he spots a potential playmate—dogs, kids, and some adults—as if to say, "Here I am. Come play with me." He has also appointed himself as my miniature protector. When he spots another male dog getting close, he positions himself between me and the other dog and barks nonstop until he's out of sight. I've tried all sorts of training techniques—ignoring the behavior, scolding him, spraying water or bark deterrent, or blowing a whistle, all to no avail. Merlin just likes to bark.

I'd moved to a new state almost three years earlier and had missed the last two Christmases with my son and granddaughters. The trips I'd made home had been by car in the summer. This year, I was determined to go home for the holidays, which meant flying with Merlin.

I hate flying. I know it's irrational, but I'm terrified of planes. I shake for days anticipating trips. All the way to the airport and throughout the flight, it's an all-around miserable experience. I'd discovered that my little buddy, Merlin, was great at calming me down. During storms or other stressful times, just holding him in my lap settled my nerves. I talked to a therapist, who wrote a letter so he could be designated as an emotional-support dog. I knew that meant I could take him with me on flights, but how would he react? I'd heard horror stories about people getting thrown off planes because their dog barked.

I took a chance, bought a ticket, and filled out the necessary paperwork for him to fly with me. In the weeks leading up to our flight, I tried to train him by taking him everywhere with me — to stores and events with lots of people. He was fine until he spotted other dogs or running children. Then he'd revert to being a crazy dog. My neighbors and family members told me I was nuts to try and fly with him — that he'd never behave in an airport or on a plane.

I disagreed. I knew he cared about me and would step up to do what I expected. However, I have to admit, as the day grew closer, I was nervous. I began to doubt the dog I had so much faith in.

So there we were at the airport. Of course, the minute we walked inside, there was another dog, and Merlin started to bark. I told him no, and he stopped immediately. That was it. All through the long baggage and security lines, he stood by my side and didn't make a peep. We boarded the plane, and he sat calmly on my lap, watching everything that was going on but not making a sound. Another dog sat across the aisle from us, and Merlin ignored it the entire trip. Upon arrival at Denver International Airport, we passed hundreds of other dogs in the concourses and terminals, but even when they barked at him, Merlin remained silent.

This wasn't the end of our trip. We had to board two shuttle buses on the trip to my son's house. Merlin was the perfect traveler.

At my son's house, Merlin reverted to his crazy, noisy self. Had it been a fluke? Would I be so lucky on the flight home? I didn't need to worry. From the minute we boarded the first shuttle on the way home, Merlin transformed to his well-behaved self. No barking the whole way home. I received so many compliments from airport employees, flight attendants, and other passengers on my well-trained dog. I shook my head in amazement.

It's hard to explain the bond between a human and her dog. Somehow, Merlin knew that taking care of me was his important job. And the best part was that I was so focused on Merlin that I forgot to be nervous. I realized that I'd completed two flights without any nerves or shaking for the first time in my life. He'd provided me with a wonderful service. I know some people question whether animals can provide emotional support, but I am proof that they really do. I can't explain how Merlin knew to behave on that trip. I'm just glad he's my best friend, and I look forward to many more trips with him by my side.

—Jill Haymaker—

Drive-Thru Dog

Dogs love to go for rides. A dog will happily get into any vehicle going anywhere.
~Dave Barry

"Want to go for a ride?" I ask. My Beagle, Lulu, barks once, which means yes. Whether we're going for a long trek to Grandma's house for dinner or just down the street to the hiking trail, Lulu loves to ride. I grab the big towel and prepare her seat while she waits patiently.

"Up, up!" She jumps up onto the front passenger seat of my car and coils her tail close around her body, knowing I'll tuck it in if she doesn't. When Lulu came to us from a shelter as a puppy, I would tuck her tail in for her. Nine years later, she knows the routine and does it herself, but I still check to make sure her tail is safe before closing the car door.

She sits regal as royalty while we back out of the garage. But by the time we reach the end of the driveway, Lulu has put her front paws up on the passenger-side door and turns to look at me over her shoulder. This is how she tells me it's time. I open her window partway, and she leans out, the laboratory of her nose deciphering all the smells: bluegrass and asphalt, lawn mowers and neighbors, insects and apple blossoms. As we gain speed, her long, floppy ears lift on the breeze. Happily, she turns her nose toward the sky, collar jingling.

First stop, the coffee shop drive-thru. I place our order while Lulu bounces on the seat, hardly able to contain her excitement. She knows what's coming. By the time we pull up to the window, she's so excited that she's almost on my lap. The cashier has my coffee and Lulu's puppy cup of cream ready. Quickly, Lulu laps the cup clean.

Still licking her chops, she settles back onto her seat while I chatter about treats and traffic. Her back is warm and soothing beneath my hand. We make easy partners and good companions.

At our next stop, Lulu leans over me again to greet the bank tellers who gather at the window to exchange pleasantries. We get down to business, and when the teller passes my finished banking through the chute, I see she's placed a small dog biscuit inside my envelope. Lulu crunches down her second treat of the morning and then sits back to watch the traffic glide by.

As soon as I climb out of the car to pump gas at our next stop, she leaps onto the back seat to keep me company through the window. I run into the store for a gallon of milk and a couple of bananas. When I come back a few minutes later, she is curled up on my seat waiting for me.

The treats at the coffee shop and the bank are special, but Lulu loves the people even more. That's why her favorite stop is the school. Now we pull into the school loading zone and settle in for a wait. Content to be out riding with me and having a tummy full of biscuit and cream, she curls into a ball on the seat to snooze while I catch up on some reading.

Before long, the school bell rings, and children come streaming out onto the lawn. Always alert, my furry co-pilot sticks her head out the car window, and kids stop by to stroke her smooth brown head and scratch her soft ears, a welcome respite after an afternoon of spelling tests and long division.

My kids make their way to our car, and Lulu licks them hello before they climb into the back seat. Time to head home.

When we turn onto our street a few minutes later, Lulu recognizes it and starts to talk. Home sweet home. Our errands have come to an end.

Even though it was just an ordinary day, Lulu's company made it special. There's no one I'd rather be running errands with. Rain or shine, any time she hears the clatter of my keys or the tread of my shoes in the back hall, she's ready to go. A car ride wouldn't be the same without my faithful companion.

—C. L. Nehmer—

Trouble in the Air

If you're uncomfortable around my dog, I'm happy to lock you in the other room when you come over.
~Author Unknown

The convulsive quaking begins in the taxi, and by the time my husband Ivan, my kids and I are in the terminal, it feels like a high-speed vibrator is in Gibson's doggy travel bag. We are hoping this is simply a case of Gibson being a first-time traveler. We gave him the puppy Xanax an hour before boarding the plane. (It turns out I could use one, too.) We feel well-prepared for his first flight to Florida. We have his travel health certificate, his stylish black-and-white houndstooth backpack, and his travel meds.

Just before takeoff, I place Gibson under the seat in front of me for what I think will be the duration of the three-plus-hour flight to Miami.

During takeoff, his shaking, heavy panting and buggy eyes are just the tip of the iceberg. Once we're airborne, Gibson begins chewing frantically at the zipper of his bag. Cujo has arrived! "Gibson, it's okay," we keep saying, but he is having none of our assurances. Soon, his gums are bloody from chewing, and he's making definite headway on tearing through the bag.

I reach down, partially unzip the bag and place my hand inside to reassure him once again, but that doesn't help. Ivan says, "For God's sake, just pick up the bag and put him on your lap." And that is what I do.

A flight attendant comes by and warns me sternly that Gibson "must stay in the bag on the floor under the seat in front of you."

"But this is our first flight with him. We even medicated him, but it isn't working," I reply. "He's chewing his bag, and the people around us are okay with him being on my lap." But she is having none of my excuses, and I dutifully put Gibson and the bag back underneath the seat.

Gibson's fearful nature and anxious temperament became evident almost immediately after we adopted him. Strangers would ask me if he was a rescue dog. "Why is he always shaking?" they asked. "What is he afraid of?" "Was he abused?"

"I don't know" was my usual reply. Sometimes, I told people that he was indeed a rescue and left it at that.

Ivan is not the rule follower that I am. He is practical and rational, not a people-pleaser. Once the flight attendant leaves, Ivan picks up Gibson in his ripped bag and places him on his lap, covering the bag with a blanket. "We'll give you our phone numbers and e-mails in case you need to show the airline that we're cool with your dog on your lap," our fellow passengers offer. They can see that Gibson needs to be held.

But that doesn't stop the flight attendant from coming back with the official airline rule book. Her face is flushed as she points to the book and threatens, "If you don't comply with the rules and put your dog back under the seat, I will need to report you."

Ivan replies, "Fine, you do that." Upon landing in Miami, the squad car is visible as we pull up to the gate.

The kids are shocked at seeing the police waiting for their dad on the tarmac. I am mortified and a little embarrassed. And yet I feel proud of Ivan. He seems unfazed as the flight attendant tells all passengers to stay in their seats as she comes to escort him off the plane. He hands me Gibson, and with a reassuring wink, whispers that he will be just fine. The houndstooth bag that I hold is no longer shaking, and Gibson is happy to be on the ground.

Ivan is escorted to a black-and-white Crown Victoria. Our two teenagers, Adam and Mia, are holding up their iPhones to video their dad being led off the plane in disgrace by two husky Miami police officers.

Ivan is taken away and locked in a small, bare-bones room in the bowels of the airport while the officers take his passport and perform a perfunctory background check. Soon, it becomes evident to all that Ivan is not a clear-and-present danger. The officers thank Ivan for his patience and tell him that he is free to go. Before being released, Ivan asks for the name of the flight attendant who reported him. The officers respond, "Well, we can't tell you her name, but her name tag may have said Diane." They all share a laugh, and my husband is finally reunited with our family in baggage claim.

As for Gibson, the Xanax has finally kicked in, and he is down for the count. Cujo is nowhere to be seen.

Later, Ivan receives a letter from the airline declaring that he is on probation for two years. We aren't certain what that means except that he is going to follow the rules from now on when he flies.

Luckily, on our next flight, Gibson and I are upgraded to first class, and we have a surprisingly different experience. The flight attendant and fellow passengers love Gibson and beg me to take him out of his carrier after takeoff. He enjoys the attention and even licks my seatmate's beer.

This is just the beginning of our many "travel tails" with Gibson.

— Tina Rafowitz —

BFFs

A good person will feel guilty even before a dog.
~Anton Chekhov

We slept in the same bed just that once—memorable because it was so unexpected: I knew Gus loved my best friend more. On the road trip up, I'd watched his eyes follow her as she walked away to take her turn at the restroom while I stayed back with him. He moaned a little as she went off without him.

We were heading north to Maine, to the Inn by the Sea, on the coast near Portland. They would welcome us to the dining room, even covered with sand after an afternoon romp in the waves, deliver treats to the room, and provide the best bedding.

That first night, Joan and I indulged our every desire at dinner: oysters, champagne, chocolate, and more. Gus did not partake, and instead rolled his eyes at the children who were showing off their ball-on-a-paddle routines for him at the next table.

Following a last morsel of mousse and the departure, at last, of the annoying children, Joan and Gus went off for a post-dinner beach walk while I went upstairs to read Dostoevsky. I felt like an idiot. White terry-cloth robe and slippers, after-dinner mints, music streaming through high-fidelity speakers, balcony, sunset view—super romantic and no companion of my own.

Joan's first marriage had lasted a lifetime, since age thirteen till death did them part. Gus was new, an attempt to fill the empty space in her heart. Gus was no Bob, for sure, though he was more willing to obey if Joan used the right tone of voice.

I claimed I didn't want the burden, and most of the time this was true. I liked my freedom. I'd been married, done that; this was a whole new phase of life, uncharted as far as I could tell, no rules for what we were "supposed to do" now. We'd gone to school, graduated, wedded, given birth, had careers, achieved, volunteered, and cared, so let the wild rumpus start! Joan and I got together as often in the year as distance allows, for locavore food, excellent wine, wide open landscapes, and nonstop conversation. But it was hard. She was east coast, I was west, plus now she had Gus, who didn't like flying.

Gus burst through the door first, windblown, lively, his energy a mismatch to the spa ambiance I'd created. Joan looked tired but happy, with the vibrant glow of cool, salty air on her cheekbones. All she wanted was a hot bath and her own terry-cloth robe.

"You look so comfy," she said to me, maybe a little jealous of my unburdened appearance, while I envied her willing ability to take on Gus and adapt her needs to his.

She went upstairs to enjoy the fantastic Inn by the Sea bathtub, and Gus moved around like a whirlwind in the room where I'd been reading my book, exciting the air around me with his good looks and dynamism.

Did I want one of these for myself?

No, I thought, *not for me.*

The room was a suite, with two queen-sized beds. Joan and I had been friends since college, so we'd slept often in the same room while traveling. We would talk late into the night until one of us drifted off to sleep.

We were doing just that while Gus did his own bedtime routine. I'm not sure which one of us fell asleep first or whether it was a dream, but suddenly I felt this body in bed beside me, its warm comfort, muscular form, a shape molding itself around mine. I shifted, conscious or unconscious, I'm not sure, making room in the bed for this unfamiliar feeling, though I could vaguely remember how it felt to be married. After my husband left, I'd slept with my cat Billy for years, but this was different, more substantial. I could feel his heart beating in rhythm with mine, the healthy breath, the desire to move closer against my resistance.

Even asleep, I could imagine Joan's feeling of betrayal if she woke up and found the two of us in bed together. Much as I may have craved unconditional love, even just for a night, I did not return the gestures of affection. Gus remained on top of the blankets and eventually started to snore at my feet. Good dog.

— Marianne Rogoff —

Coast to Coast Canines

The theatre is so endlessly fascinating
because it's so accidental. It's so much like life.
~Arthur Miller

We were filled with enthusiasm and energy, a troupe of stage-struck, starry-eyed and—though not one of us would admit it—slightly homesick singers, actors and dancers. Our bus and truck company of *Fiorello!*, a Tony Award and Pulitzer Prize–winning Broadway musical, would play 101 cities across the United States and Canada. After months of one-, two- and three-night stands, our cast and crew settled in Los Angeles for a six-week run. Furnished apartments were rented, clothing laundered, food home-cooked, and acting, dance and vocal classes booked.

My husband rented a car, and one day our leading lady asked for a ride to a Toy Poodle–breeder located just outside Los Angeles. Five of us thought we were going along for the ride, but each of us ending up falling in love that day.

My husband, an ex-dancer who became a stage manager, lost his heart to an energetic, six-pound white Toy Poodle with a freckled nose and ears that stuck up and reminded us of Jacqueline Kennedy's bouffant hairstyle. Naturally, we named her Jackie.

One of Jackie's kennelmates, the elegant Missy, enchanted our leading lady. Sweet and cuddly Debbie beguiled the dance captain, and the smallest Poodle, Big Daddy, made off with her partner. Mimi, a black-and-white mischief-maker, reeled in the tenor—they made beautiful music together. When the other members of our troupe met our puppies, they too were smitten. Within a week, Mr. Kelly, a Sheltie, and Ming Toy, a Pekinese, had joined the company.

By the time we left Los Angeles, a Yorkshire Terrier and two Dachshunds had been added to the entourage. All the puppies were small breeds able to adjust easily to hotel rooms and sit comfortably on the trains and buses we used for transportation. Our wardrobe trunks now held dog blankets, sweaters, squeaky toys, cans and boxes of dog food, and boots to protect paws from salt when we hit the snows of winter.

"Look! A dog show!" Friendly smiles greeted us every time the tour bus paused for a break. Our star performers were ignored as puppy after puppy left our bus to investigate and rate each rest stop.

When the curtain came down at 11 p.m., we'd return to our hotel rooms, unlock the doors and stand back.... The race was on. Puppies challenged and raced each other up and down the hotel corridors, in and out of rooms, around and over furniture and through our legs. Missy — the one exception — would slow down and devour any leftover dog biscuits.

While performing the musical in Washington, D.C., we met a troupe of touring Russian ballerinas. Although the Cold War was far from over, pats and endearments sparked conversations until bodyguards hustled the dancers away. For a few precious moments, puppy love played a small role in improving relations between two nations.

Jackie, a dancer's companion, became the Pavlova of Poodles — though too shy a dog to tread the boards professionally — and she developed the ability to leap from one side of the bus to the other.

Our dogs were the family we needed on the road. They brought the company closer together and made us less homesick. The cast and crew exchanged feeding and training tips, admired newly clipped and shampooed puppies — although I admit to a few tears when Jackie's puppy fur was gone — celebrated birthdays, and established enduring friendships.

Jackie continued her travels after *Fiorello!* closed, accompanying us as we traveled with national tours and industrial shows. She visited

Wilmington, Delaware during Broadway tryouts; watched soybeans grow in Waterloo, Iowa while we stage-managed a show that featured dancing tractors, plows and earth-moving equipment; and suffered a severe case of indigestion in Hershey, Pennsylvania when she mistook a bar of chocolate soap for a slab of candy.

She was offered a spot in a production of *Wonderful Town,* but she tended to be shy, and I realized she would suffer from stage fright. At home, she would sit by the piano and lend her voice in support as someone reached for a high note.

Between jobs, Jackie practiced grand leaps. If we left the dining room to answer a phone call, our budding gourmet would spring to the table and pull off a bowl. Then she'd devour homemade baked beans or rice pudding—her favorite dishes. On our return, we'd find a happy Poodle stretched out next to an empty bowl, grinning at us and belching indelicately.

Although her entire life was spent in theatre, Jackie remained a morning dog. If the rising sun and washing of our ears didn't wake us, a quick nip on the derriere would.

In 1976, we were rehearsing a musical in Seattle when Jackie, almost sixteen years old, passed on. We were consoled by members of the company who had loving relationships with their own companions—dogs who understood the adventure to be found on the road in different towns, cities and states. They were show-business gypsies with four paws and hearts full of love.

—Elise Warner—

My Dog Can Smile

The best dogs are the ones who possess every character trait you wish to see in your fellow humans.
~Amy Newmark

After my wife, my dog is my best friend and constant companion. She goes with me everywhere, usually with her head outside my truck window and her ears flapping in the wind. She looks like Yoda with a wet nose.

She waits patiently when I go into a store and greets my return with a wagging tail that says I was terribly missed even though I was only gone a few seconds.

She also makes a curious guttural sound that sounds a lot like she is saying, "How are you?" More than once, this has prompted an answer from a stranger next to us at a red light.

I am not going to push the issue here by saying that my dog can also talk (even though I know she can), but I *will* stick with the smiling story.

When I tell people that she can smile, I get that roll of the eyes from people who do not own a dog, and a nod of comprehension from those who do. And it really doesn't bother me that everyone in the neighborhood knows her by name but just refers to me as Dad.

I must also plead guilty to anthropomorphizing, which is a fancy word for assigning human traits to an animal. I will start conversations with her in which I answer for her with what I think she would say, while she sits there smiling at me.

To me, she is a gift from the Almighty who loves me unconditionally and asks nothing in return. This love has gotten me through some very hard times.

Recently, I was stopped by a policeman as I had clearly committed a moving violation by driving on the shoulder of a freeway off-ramp as I hurried to my destination.

I handed over my driver's license while answering his questions, freely admitting my guilt and asking for no mercy.

He stared at us for a moment before closing his ticket book and saying, "I was going to write you a ticket, but I can't do it with that dog smiling at me. Drive safe and have a good day."

I turned to my dog and gave her a pat on the head. She smiled at me as if to say, "I took care of that. Now, what's next?"

—James Michael Dorsey—

Flight Training

We should remember that good fortune often happens when opportunity meets with preparation.
~Thomas A. Edison

Jake didn't know it, but we were flying from Oregon to Georgia and he'd be on more than one flight. I wasn't sure how he'd do, but he does have the temperament for travel. He adapts easily to new situations. Part of the credit goes to his breed, Cavachon. That's a fancy mutt term for a Bichon Frise and Cavalier King Charles Spaniel hybrid.

This was a lot to ask of him, though. And I wasn't my normal self. Normally, I think of myself as resilient and adventurous, but my world had unraveled. A year earlier, Matt, my amazing husband of thirty-four years, had died suddenly in an accident at home. Five weeks later, a windstorm hit, dropping towering evergreens on my front porch and garage. I knew one person couldn't manage the hay meadow and five-bedroom home. I sold and moved to a small rental. It is lovely, but the downsize was grueling.

And now, my son Jack was deploying to Iraq. We were going to visit him, his wife Samantha and brand-new baby girls, Madison and Gracie. Yep, twins.

I did research on the airline's webpage and spoke with the local veterinarian, gleaning some advice and information about requirements and restrictions for pet-in-cabin travel. I made sure Jake's vaccinations and other health information were current, and then scheduled an appointment for his vet check and health certificate. Finally, I talked with an airline representative to be sure I hadn't missed anything before making my reservation.

Logistics handled, I focused on making the trip comfortable for Jake. Practice airplane rides weren't possible so I did the only thing I could think of: We started working with his soft travel crate. I chose an airline-approved model and size that fit Jake's needs. Then I purchased some really stinky treats—well, stinky to me, irresistible to him.

By the time we were done with "ground school," he would enter willingly, turn around, lie down and scoot backward on request—sometimes, all at the same time and without the request. He thought that crate was a treat dispenser.

A back injury and my sixty-something age made it unwise to lug Jake, crate and other necessary items around while navigating three airports. Instead, I began training him to ride on top of my four-wheeled roller suitcase. With Jake zipped into his soft home away from home, I secured his carrier to my luggage.

I unzipped the half-door and out popped a furry, familiar face. I gave him a treat, and then rolled along a few feet. Another treat, another few feet. Soon, he was curiously taking in the house from a new altitude.

Rolling sessions continued, as did "zipped-in" periods. He would need to be fully within the crate during the majority of travel. The training was going well, but we also weren't at 37,000 feet going 500 miles an hour in a confined space.

As I packed, my anxiety ratcheted. Jake took it all in stride. He still gave me the time-to-play-ball stare, faked potty requests so he could enjoy a sniff patrol in the front yard, and cozied up with me in our favorite chair at day's end. I thanked God for such an amazing companion and asked friends for prayer.

Jake and I have an agreement. I don't make him come along unless it is fun for both of us. Was it kinder to take him or leave him? The question plagued me. He'd offer much-needed comfort and companionship, but I couldn't ask that if it was at his expense.

The only thing I could think to do was watch his reactions to the crate closely. So, I repeated the training. He seemed more relaxed, which was reassuring.

Our travel day approached, and Jake's vet screening went well. A health certificate was issued, and the vet suggested a calming collar containing pheromones. I got one for Jake and considered one for myself. It was only wishful thinking; they don't work on humans.

We arrived early at the small airport, checked in at the ticket counter—a must with pet-in-cabin travel—and made it through security. The short hop to the larger airport was, thankfully, uneventful. But I still had concerns over a longer layover and flight.

Once in the bustling international airport, we found the pet-relief area, and Jake stretched his legs and watered the red plastic fire hydrant.

I wheeled him out into the terminal, his soft, fuzzy head leading us like a fur-covered hood ornament. He looked all around, fascinated. People did double takes. Others smiled as they passed by. Many stopped and talked, asking permission to pet him. He soaked it up. As we continued, Jake searched people's eyes, looking for that certain one who needed his special breed of attention.

The more we rolled along, the perkier he got. Then it hit me. The little dog was now hip-high; he could see everything and participate!

"Jake," I said, "you're a big dog and running with the pack!" His happy ears confirmed my observation, and he seemed to say, "I see faces and hands not shins and shoelaces. Yup, and nobody's stepping on me."

When we boarded our next flight, he was ready for a nap. I slid his crate under the seat in front of me and slipped my shoeless foot in alongside to keep tabs on him. He stayed curled up and quiet the entire four hours.

We've flown several times since, and Jake still loves the terminals. He's zipped in when safety or rules require. We try to be courteous, alerting people to his presence, and asking if they mind sharing the elevator and such. Folks are so kind. I've been blessed in my grief as others share their stories while gently stroking Jake's soft locks.

So, please, the next time you're in an airport and see a fluffy little brown dog happily perched on a roller bag, come on over and give Jake an ear scratch. You'll make his day, and I'd love to visit with you, too.

— Nancy Fine —

A Nose for Trouble

One way to get the most out of life,
is to look upon it as an adventure.
~William Feather

We were walking on an abandoned logging road in the Mt. Hood National Forest, heading back to the truck, while I glanced occasionally over my shoulder. Murdock, my chocolate Labrador Retriever, had a long history of getting involved in bizarre and sometimes dangerous situations, but today was one I would not forget. Fifteen minutes earlier, he had barged through the brush surrounding a downed tree and confronted a sow black bear with cubs. Immediately, she sent her little ones up a Douglas fir, but she stood her ground at the base of the tree, popping her teeth and emitting loud huffing sounds.

This was not Murdock's first close encounter with a bear. The preceding September, we had unexpectedly met a large bear at a bend in the trail. However, that bear was quick to flee, and my 100-pound dog seemed to be expecting the same reaction this time. I knew that wasn't going to happen. My commands to "come here" went unheeded, but it certainly appeared the bear might oblige. I had to act quickly.

Murdock's history of creating adventure spanned many years. When little more than a pup, he had flushed a bobcat and three ruffed grouse from the same patch of brush, each going in a different direction. Clearly, the cat's plans for a grouse dinner had been spoiled. Murdock was as surprised as I was, and simply stood swiveling his head as he watched the cat and birds disappear.

Other times had been less amusing. Once, on a wintry walk, Murdock suddenly left the road, jumped down an embankment and disappeared into the brush. Almost immediately, the cold, still woods were split with his piercing cries and the sounds of wrestling in the brush. Plunging down the embankment, I saw that a steel trap had a firm grip on his powerful foreleg. Despite his strength, he could make no headway against the trap, which was chained to a log buried in the ground. The dog was frantic. Kneeling, I reached for the trap as he seized my wrist in his mouth. I spoke his name, and he released me unharmed. Using both hands, I was able to release the pressure, and he pulled free. He was able to walk away without a limp, but we still had to make a trip to the veterinarian due to a broken tooth from biting the steel jaws.

But the excited and angry sow presented a different problem. She would never back down with the cubs in her care, and Murdock was, of course, oblivious to the dangerous situation he had created. With the dog ignoring my exhortations, I had little choice but to step forward, bend down and grab his collar. This calmed Murdock, and we backed away, while I spoke softly to the bear, telling her what a fine mamma she was. Once on the other side of the uprooted tree, we quickly left the vicinity.

That night at home, I watched him sleeping, limbs twitching, and occasionally barking softly. I can only hope his dreams were pleasant as he relived our adventures.

—Robert E. Boertien—

Welcome to Canada!

Why does watching a dog be a dog
fill one with happiness?
~Jonathan Safran Foer

"STOP on the White Line," the sign read as we approached the U.S./Canada border. It was my first trip to Canada in thirty years, and the first border crossing for my husband. We had our Cocker mix, Gypsy, with us as well as our two recently adopted Toy Poodles.

"The papers! Have you got the dogs' papers?" my husband asked with a tone of panic in his voice, as though we hadn't checked on an almost hourly basis to make certain that the dogs' official vaccination records were readily available.

"Yes, Larry, they're right here," I answered soothingly, patting my tote bag. "Hey! Watch where you're going!" In front of us, brake lights were flickering as the line of cars inched toward the guard station. Evidently, the thought of a border-crossing inspection had my husband a little edgier than I'd realized.

I glanced back over my left shoulder. Gypsy was looking out the side window attentively, studying the other cars and their impatient drivers. In contrast, the two Poodles, Teddy and Sandy, were enjoying their usual post-breakfast snooze.

When we were finally first in line, Larry drove forward at what I thought was a perfectly acceptable speed. The border guard, however, was of a different opinion. Raising her right palm forward in the international sign for "HALT," she pointed with her left hand toward the "STOP on the White Line" sign. Then she marched forward, toward the car window, with an accusatory glint in her eye and her mouth set in a grim, no-nonsense line.

"Can you not READ the sign?" she inquired sarcastically with a French accent.

Larry shrunk behind the steering wheel, and at that moment the Poodles began to rouse themselves from their slumbers. Two sets of sparkling black eyes blinked open, and two tiny pink mouths yawned in unison. Identification tags jingled a jaunty tune as Teddy and Sandy shook themselves awake.

The noise or the movement must have caught the ever-alert eye of the border guard. She peered suspiciously into the back seat. Then, before our astonished eyes, she suddenly transformed. "A-a-a-ah! *Les chiens*!" she enthused, clasping her hands across her heart.

Still in shock, I grabbed the dogs' veterinary records, assuming she was overjoyed at the possibility of barring us all from her country due to insufficient canine health documentation. By this time, she had advanced to the rear window and was peeking in through the three-inch opening for a closer inspection of *"les petits."*

"Ma'am, here are the dogs' vaccination certificates," I ventured timidly, holding the folder out to her.

With a flutter of her hands, she waved away my offer. "*Mais non!*" she responded, with an air of one insulted. "Anyone can see that they are the picture of health." As if to verify her pronouncement, Teddy reached up, grasped the edge of the window glass with his front paws, and stuck his quivering black nose through the opening. His tongue gave one quick but effective lick to the guard's outstretched fingers.

"Eh! Bienvenue, mon petit chou," she chirped. *"Bienvenue!"*

By this time, the drivers backed up behind us were demonstrating their impatience. Beep-beeps and honk-honks filled the air. One particularly rude blare from a nearby semi reminded the border guard where she was and what she was supposed to be doing.

"Ahem." She straightened up and resumed her officious demeanor. "Yes, everything seems to be in order. You may proceed."

Larry stared incredulously in my direction. I shrugged my shoulders. Then he turned back toward the guard. "Thank you very much for your help," he said politely as he shifted gears.

"*Mais ç'est moi qui suis enchanté*," the border guard insisted, her eyes turned toward the back seat.

So, we proceeded. Larry and I looked at each other. The tension dissolved away into smiles of relief and then, the more we thought about it, into giddy laughter.

"Thanks for your help, pups — or should I say, *merci beaucoup*?" I reached back to give our French Poodles a quick pat. "*Mes chiens*, welcome to Canada!"

— Joyce Styron Madsen —

A Creature of Habit

For me, a house or an apartment becomes a home when you add one set of four legs, a happy tail, and that indescribable measure of love that we call a dog.
~Roger Caras

"Mom, can Piper ride to school with us?" my seven-year-old son, Nathan, asked. Piper was our new puppy, and Nathan could hardly stand the thought of being away from her. "If she rides in the car with us, it will be less time for us to be apart."

Sadly, I shook my head. "After I drop you off at school, I have to go to the grocery store, so that wouldn't work out," I answered.

The next morning, Nathan asked again if Piper could ride along when I drove him to school.

"I'm meeting a friend for coffee after I drop you off," I said.

He sighed but didn't argue.

The next morning, Nathan said, "Mom, are you going anywhere after you take me to school?"

I shook my head and grinned. "Piper can ride in the car today."

Nathan scooped her up in his arms and happy-danced. "Do you want to go to school today?" he asked her in a baby-talk voice.

I got Piper and Nathan secured in the back seat, and we took off for school.

Nathan sang to the puppy all the way there. When we entered the drop-off line, Nathan said, "I hate to leave you, Piper, but I have to go to school now."

He kissed the top of her head and then kissed my cheek. "Take care of Piper until I get home, okay?"

I promised to look after "his" puppy while he was away.

The next morning, I fully expected Nathan to ask if Piper could ride along in the car again. What I didn't expect was that Piper would ask as well.

As I did every morning, I took Piper outside for a potty break and then filled her bowl with food. She usually wolfed down her breakfast, but not this morning.

She was sitting in our mud room, right in front of the door to our garage — the door Nathan and I used to leave for school every morning.

I shook her dish and called for her to come and eat.

She just looked at me from the door. It was clear she wasn't moving from that spot.

If she didn't move, Nathan and I would have to step over her to leave or pick her up and take her with us. It was clear what her preference was.

Because she is incredibly cute, we took her with us.

And from that day on, Piper made a new morning routine for herself. Instead of eating, she parked herself in front of the door to ensure she would get an early morning car ride. It was clearly more important to her than her breakfast.

So, Piper started riding to school each morning.

A few weeks later, I needed to run errands after taking Nathan to school. We stepped over Piper who was sitting in the doorway and left. When I got back, she lay on the couch and wouldn't come to me when I called her. She even refused to look at me.

My dog was pouting because she didn't get her way.

While I'm not proud of it, I rearranged my schedule and stopped running errands after taking Nathan to school — all so Piper could have her early morning car ride.

I'd love to say that Piper only dictated what my morning looked like, but that's not really true.

One time, I took Piper on a walk down our driveway to get our mail. The next day around the same time, Piper brought me her leash. I took it from her and said, "Honey, I'm busy right now." She stared at me and whined until I finally took her for her walk.

Now, every day, she watches for the mail lady to drive by and deliver our mail. As soon as she sees her, she grabs her leash and brings it to me. And I have no peace until I drop whatever I'm doing and walk her to the mailbox.

One time when I was making a peanut-butter-and-jelly sandwich, I let Piper lick the knife when I was done. Now no one in the house can make a peanut-butter sandwich without sharing with Piper.

If my kids make popcorn, the second Piper hears that first pop, she runs and parks herself in front of the microwave to make sure they share with her. Same thing if she hears someone open a piece of string cheese.

Our entire family has come to accept that our dog outsmarts us on a regular basis. Piper loves her schedule, and she insists that we stick to it. If we do something once, Piper remembers it and does whatever she can to ensure that the new experience becomes a part of her daily routine.

Piper is a creature of habit, and she makes sure that the rest of us are, too.

I might feel manipulated if she weren't so cute. As it stands, I just love to see her happy.

—Diane Stark—

Changed by the Dog

My Buddy

There is no psychiatrist in the world
like a puppy licking your face.
~Ben Williams

"If you can gain ten pounds, we'll get you a puppy." It was a bargain born out of desperation. We were one year into my outpatient treatment for anorexia when my parents made this announcement. In hindsight, I'm relatively certain bribery is not a recommended therapeutic tool; then again, nothing else seemed to be working.

Even as I agreed to the terms, I thought to myself, *I want a puppy, but even if I can gain the weight, I know I'll give in to the eating disorder again eventually.* I was so mired in the obsessive thought patterns and destructive behaviors attached to my anorexia that a future without it seemed impossible.

Yet, thanks to my parents' constant supervision and the help of my outpatient therapy team, I did gain enough weight to earn my reward — a tiny black Cockapoo puppy I named Buddy. We had owned many dogs before — German Shepherds, Labs, and other medium-to-large breeds — but this was the first dog that was truly mine. I wanted a small dog, something I could cuddle when the eating-disorder demons inevitably crept back into my head.

Buddy and I bonded as quickly and firmly as if we had been attached to each other with magical Super Glue. He slept in my room every night, and nearly wiggled himself to pieces with joy every afternoon when I came home from school. From the very beginning, all I had to do was sit cross-legged on the floor and pat my legs, and he would stop whatever he was doing to run over to me and settle instantly in my lap.

Wanting me to take full responsibility for my furry (and, at times, slightly rambunctious) companion, my parents encouraged me to take Buddy to puppy kindergarten. He was by far the smallest dog there, but that didn't stop him from becoming best friends with a giant Newfoundland. Even though my dog looked like something the other dog had coughed up after grooming itself, the pair refused to do their exercises unless they were side by side. Buddy was as determined as he was diminutive.

The first few weeks of training weren't exactly a walk in the park. I was still weak from the eating disorder, which continued to sap my mental and physical health. And Buddy… well, Buddy was still nervous-peeing every time the instructor came near him. However, with time, patience and more than a few pairs of wet shoes, both of us started to make some progress. Buddy learned to sit, stay, and walk at my side, with or without his lead. For me, cracks of light began to break through the darkness that had hung over me for nearly two years. Watching Buddy grow from a trembling dust bunny into a happy, well-behaved dog reminded me what it was like to feel joy. I wasn't cured, not by a long shot, but the idea no longer seemed as impossible as it once had.

Upon his graduation from puppy kindergarten, the instructor approached me and asked if I was interested in trying to get Buddy certified as a therapy dog. "He's the perfect size to sit on the lap of a wheelchair-bound patient at one of the hospitals or nursing homes where our local chapter volunteers," she said, giving Buddy a scratch between his floppy ears. "It would mean more classes and a commitment to volunteer a certain number of days each month. Does that sound like something you guys could do?"

I balked at the idea at first. Something like this was completely out of my comfort zone. Anything that triggered my anxiety increased the risk of backsliding further into the false security of my eating disorder. But when Buddy looked up from my lap with his round black eyes, I knew there was no way I could say no. After all, he had brought so much comfort to me. It seemed wrong not to share that with other people who could benefit from his incredibly sweet nature and adorable bouncing gait.

"We're in," I replied, with more than a little trepidation.

The training was extensive and required participation at several public events to ensure that Buddy could tolerate crowds, noise, and lots of distraction. Sometimes, he had a hard time keeping up with his Newfoundland pal, who was training alongside us. During one parade, I picked him up and carried him the last stretch of the route as his little legs began to teeter precariously. However, not even the limitations of his stature could contain my sweet Buddy's lionhearted persistence, and both of us gained the certification by the time I turned sixteen.

At least one Saturday per month, we committed to visiting the local nursing home with the therapy-dog chapter. I was nothing short of petrified the first time we walked in to visit the residents. Everything smelled and looked so… sterile. What if Buddy slipped back into his old habits and peed on the floor? What if I didn't know what to say to the residents? Feeling out of control was a key factor in my anorexia, and this was a huge challenge to my recovery.

As usual, Buddy put my anxieties to rest within an instant. He trotted in wearing his therapy-dog cape as proudly as a standard-bearing knight. We wandered between the wheelchairs, stopping periodically to ask if someone was a dog person, and if they would like Buddy to sit on their laps. For the most part, the residents lit up as soon as their hands touched his soft, curly fur. Then it would be time for the dogs to perform a little show, and Buddy nearly brought the house down every time he executed his signature trick—standing on his hind legs and dancing in a circle. The joy Buddy brought to others gave me something to hold on to besides anorexia: hope. I knew now that I had more to give the world, something worth fighting back against the voice inside my head that told me, "The only thing you're good at is disappearing."

It took a miniscule black dog with love and gumption that belied his size to teach me to love myself.

Years later, even after I went away to college, and Buddy's wooly onyx coat developed a silvery tinge, he remained my faithful friend. No matter how many years passed, all I had to do was sit on the floor and pat my legs, and he would be there, his eyes shining up at me like I was the only person in the entire world. Even at my most fragile, just being there had always been enough for him, and he was so much more than enough for me. He was my miracle, my hope. My Buddy.

— Laurie Batzel —

Cured with Love and Licks

Every puppy should have a boy.
~Erma Bombeck

When my son was diagnosed with Asperger syndrome, verbal and physical dyspraxia, dyslexia, epilepsy and severe hypersensitivity disorder, my world was shattered. How was my beautiful little boy ever going to cope? While the other children jostled for the ball at playtime, yelling and shouting with joy, Rufus would sit silently watching from the sidelines. He struggled to speak and therefore became an elective mute since this was easier than being bullied for slurring his words. With two left feet, he couldn't keep up with the fun and games, so his teachers let him stay indoors alone, quietly colouring pictures of animals. It was a desperately sad situation that neither my family nor I knew how to handle.

Birthdays had always been rather traumatic for Rufus. He hated to be the centre of attention, couldn't cope with being cuddled or touched, and found it difficult to communicate his feelings. At the same time, nobody was sure what to buy this solemn, silent boy. Each year, I suggested books about animals, something that he was fascinated by, but on his tenth birthday I decided he should have an animal of his own. The problem was I had no idea what sort of pet he could handle.

This was a lad who couldn't organise his own clothes or cut up the food on his plate. What he needed was a friend who would play with him, wouldn't become frustrated by his lack of verbal communication, and would offer him unconditional love.

I decided the right pet would be a puppy. I accepted the fact that I would be feeding, walking and cleaning up after our newest family member, but the love would all belong to Rufus. Maybe, just maybe, this would bring him some happiness.

On the morning of his birthday, Rufus's "gift" woke him up to wish him many happy returns. Autistic faces tend to remain neutral, rarely betraying their internal feelings, but there was no mistaking the sheer elation in my son's eyes. The puppy was a wriggling sausage of smooth black fur, chocolate-brown eyes and whirling tail. He was half Dachshund, half Jack Russell, and one-hundred-percent mischief.

Initially, I was panic-stricken when a long, wet tongue wiped itself across Rufus's face. His OCD manifested itself in the form of a crippling fear of germs, but far from upsetting him, the puppy seemed to override all his debilitating symptoms. After a couple of "accidents" on the carpet, I explained to Rufus that his new best friend would need to be taken out into the garden after every nap and meal. I expected this to become my job, but the role of puppy protector was guarded jealously by Rufus, who insisted on accompanying his new friend outside each and every time.

It took Rufus less than ten minutes to decide upon a name, Maximus (Max for short). From the very start, Max worked his doggy magic on my boy. The first positive signs consisted of whisperings in the bedroom. From beyond his closed door, I could hear my previously silent son chattering away to a puppy who listened attentively to his master's words as they tumbled out. As his confidence with talking grew, Rufus started bellowing Maximus's name from room to room — not that his little black shadow was ever more than a few feet away.

Other wonderful changes followed. Rufus gladly took on the responsibility of feeding Max, and when the pup had completed his course of injections, Rufus took him for regular walks. The outside world was no longer a place to fear, not when he was accompanied by his furry friend. When strangers stopped us in the street to compliment us on such a cute puppy, I would open my mouth to reply, but was invariably cut off by Rufus, who proudly discussed Maximus's unusual parentage and undeniable doggy skills.

Other changes were far subtler but no less magnificent. Although still quite shy and reserved, Rufus began to make friends at school. He still couldn't kick a ball and didn't want to join in with any rough-and-tumble games, but he was happy to discuss his love of animals with other quieter members of the class. He started sharing his animal books and brought in photographs of Maximus to show the other children. In turn, they showed him pictures of their cats, birds and rabbits. Thanks to Maximus, Rufus had connected with the outside world.

Gradually, the responsibility he accepted for Maximus widened into other areas. He started choosing his own clothes to wear (including some pretty outrageous colour combinations). Just as Max ate what was given to him without making a fuss, so too would Rufus, even peas and carrots! Every day was met with joy, not trepidation, and laughter filled our house, which had once been so quiet.

When Rufus was young, specialists informed me that he would never achieve academically, ride a bike, learn to swim, read properly, or break out of the sombre world that he had inhabited from birth. Apparently, there was no cure, just a life of "managing the situation."

Well, I'd like to introduce my sixteen-year-old son, Rufus. He is incredibly tall — six feet, four inches, to be precise. He is handsome, charming, extremely raucous at times, hysterically funny, popular with his peers and, right now, is writing an essay on evolutionary biology. He is a supremely intelligent young man who still adores all forms of wildlife. To this end, he is preparing to study sciences at A Level so that he can go to university and obtain a degree. Long term, he wants to protect our planet and all the creatures that inhabit it. He made lots of friends at high school, but his best friend hangs around the house, waiting for him to come home at the end of the day — that mixture of half Dachshund, half Jack Russell, one-hundred-percent mischief, Maximus.

I don't know what would have become of Rufus if he had never met Maximus. I really don't want to think about that. What I do know is that this wriggling bundle of fur brought genuine magic into all our lives. With love and licks, he found the cure that no other could have given.

—Joanna Elphick—

Just Right

Sometimes, the bravest and most important thing
you can do is just show up.
~Brené Brown

Years ago, I limped away from an eight-year roller coaster of a relationship. I knew if I stayed in our shared home while we unbraided our lives, I might never go.

So, late one evening, I loaded the back of my car with my laptop, clothes, shoes and a few other necessities and headed over to my friend's house.

Jen and her dog Rocky greeted me at the door. We walked past her teenagers doing homework in the kitchen as if it were normal that I was lugging a laundry basket full of my life into their basement.

Rocky, a mini Labradoodle, was quietly attentive. He followed us downstairs and back up again as we made a couple of trips to the car. He nestled into the corner while we hung some things in the closet.

It was getting late. When Jen left me alone in her guest room, I took a deep breath and wondered if I was ever going to feel okay again. I was heartbroken.

Somehow, Rocky understood. After all, he embodied the gentle spirit of a wise, all-seeing elder. If personified, I imagine he would revel in life's simple pleasures, never finish anyone's sentence, and find quiet ways to bring kindness to strangers.

Sensitive souls, like Rocky and me, know how to find each other.

The next morning, I woke to the sound of Jen pacing upstairs, calling for Rocky. I leaned in and realized he was snuggled in with me. Apparently, he wasn't the type to venture to the basement without his people, so my friend had no idea where he was. He glanced at me and then at the door, as if to say, "If you're okay, I better be going." So, I opened the door, and off he went, with more pep than I would expect from an older dog.

On my first night alone, as it turned out, I wasn't alone. Rocky innately knew what I needed most. He stayed with me through the night, as if to say he might not be able to fix the mess that was my life, but he could do one thing: show up for me.

As the days passed, Rocky showed me he was willing to stand in the mess with me. He didn't require an explanation. He didn't tell me what to do next. And, best of all, he didn't expect me to pull myself together. I could just be as I was, up past 2 a.m., binge-watching *Friends* or in bed with the covers over my head in the middle of the afternoon. He'd simply lie nearby with an occasional sigh as if to say, "Yeah, this is tough. I'm here. Let's just breathe."

I began to question why I did so much talking, offering wise words and "helpful" suggestions, whenever my loved ones struggled. Maybe all they really needed was my quiet presence and an occasional sigh to let them know I was with them in their pain.

Over the next couple of months, I grew stronger. Rocky wasn't watching me quite as closely. He seemed to know that I was going to be okay. Eventually, I came to realize it, too.

Soon after, I moved from my friend's basement, found my own place and began settling into my new normal. One afternoon, with my daughter home from college, we went to see some puppies that were available. We met a handsome little Lhasa Apso with a patchwork coat of cinnamon and white who played and played until he fell asleep in my hands with a mini tennis ball still in his grip. Unable to set him down, I paused for a while and watched him sleep. Then I did the only thing I could: I took him home with me. Recently, he turned four.

He's grown so much in these years together. And so have I.

— Mindi Ellis —

Me Time for Two

When the world is at its dismal, dullest or darkest,
your dog will insist on his walk —
and cheer you back to sanity.
~Peter Gray

I had already been facing a few problems before COVID-19 came along. Even before March of 2020, my freelance editing work had dwindled down to virtually nothing. Without warning, the work-from-home career I had built over the past ten years had vanished. I still worked part-time at my kids' school, however, so matters weren't desperate… yet.

By the middle of March, though, the school closed for the rest of the academic year. Now I had no job, plus I had three kids home full-time who needed help with remote learning, and I still needed to do all the household chores and finish the last semester toward my MFA degree. My husband, an in-home healthcare provider, still had work, but my unexpected lack of income weighed heavily on me.

I needed something to keep me occupied, or I feared I would fall into the depression that had marked my teenage years. I knew just the thing. For years, I had wanted to plant a vegetable garden. This was the perfect year! Spending time outside would give me exercise and, more importantly, some personal space.

After waiting out a few rainy days, I headed into our back yard on the first sunny afternoon to do some weeding and planning. As soon as our dog Saffy saw me, she began barking for attention and wagging her tail wildly.

Inwardly, I groaned. Saffy had been a member of our family for five years, but I considered her my husband's or the kids' responsibility. Not mine. I had to keep on top of everything else in the household, didn't I?

I ignored Saffy's barking as I pulled on gardening gloves and got to work. She began whimpering and scratching at the fence that kept her out of the area where I was working.

I stepped into the house and called out, "Can someone take the dog for a walk?"

My younger son was in the living room playing with the kitten he got for his birthday several weeks earlier. "Mom, I take care of the kitten, remember?"

I went to my daughter's room. "Can you take Saffy for a walk?"

She shook her head. "I've got homework. It's so hard without being able to ask my teacher questions about chemistry." I couldn't help her there. I was ready to help her with questions about English, but chemistry was not my forte.

"Why don't you call your cousin? She took that class last year," I suggested.

I went to find my older son to ask him to walk the dog, but he had just stepped into the shower.

"Fine, I'll do it," I muttered to no one as I headed back outside. "Just this once." Then I'd be able to get something done.

Saffy jumped and licked my hands as I leashed her. She led me straight to the gate, and I trotted to keep up with her excited pace as we stepped into the front yard. We walked the length of several houses, stopping frequently so she could sniff a bush, mailbox or random spot on the sidewalk.

We reached the end of the block, and I guided Saffy toward a large field that stretched across a couple of acres. Leaving the road behind, we began to follow a path that wound around the field. Grass grew knee high in some patches, while other areas had been plowed recently. Ground squirrels scampered about, standing tall and letting out warning chirps, disappearing into their burrows before we got too close. A couple of doves flew up from a place in the field where they were likely nesting.

The sun had begun its descent in the sky and cast sharp edges upon shadows as Saffy and I walked. We reached the end of the field and followed a road toward an area that had been a field a few months earlier. Now, nearly a dozen new houses stood unfinished. With their frames unpainted and no windows or doors, I could easily picture them as old and abandoned. Saffy trotted alongside me as we walked the length of the building site, my imagination running alongside as well, alive and active for the first time in weeks.

Our shadows rose in front of us as Saffy and I set off toward home. I breathed deeply and felt more aware of the sights and sounds around me. Buds on rosebushes in a neighbor's front yard. A cat hidden in shadows at the base of a fence, watching us warily. A neighbor power-walking toward us, nodding her hello as she passed (keeping her social distance, of course).

When we got home and entered the back yard, I unhooked Saffy's leash. She raced straight to her fenced-in section. I closed the gate behind her, and she watched quietly while I pulled on my gardening gloves once more and began to pull weeds and hoe a patch of ground. Saffy seemed content after our walk together. She wasn't the only one.

The following afternoon, instead of calling on one of the kids to walk the dog, I pulled my hair into a ponytail, put on my sneakers, and set out with Saffy once again. This time, we followed a path that took us past a reservoir. We watched a dozen or so Canadian geese swimming in the reservoir and sauntering around the fenced area, chattering amongst themselves while keeping a careful eye on me and the dog.

Once again, after returning home, Saffy watched contentedly while I worked in the yard and planted rows of cucumber and zucchini seeds. I felt energetic and inspired.

Every day since, as we continued sheltering in place, I took Saffy for an afternoon walk. Sometimes, one of my kids joined me and the dog. We pointed out sights along our path — grapevines growing thick with young, green leaves or a weeping willow at the end of our block sweeping its branches all the way to the ground.

Saffy still barked and whined when she saw me step out into the back yard, but I didn't groan about it anymore. She was not the only one who anticipated our walks together. They became a time I looked forward to as much as she did, finding peace and inspiration along the paths we took.

— Bonita Jewel —

A Gift from Heaven

Perhaps they are not the stars, but rather openings in Heaven where the love of our lost ones pours through and shines down upon us to let us know they are happy.
~Author Unknown

We've all heard the saying, "All dogs go to heaven." All dog lovers want to believe that their pets do indeed go to heaven. But what if a dog was sent to us through divine intervention? I believe our dog Bella was just that gift.

On August 21, 2017, two weeks after my only child Rachel arrived in Japan as a brand-new sailor in the U.S. Navy, we tragically lost our cousin Kevin Bushell on the USS *John S. McCain*. Ten sailors died that day when their ship was hit by an oil tanker off the coast of Singapore. Kevin had been advising my daughter about the Navy for the previous three years with tips about joining, how to get through boot camp, and how to pick a good job after boot camp. He was the driving force behind her joining shortly after high school. Kevin would send me countless messages on Facebook answering all my Navy-related questions. He was so excited when he found out that Rachel was going to be joining him in Japan, and they would be stationed at the same naval base!

When our family received the news that Kevin was one of the missing sailors, my heart sank, and my world fell apart. Two months prior, in June 2017, seven sailors had died tragically aboard the USS *Fitzgerald*, and Kevin had told me it was a fluke, an accident that could never be repeated. But it was repeated, and this time he was one of the missing. As soon as I heard Kevin was missing along with nine other shipmates, I knew that he was gone.

My grief and worry hit an all-time high when Rachel was sent out on a ship just two weeks after Kevin's death. I could not sleep and was tormented night after night by horrible nightmares about her dying the same kind of horrific death that Kevin did. I had chilling dreams that her ship was hit and sank to the bottom of the sea.

Kevin was buried at Arlington National Cemetery on October 5, 2017. One month later, on November 4, 2017, our sweet Bella was born in Findlay, Ohio to a fellow Navy family that I befriended right after Kevin's death. Kristen was a Navy veteran and had two sons on active duty in the Navy. Her sons owned the male and female dogs that produced Bella and her eleven littermates. It was an "oops" litter, a completely unexpected but undoubtedly welcome surprise.

Bella was the ninth puppy born, and at the time of her birth, she was not breathing. Kristen worked desperately on Bella to get her to breathe, massaging her chest and rubbing her to stimulate air flow. Finally, after thirty agonizing minutes, Kristen got Bella to take her first breath. For several hours, it was touch and go as to whether Bella would survive.

There were twelve puppies born, and all were named after Navy ships. Bella's original name was "Pearl," named after the USS *Pearl Harbor,* but we changed her name to Bella when we chose her in December. Bella was the perfect name for her; she was beautiful and majestic, a gorgeous bi-color German Shepherd/Rottweiler mix with silky black fur and just a touch of brown on her legs. She came home to us on January 6, 2018, at nine weeks old, just a few days before my wife's birthday. We got Bella for my wife, but she was really for me, too. I just didn't realize it at the time. I never knew how much I needed that puppy and how therapeutic it was to have her.

I believe our loved ones who have passed are still with us. Bella was not supposed to live, but I feel that Kevin must have channeled down some of his energy and made sure that Bella survived. He knew she was going to be my emotional-support dog, even though she was supposed to be my wife's birthday present. Bella had a dual purpose when she came into our lives. Of this, I have no doubt.

I had not trained a puppy in over thirteen years. Getting Bella was secretly the best medicine for my pain and grief. Much of my time was spent training her, so I was able to redirect my sadness into love. I had little time to sit and worry about our daughter and what might happen to her while in the Navy.

Until we moved into our new home with a large, fenced-in yard, Bella spent the first few months with us in a small apartment. I lost track of all the times I spent leashing her up and taking her out to do her business, rain or snow. We spent the winter nights playing laser tag with her in the small apartment and watching her do zoomies to expend that bottomless well of puppy energy. Dog training and food selections were a standard part of my day, along with coming home at lunch to let her out while praising her accident-free moments in the dog crate. My mind was so consumed by shaping Bella into a sweet, obedient, and loving dog that I had little time to be sad.

Kevin was an avid animal lover like me. He had saved and rescued all kinds of animals from the time he was a little boy all the way up until his death. The synchronicity of events is not lost on me. I needed Bella and, in some small way, I believe she needed me as well.

After all that Bella did to heal my heart, it was time to give her a gift. In March 2019, we had a rare opportunity to adopt one of Bella's littermates, Piper. Bella and Piper remembered each other and bonded instantly. They now spend their days chasing balls and bubbles in our back yard.

— Michelle Padula —

My Boy, My Pride and Joy

Animals keep you company when you're really lonely.
It helps because when you have a friend around
who always likes you no matter what—
it's harder to feel bad or down.
~Aaron Carter

I remember when I realized that my dad had abandoned me. A nice lady was showing me around the shelter home. She asked, "Do you want a piece of candy?" I smiled as I followed her to her office, but my smile didn't last long. As I reached for the candy, I looked out the window and saw my dad getting in the car to leave. I started to cry and scream out to him, begging him to come back and not leave me.

The candy in my mouth was no longer sweet. All the crying and screaming didn't do any good. The nice lady pulled me into her arms, but I just wanted to know why no one loved me. All I wanted was to be loved.

I tried to think of reasons why no one wanted me. I was just a little boy. What could I have done that caused people to hate me? So, I learned to hate myself. If no one wanted to love me, then I wouldn't either.

I started to steal candy from stores, but it was no longer sweet.

It was bitter, and so was I. All I wanted was to go home to my mom, dad, and siblings. Instead, I started getting into trouble and wound up in a boy's reformatory school. Because of the bad choices I made, I wouldn't be going home again.

In the reformatory, I really felt all alone. I was so young and small that the other boys picked on me a lot. At night, I would cry myself to sleep, praying my dad would show up on visiting day. I would sit by the window in the cottage all day watching for him to show up, but he never came. The other boys who didn't get visitors would play outside, but I just sat there by the window, alone and withdrawn.

When I became an adult, I ended up in the Department of Corrections. For the past twenty years, the adults in custody have been my family. But I couldn't love them even though I have been looking for love all my life. I just wasn't worth loving. That was, until Felix.

Felix is a dog who was abandoned when he was a puppy at the shelter where he was going to be euthanized. But someone saw potential in him and rescued him from certain death. They sent him to a dog program at the same boys' reformatory where I was incarcerated years earlier. When I was there, no such program existed. But as fate would have it, we were destined to meet — two of God's creatures just looking to be loved and to give love in return.

In my years spent in the Department of Corrections, people began to teach me ways to love myself — to stop hating myself and appreciate the good in me, and the good things I have done in life. Being incarcerated most of my life, I never got married or had children. I could not express love. But I've been able to learn how to give and receive love, and to know how it feels. However, even though I was learning to love and like myself, I still felt alone.

When Felix completed his work at the boys' reformatory, the Oregon State Penitentiary adopted him for a first-time dog program. I was at the penitentiary and saw him out and about as his trainer, inmate Ralph, walked him around. I was able to pet him, and give him hugs, kisses, and a treat now and then. Being able to do this really brought out the kid in me.

I thought I could never be a dog handler because you had to be someone special for that. I was still struggling to see myself that way and never thought the institution would even give me that chance. But, as fate and tragic circumstance would have it, I was predestined to be Felix's handler.

Ralph got sick with cancer and ended up in the infirmary. To my utter surprise, I was asked to fill in for him. I jumped at the chance to be one of those special people. I was sad to see what Ralph was going through, but I was also experiencing a warm and wonderful feeling inside. For what seemed like the first time in my life, I was happy. It was as if candy tasted sweet again.

I would take Felix up to the infirmary to visit Ralph and learn all I could about how to care for him. Eventually, the cancer got the better of Ralph, and he passed away. Felix and I were at his bedside. As I was there for Ralph, it was now my responsibility to be there for Felix.

Since day one, Felix has been my boy, my pride, and joy. Finally, at the age of fifty-three, I knew what it meant to love something and to love life. The Pooch Program rescued Felix from being euthanized, but it saved my life as well.

Felix has touched so many lives here at O.S.P. In return for his life, Felix has given back 100 percent. Originally, he was brought to O.S.P. to manage our out-of-control geese population. But when he's not chasing geese off our recreation yard, he's giving so much more to our community. He is like a hospice program, visiting the sick and injured patients in the infirmary. We go up daily to visit the patients, bringing them joy in an otherwise depressing place. I also take Felix out to our mental-health building for the guys there. Like he has done for me, Felix brings joy to so many lives here in the penitentiary.

Felix is also self-supporting. A whole photo program has been built up around him. Inmates and staff alike can have photos taken with him, which they can keep or send home to a loved one. The men love having their pictures taken with Felix, at times in different costumes for the holidays that they can send home to their children. It is a great way to help the family bond. All the proceeds go to Felix's health and wellbeing.

Felix helped me with my loneliness. He has literally become a bridge to my social life. Before him, I always felt left out of people's lives. Now I am a part of this community here at O.S.P. He has also been the inspiration that motivated me to work on my anger issues. In order to remain his handler, I had to learn new ways to express myself.

Because I always felt left out and alone, I was depressed a lot. Having Felix to love and care for keeps my depression at bay. Sometimes, I still get feelings of anxiousness, which can lead to feeling down. In times like these, I hug Felix, feel his breathing, and calm myself down.

Mentally and physically, I was a mess before Felix. But having the responsibility of caring for another living thing has helped me care for myself. Having to be concerned with his diet and exercise, I realized I had to take charge of my own health in order to continue to care for him. In more ways than I have described, caring for Felix has taught me how to give back, and I will be grateful forever for the opportunity.

My days are getting shorter, and my release is on the horizon when I will be back in society. Joining them as an older and more mature man, I will be able to share my story with all those who cross my path. As someone who now loves himself and life, I'm able to give love to those who need it. I can only hope and pray that the Department of Corrections will let me take Felix home with me. We are companions who have shared our lives together. Buddies! Over the years, he has also gotten older and is in need of more care. He needs me to continue to hold him while he rests his head securely in my lap as we finish our journey together.

Before our lives crossed, our futures were uncertain. But now, together, we can care for those in need who are lonely and need a touch of love. We are a team, and life is sweet.

My boy, my pride and joy, Felix.

— Steven Johnston —

My Perfect Friend

The unconditional love you get from a pet is something you carry with you for the rest of your life.
~Kyra Sedgwick

As soon as this fluffy little creature with huge, intelligent eyes looked up at me, I felt a totally new kind of love. It was poignant, protective and fiercely intense. I knew instantly that we belonged together.

Maisie was the outsider of the litter. The other three puppies were piled in the middle of the floor, playing and rolling over each other. Maisie trotted calmly around the perimeter, surveying them solemnly before coming back to sit at my feet. It was the first time we met, but our lives were destined to be intertwined.

I was an outsider, too. I had battled clinical depression since childhood, culminating in a full-blown mental breakdown in my late thirties that nearly cost me my life. I was now forty-one and single. I couldn't have children. But what I did have was a moderately successful business working from home and a heart absolutely bursting with love. The time was right to fulfill my lifelong ambition of having a dog of my own.

When the day finally came for me to take this little puppy home, it was a daunting experience. I had never owned a dog before, and even though I had read everything I could find on the subject, nothing prepared me for the reality. I had sole responsibility for this precious life, and I was determined to do my best to give her the happiness she deserved. Was I good enough? Could I cater to her needs? Most worryingly of all, would she love me? I put these thoughts to one side and carried her gently into my home, my heart pounding with the awareness that my life had changed forever.

Maisie woke me up in the middle of the night — not crying for her mum, as I had been warned to expect, but jumping onto my pillow, wagging her tail, wanting to play. We played with a squeaky toy until it went light, and I thought my heart would burst with love every time I looked at her. I probably imagined it, but she seemed to be smiling. So far, so good. I'd made a friend of my new little girl.

I wasn't the only one who fell under Maisie's spell. My family and friends adored her from the outset, falling in love with her adorable looks — huge brown eyes, little black nose, and reddish-brown fur with patches of black and white. And she loved everyone back, making it clear she was confident and friendly, relishing the attention. The outsider of the litter was rapidly becoming the queen of her new social group, and it was wonderful to watch.

However, it wasn't all smooth sailing. I cried every day for the first two weeks as self-doubt kicked in. Raising a puppy was harder than I had bargained for — sleepless nights, potty training, teething. She bit holes in all my clothes, as well as my skin. Sometimes, it seemed she was deliberately doing the opposite of what I said. There was one memorable incident when she went to the toilet on her puppy mat before running off with the mat, dragging it behind her between her teeth. I didn't appreciate having to clean up the mess at 6 a.m., but I couldn't help smiling at her innocent expression.

There were so many new things to get used to in those early days. She howled when she had her first injection, and I thought my heart was going to explode with sympathy. I took her for her first walks, and she was terrified of the traffic. But she was great with people and other dogs, and it was amazing how many people I ended up speaking to, whom I had never seen before. Maisie captured everyone's hearts the way she had captured mine.

At puppy-training classes, she became the star of the show, her gregarious personality quickly establishing her as the joker of the group, and her cute looks making even the trainer fall in love with her. She passed the course with flying colours, and from that point on she was much easier to handle.

But it was a steep learning curve for me, too. Naturally shy and sensitive, I found that having a dog was gradually bringing me out of myself, encouraging me to talk to people. I started feeling more confident due to the dog-owning experiences I shared with them. Maisie seemed healthy and happy, so I felt reassured that I couldn't be doing a bad job of raising her.

Maisie was doing wonders for me. She gave me a reason to get up every morning, and a thousand reasons to smile each day. I felt my love being returned, and every time she looked at me with her huge brown eyes, a little more of the hurt of my previous life melted away. She listened when I spoke to her and gave me kisses filled with love. When I cried, she jumped up and licked away the tears. I couldn't stay sad for long, and my depression was dormant, hopefully extinct. Now I truly understood why it was said that a dog was man's — or woman's — best friend.

As I write this, Maisie is almost two and a half years old, sleeping by my feet. She's the most beautiful dog I've ever seen. She's confident, outgoing and playful, and she brings those qualities out in me, too. But it's more than that. She's loyal, clever and overwhelmingly loving, and she gives me hope and optimism as I look to our shared future.

— Amelie J. Rose —

Lost and Found

Courage is being afraid but going on anyhow.
~Dan Rather

I had to learn to be an Army Mom. Twenty-three years earlier, I'd had to learn to be an older mom. Doctors had a term for my condition: geriatric pregnancy. Giving birth at thirty-five to a ten-pounder was unusual in 1981.

I had to learn to be Brad's mom. He never walked — he ran; he never played with a rattle — he bounced balls against my once white walls; he never took up golf or swimming — he gloried in contact sports like football and lacrosse. As a teen, he killed a javelina with his compound bow and learned how to field dress it to smoke jerky. My family members were not hunters, so I had to learn to be the mother of a hunter.

I had to learn to accept Brad's decision to sign up with ROTC. Upon commissioning as an Army officer and college graduation, he'd owe our country four years. When graduation day arrived, I learned of Brad's further goals: Ranger, Airborne, Paratrooper.

I had to learn where Iraq was, the place where he'd deploy for fifteen months. I hugged him, clung to him in the airport, and cried and beat the steering wheel as I drove home alone. My known world had stopped, but the rest of the world raced about normally. A friend said to me, "Your son? In the Army? Why? Your family isn't poor." I stopped myself from slapping this person. I walked away and never spoke to him again.

I had to learn not to spend all day and night worrying about Brad, a lieutenant, leading his platoon to clear roadside bombs. I never mastered that, especially when I read a newspaper article about Brad and a young soldier, who suffered an explosion together. With shrapnel in his leg, Brad raced in under sniper fire, climbed up a bombed-out Bradley Fighting Vehicle, and pulled out his soldier, who was stuck in the turret, both splattered with fuel, dirt, oil, and blood. The saga of the young soldier's recovery in a Texas hospital was amazing, but the mom reported that her son's turning point involved his lieutenant — Brad.

Her son, a champion basketball star, had remained silent since he'd heard of his impending leg amputation. Then, a call from Iraq came through from his lieutenant. Brad had phoned to challenge this young man to get used to his bionic leg quickly to see if the kid could still whip his lieutenant on the basketball court. I wept tears of a new salt — the salt of truth that a soldier is indeed a brother forever to his fellow soldiers.

Finally, I had to learn how to get to know this son all over again when he came home with a Purple Heart and Bronze Star. He suffered from post-traumatic syndrome disorder and traumatic brain injury. This wasn't the same son who'd set out for war.

He had to face toward a door, a way out, all the time, at home, at restaurants, anywhere. He could not be in a crowd, at a mall, let alone in a dark movie theater or a sports arena. He jumped and yelled when a car backfired or a plate broke on the tile floor.

He had nightmares every night. He'd thrash about and yell and sweat and shiver.

It brought back memories of the little boy who was frightened by the cruel, wicked Cruella de Vil in *101 Dalmatians*, his otherwise favorite movie. I cried for my twenty-eight-year-old man-child.

Oprah highlighted Puppies Behind Bars, a program in which prison inmates raise service dogs for wounded war veterans and first responders. Brad applied and was flown out to meet with incarcerated women who received eight-week-old puppies and raised them for twenty-four months. Brad sat in a circle of others wounded with PTSD while these specially trained dogs sniffed about and settled by someone. A white Lab, a cute runt, chose my big, muscled son. Her name was Bettine. He trained with the incarcerated woman who had taught Bettine sixty-five commands.

On graduation day, Brad spoke with Glenn Close, who had sponsored this little dog and named her after her mother. Brad couldn't believe he'd met the voice of Cruella; this story had come full circle. Brad learned about a new kind of courage — the courage to go forward with Bettine.

Brad came home with the adorable dog that wore her service jacket proudly. She slept by Brad, and his brain rested and began to heal. Bettine and Brad visited classrooms, and he explained about not petting Bettine when she wore her vest because she was working. He learned to be open, even when his voice shook speaking to kids about PTSD and TBIs. He explained that he'd responded to an abnormal situation in a normal way and had to learn to live with PTSD and beyond it. These conditions were part of who he was, part of many soldiers, firefighters, men, women and kids. In teaching others, Brad taught himself and learned to reenter the working world.

One evening, my soldier son patted me on the shoulder and said, "Mom, I think you might have caught my PTSD."

"No doubt," I said. "It's something Army moms catch."

I turned back to cooking dinner and reflected on seeing a group of young soldiers the day before. Such chance encounters seemed to happen often, or perhaps I was just now being drawn to soldiers. I moved closer to this group, and our eyes engaged. I nodded, and they paused mid-step and gave a quick nod. But one soldier's eyes lingered; perhaps he was thinking of his own mom because now my eyes glistened. We both smiled, and then he joined his buddies.

Rain started tapping the kitchen window, and I heard Brad shout from the family room, "Mom, you're burning the rolls!"

I grabbed a potholder and thought about talking further to Brad about PTSD. I took a deep breath. All the grandpas, grandmas, moms, dads, sisters, brothers, wives, husbands, and kids who love their soldier-men and soldier-women — they, too, would forever belong to the Army.

I had learned to stand as an unwitting, fearful sentry when my Army son lived the thrilling ups and downs of Army life. I said a thankful prayer that I still had this son, who taught me about taking baby steps, one step at a time, sometimes forward, sometimes backward — but always together with the healing power of Bettine.

— Barbara Bolton-Brown —

A Dog's Plan

Dogs have a way of finding the people who need them and filling an emptiness we didn't ever know we had.
~Thom Jones

Travis and I didn't leave the dog rescue with the puppy we chose, but with the one that chose us. I cradled the squirming bundle of shiny black fur as my new husband and I walked to the car to escape the blazing August sun. The thick, humid air reminded me of the summer evening we met two years earlier. A dog also changed my plans that day—and led me to Travis, changing my life.

It had been a scorching July night, and the Café 210 West patio was packed with Penn State alumni returning for Arts Fest. I took this week off from my job in corporate communications for a beach vacation to avoid these crowds. I returned home early when my family dog Gidget's health deteriorated. Knowing how heartbroken I was at the loss of my beloved thirteen-year-old Jack Russell Terrier, my friends convinced me to brave the crowds.

While I searched for an empty chair, a handsome stranger offered me his. The gesture turned into a conversation that quickly led to my emotional story. He listened intently as I shared poetic words I heard that day: "The best way to honor the dog you lost is to save another."

I loved this message and declared that as soon as I owned a home, I would rescue another dog. It was surprising to feel comfortable sharing personal feelings with someone I had just met, but his thoughtful brown eyes were instantly comforting. We talked until the patio closed, and his sweet, secretive smile conveyed that he knew something I didn't. A year later as he proposed, Travis said he knew that night he had met his wife.

Two summers later, we returned from our honeymoon to a house with a yard in suburban Philadelphia. The first e-mail I opened was a photo of Beagle/Terrier puppies my brother saw at a rescue. Travis and I chose "Archie" because of his strong build and brown tri-colored coat. We completed an application and were approved to adopt.

A herd of dogs raced by as I sat there beckoning them. Suddenly, the smallest one darted from the group and charged my lap, furiously licking my chin. The harder I laughed, the fiercer she kissed. Wherever I moved, this affectionate black puppy with a Jack Russell Terrier face found me. She had a white stripe down her nose and white paws, as though she had walked through white paint. We learned that "Archie" had other applications, but this feisty runt of the litter had none.

As we talked, the chin-kissing puppy pounced onto my lap again and playfully nuzzled her nose under my neck. We thought we went to get Archie, but this little girl had other plans. I gave Travis a smile that said, "I can't leave without this little black one."

"Nittany" needed the strength of a Penn State linebacker and an experienced veterinarian to overcome health ailments. Dr. Madden was an older gentleman with a thick Irish accent who practiced out of his Victorian home on a quiet street. When he met her, his eyes lit up as he recalled a special dog from his past. "She reminds me of my old Spike," he would say joyfully at each appointment for the chronic conditions he expertly treated her for.

Nittany's health needs prepared us to become parents, and she turned out to be a natural assistant. When Kyle and Tyler were sick, she slept vigil by their cribs. As they grew into active little boys, she handled roughhousing with love. They doted on her, snuggled as they watched TV, and always tucked her into a favorite Spider-Man blanket. We held backyard birthday parties for her every summer, complete with party hats and Frosty Paws (doggie ice cream).

We never thought the sick runt of the litter would reach her fifteenth birthday, so Kyle, age ten, and Tyler, age six, created an extra special celebration.

Soon after, Travis was preparing to leave for a business trip when he stopped suddenly at the sight of Nittany collapsing, He gave her a long, quiet goodbye before reluctantly leaving for the airport.

When she couldn't walk, the boys and I carried her outside to lie in the glorious summer sunshine she adored. We spoiled her with special treats, toys and Frosty Paws. They took turns holding the ice cream to her face as that fierce tongue furiously licked the cup dry.

All week, they sat vigil by her side just as she had for them. When she stopped eating, I explained that euthanasia was the compassionate choice. Tyler cried, unable to accept "deciding she would die." Deepening his sorrow was his intense fear of all other dogs. My heart broke for my sensitive boy who was convinced he'd never be able to have a dog again, but also for Kyle who desperately wanted to fill this void by saving another.

Kyle fought back tears as he left for baseball camp, and I scheduled the dreaded appointment. Tyler helped me carry her to a favorite spot in the yard and said a sweet goodbye before running inside, inconsolable. My parents were on their way over to stay with him. I thought it was best for him not to come, knowing how much he was struggling with the "decision." Somehow, Nittany knew, too.

I stroked her soft black fur in the bright summer sun, and her tired gray eyes told me she had nothing left. I hugged her in my lap, wishing she had the strength to furiously lick my chin. As I nuzzled the white stripe down her nose, I thanked her for being my first baby, for teaching me how to be a mom. And I thanked her for choosing us.

Minutes later, she took her last breath. It was my final gift to Nittany to comfort her at that moment. It was her final gift to us that there was no "decision" to make.

Covered in the Spider-Man blanket, I held her close on that walk to the car, just as I did fifteen summers before as a newlywed starting my family.

That walk down the driveway of the rescue, cradling her that first day, is one I will always remember. The walk down the driveway of our home, carrying her that last day, is one I wish I could forget.

I met the vet technician behind their office, robotically completed the paperwork and ordered a paw-print plaque. She asked for a date to be engraved. "Please use 8-24-02," I answered, "the day she chose us."

As the vet tech prepared to take her away, her beloved Dr. Madden came out instead. It was immensely comforting to hand her to him when I said my final goodbye.

As I lay awake that sleepless night, I prayed for a sign.

When I turned on my phone the next morning, a photo of Terrier/Hound puppies from a rescue appeared in my Facebook news feed. Both were black, with a white stripe down their nose and white paws that looked like they had just walked through paint. They were slightly larger, but the resemblance to Nittany was uncanny. Travis returned home and shared my disbelief. The energetic female was adopted but the mellow male was available.

Cautiously, we attended the rescue event and donated leftover dog food. Twenty puppies barked and jumped while Tyler hid behind my back. But, in the chaos, one basked peacefully in the bright summer sun. The very same black puppy with white markings that mysteriously appeared in my news feed was the only calm and quiet dog in a sea of wild, loud ones. As we placed him in Kyle and Tyler's laps, he snuggled in for a nap as if this was the plan. And, obviously, it was.

—Jennifer Kennedy—

Four-Legged Friends

An Unlikely Pair

Animals are such agreeable friends — they ask no questions; they pass no criticisms.
~George Eliot

Our daughter was three when we brought Sabrina home on a cold winter's day. All legs and floppy ears at six weeks of age, she was already as big as many adult dogs. My husband Bill stopped weighing her when he could no longer pick her up and stand on the scale. At that point, at only eight months old, Sabrina weighed 185 pounds. By the time she was a fully grown Great Dane, though, she stood over six feet, three inches tall with her front paws on Bill's shoulders.

Over the years, when I would answer the doorbell, Sabrina always joined me. It was one of her duties to inspect anyone who might want to enter "her" domain. What a sight: She stood quietly but impressively next to me, black ears pointed high, with the back of her large, firm body at my waist. Unsuspecting strangers would start out smiling, then gasp when they looked down. I think both Sabrina and I looked forward to their reactions.

However, the most surprised individual was our six-inch-tall squirrel monkey, Samantha. Sam was five years old when we brought our puppy home. From the moment this gentle, loving, vigilant dog came into our lives, she bonded with Sam. More precisely, Samantha bonded with Sabrina — the only animal bond Sam allowed in her twenty-five years of turning our world upside down.

Their bonding occurred shortly after our Dane grew too big to sleep in an open suitcase or under our daughter's canopy bed. Sabrina started taking long naps in front of the fireplace, where Samantha decided to join her. This tiny monkey, curled up and tucked into the chest of this massive Great Dane in front of a large fireplace, was an image that will be (as my grandfather was famous for saying) "forever green in my garden of memories." They were both warm-blooded animals with very short fur. So, the roaring fire we built every day during the cold months in Las Vegas was a perfect solution for them to keep up their body temperatures. Snuggling was optional.

Soon, Samantha relinquished household control only to Sabrina, and Sabrina was the only one who could punish Sam without facing any retaliation. Monkeys tend to lose control when something doesn't go their way—and the list of offenses is a long one. If Sam was mad, she'd jump up and down while emitting a long, high-pitched "squeak"—usually while sitting on the arm of a couch or her favorite, the overstuffed chair. After watching Sam go into her tantrum, Sabrina would calmly raise a large paw up over Sam's body and bring it down with a gentle but firm plop onto the back of the small monkey. Sam would be flattened against the chair's arm—two arms and two legs spread out flat.

Sitting down close to Sam, Sabrina's head was at the perfect level to look directly into Sam's eyes. Still spread, head resting on her chin, Sam would look back. Then she'd sit up, shake her head slightly, and appear to be thanking Sabrina. You could almost hear her saying, "Thanks, I really needed that." It was an unbelievable sight. In anticipation of what was to come, it was hard not to laugh when Samantha had a meltdown.

Sabrina also seemed to know when Sam needed a back rub. We'd come across the two of them—often lying by the pool in the warm sun—only to find this six-inch squirrel monkey lying flat-out while this 185-plus-pound majestic Great Dane was chewing rhythmically (gently with her front teeth) up and down Samantha's small back. Sam's eyes would be half-closed, apparently in some sort of monkey heaven.

Samantha joined all of us in abiding respect for Sabrina. And if

Sabrina could have answered the phone over the years, we never would have had babysitters for our young daughter and son.

Sabrina was only two when our son was born. And, having just become a full-grown adult dog, she increased her protecting to a new level. It was serious business now. Still preferring to sleep in our daughter's room at night, as soon as she'd hear me in the kitchen warming a bottle, she would seek me out and gently follow me from the darkened kitchen into the quiet nursery. There, she would settle down next to the rocking chair until I put the sleeping baby back in his crib. Then, only after she did a complete check of our resting son, would she leave the room with me. Her nose was mattress height, making the official examination easy for her.

Years moved on, and we built a lovely new home in California's Malibu mountains just after our son turned three. With brand-new construction and no fences yet separating the homes on Castleview Court, Sabrina took charge immediately, overseeing ours and all the neighbors' children playing in the cul-de-sac. With ages ranging from three to ten, no one was beyond her protection, no matter how old they got.

Sabrina reigned over Castleview Court until she left us at age nine. Sam never forgave us—actually, *me*. Apparently (in this little monkey's mind), as the mother of the family, I controlled everything. So, I seemed like a good person to peg this tragedy on. One sunny day, I had taken an unusually quiet Sabrina away… and she never returned.

I have no doubt that this highly intuitive monkey knew that Sabrina was "someplace else"—even feeling Sabrina's presence in the years following—but I was going to pay anyway. Samantha continued being the boss of all she surveyed in Sabrina's absence. It would be another eleven (long) years before Sam could join her best friend.

They are in a place where Sabrina and her beloved, rebellious Samantha can once again share the warmth of their spirit together. Their fireplace is always flickering gently.

—Diane Dowsing Robison—

Tag, You're It

The main difference between play and playfulness is that play is an activity, while playfulness is an attitude.
~Miguel Sicart

We had recently moved our mobile home to an acreage about ten miles from Hysham, Montana. About the same time, we adopted a dog named Wally, a longhaired Dachshund, which was a new breed for me.

I worked at our hardware store five and a half days a week, so I didn't get to know Wally very well at first. One Saturday afternoon, though, I was doing yard work during my only free time. I heard a noise behind me where Wally was lying. I spun around to see Wally disappearing up the coulee to the north.

I called and called, but Wally didn't come back. I was hot under the collar as I proceeded into the house. My wife, Linda, asked me what was bothering me, and I told her about Wally disappearing. She assured me everything was going to be alright, but I wasn't ready to hear that.

I grabbed a glass of water and went back to my project, still steaming about the senseless dog. As I came around the house, I noticed the horses were all staring at the hill to our east. My eyes caught a strange sight. There was Wally with a doe antelope hot on his heels.

They rounded the hill and disappeared out of sight. I was about to go back into the house and tell Linda about it when the antelope reappeared, running along the hillside in the opposite direction than she was before. Close behind, short-legged Wally ran for all he was worth.

My jaw dropped in disbelief at the strange sight. *What was happening?* I continued to watch as Wally ran down the side of the hill again, but this time the antelope was in pursuit. I stood there wishing I had a video camera as this was long before cell phones with cameras. I was sure I could have won *America's Funniest Home Videos* with the scene playing out before me.

This happened three more times. First, Wally chasing the antelope, then the antelope chasing Wally. The antelope should've been able to outrun Wally with ease, but she stayed within a few yards of him.

Wally soon got tired and returned to the yard panting. With his short legs, it must have been challenging to try and keep up with that antelope. As he lay there exhausted, the antelope came closer and closer to the yard where I stood, until she was about twenty-five yards from me. She stood there eyeing Wally, and then she stomped on the ground and whistled.

She ignored me as if I wasn't even there until Wally jumped to his feet and ran out of the yard. The antelope spun around and raced up the coulee, just a few feet ahead of Wally.

Again, as I watched, the same scenario played out before me. I had never seen anything like this before. I went into the house to get Linda and the kids. We all stood there and watched the two very different animals play with each other like they were good friends playing a game of tag.

I'm not sure how many times that summer this happened, but we did observe it at least a half-dozen times. One time, the doe brought her fawn close to the house as if she wanted us to see it.

For the next three or four years, this doe showed up to play tag with Wally every spring. They would always run along the base of the hill to the east, first one direction and then the other. It brought joy to our hearts to see these two playing tag together. We talked time and time again about how this would have made a great video, but we never acquired a camera. Maybe if we had started filming them, they wouldn't have played together anymore.

After three or four years, we never saw the doe antelope again.

We're not sure what happened, but I would guess she got old and didn't make it through the winter.

It was a great lesson in creativity and cross-species friendship. And it sure kept our little Dachshund in good shape.

— Lee E. Pollock —

Gentle Gracie

The average dog is nicer than the average person.
~Andy Rooney

Princess was the kindest dog we ever had. My son had found her in a blizzard and brought her home. She was never claimed, so we kept her. After she died from cancer, we decided to get another dog but couldn't imagine finding another one like her.

After about a month, we went to the shelter. All the dogs were barking and wagging their tails. One dog in particular was barking hysterically and jumping high against the cage as if to get our attention. She was a Pit Bull mix named Gracie and she'd been found wandering the streets of a rough neighborhood in the city. She seemed insistent that we take her.

Gracie had been adopted once and brought back. I had some doubts, wondering if she might be aggressive. But after some discussion, we decided we'd give her a chance. They would not let us take her, though, because her eye was swelled shut. We had to wait a week until her eye cleared up. We left, and her crying and whining as we left her behind haunted me.

A week later, we returned to pick her up, and she was facing the corner of the dog pen, not greeting us. She seemed very depressed. Apparently, she thought she had been abandoned for a third time. We took her home and introduced her to all the cats. She accepted them all as her family and they slept with her every night.

Gracie loved watching the action at the various bird feeders we had. She'd sit there for hours barking at the birds. I didn't know if she was saying hello to them or trying to scare them away. I just hoped she wouldn't hurt any of the birds who stopped frequently in our yard to drink from our pond.

One day, as I was in the bathroom, I looked out the window and saw a small sparrow struggling in the middle of the pond. Gracie happened to be outside. She loved to run around the fenced-in yard with all the trees and the big pond full of fish.

Suddenly, Gracie jumped into the pond and started swimming toward the bird. I yelled out the window, "Gracie, *no*!" I thought she was going to kill the little bird. But, to my surprise, she scooped it up gently in her powerful jaws and swam back to the bank. When she got out of the pond, she gently laid the bird on a large, flat rock. Then she sat down next to it and waited.

It was hot that day. The bird's wings dried quickly, and it flew away. Only then did Gracie get up and come back onto the porch. She had waited patiently and protected the bird until it was strong enough to fly away. She did not abandon the bird, like she had been abandoned so many times. She was our sweet and gentle Gracie, the kind dog we had hoped to find.

— Sonia A. Moore —

Part-Time Retriever

Protecting yourself is self-defense.
Protecting others is warriorship.
~Bohdi Sanders

My aunt needed a dog walker, and I needed the money. I was thirteen.

When Aunt Lee opened the door, I was hit by an explosion of love. A wild streak of gold dived into me, knocking me to the floor. We rolled and rolled in a delightful frenzy. I laughed until the tears covered my face, and that crazy dog licked them all off.

Two older kids were also there applying for the dog-walker position. They sat on the couch, looking so professional and confident. I took my place beside them.

"What should I call my new dog?" my aunt asked us.

"Goldie" and "Taffy" were the suggestions. The dog reacted with a blank stare.

I threw a ball across the room and yelled, "Fetch." The dog ran to the couch and jumped into my lap, her tail slapping me furiously. She never retrieved the ball, but she did show Aunt Lee that she liked me better than the other applicants.

I got the job, and the dog got her name: Fetch.

She was a beautiful four-year-old rescue who was part Golden Retriever. The only thing I remembered her retrieving, however, was a hamburger off my plate.

I never held that against her. My love for her was childlike and pure. A hamburger was simply meat. Fetch was LOVE.

She wasn't my dog, but she didn't know it. She loved me more than her real family, and the feeling was mutual.

Every day after school, I ran joyfully over to Aunt Lee's apartment. After a bunch of tail-wagging and sloppy kissing, Fetch and I would go for a walk.

On our walks, we'd see the neighbor's cat, Droopy, whose eyes gave him his name. He must have known our schedule because he was always sitting in the window next door, as if waiting for us. I'd heard that Retrievers liked cats. Well, no one told Fetch. She didn't. She'd drag me to the window to terrorize the kitty with her intimidating bark. Droopy's eyes would droop even more. Then he'd have a hissy fit, slap at the doggie in his window and escape inside the house.

One day, Droopy was nowhere to be seen. Fetch ran to the window, expecting a good fight as usual, but no cat.

Thankfully, we'll avoid a scene today, I thought.

We continued our walk. It was a cool autumn day, and it was starting to drizzle. I wondered why several kids were gathered around a sewer or storm drain — that hole in the ground by the curb where excess rainwater runs off the street. Some kids were sitting on the ground, and a couple of them were down with their bellies on the pavement, peering into the sewer opening.

Of course, Fetch was curious. She tugged on her leash, and I gave in to her wishes, as always. We went to the sewer to investigate.

"What happened?" I asked.

"It's Droopy! He fell in!"

So that's why the cat hadn't been at the window.

"Keep that dog away!" the kids yelled.

They didn't have to tell me. I took Fetch across the street and secured her leash to a fire hydrant. "Stay, Fetch," I commanded. "Good girl. And be quiet."

Good luck with that! She loved me, but that didn't mean she ever listened to me.

I returned to the sewer. I could see Droopy sitting below. There was a layer of moisture on the ground where she sat.

Oh, please, don't let it rain, I thought. I didn't want Droopy to be swept away.

The poor kitty's back was arched, and his tail was all fluffed up, typical for a cat who is scared to death. The kids hanging around the sewer kept trying to reach him, but their arms weren't long enough, and he kept pulling away in fright.

"We should call the police," someone said. But no one had a cell phone in those days.

Being the eldest kid there, I decided to use my thirteen-year-old common sense.

"We should all leave. Droopy's too nervous to come out with all of you yelling and screaming. He got in by himself, so he'll come out by himself. Cats are resilient."

Suddenly, the rain started coming down hard. In what seemed like a few seconds, I could see Droopy's little paws almost covered in water. As a last resort, I lay down frantically on the sidewalk and stuck my head and arms into the sewer, reaching for the cat. This terrified him even more, and he pulled farther away.

Meanwhile, back at the fire hydrant, Fetch's barking kept getting more intense. When she saw me on the ground reaching into the sewer, she somehow yanked her leash off the hydrant and ran to the sewer. I guess she thought I was in danger, so she went into protective mode, trying to rescue me. Quickly, I pulled myself out of the hole, but she took my place, squeezing her head and half her body into the sewer. I lunged onto her lower body, trying to keep her from falling into the hole. No way was I going to lose the best dog I had ever known.

Everyone was yelling, "No, Fetch, no!" I tugged on to the dog and, with everyone's help, we managed to pull her to safety.

And then we saw a beautiful sight: In Fetch's mouth, hanging by the nape of his neck, was Droopy.

Fetch let go of the cat. Droopy rubbed his face against the dog, briefly forgetting their past differences.

Fetch had finally retrieved something more valuable than a hamburger from a plate. She was a true Retriever after all.

The cheers from the kids for Fetch and Droopy could be heard blocks away. Fetch barked in appreciation as if she had been chosen Best in Show at the Westminster Kennel Club Dog Show. Droopy took off in the direction of his home.

After that adventure, Fetch still stopped by Droopy's window each time we went walking. The barking and hissing continued but with less intensity. I think they had gained a mutual respect for each other, but they still wanted to prove that dogs will be dogs, and cats will be cats.

— Eva Carter —

COVID Comfort

Laughter is the corrective force that prevents us from becoming cranks.
~Henri Bergson

Normal dogs like to chew sticks. Our dog protects them from danger. If we burn sticks in the yard, Rusty tries to pull them out of the fire. He wants to take these cherished sticks for a walk. Seriously. When I get the leash, he gets a stick.

Normal dogs chase backyard critters. Rusty greets them like family—all bounding happiness and unfettered adoration. Sure, these critters flee in terror, but only because they don't understand.

It's not a hunting thing. It's a friendly thing.

Once, he greeted a vole too exuberantly, causing it to cry out. Rusty stared at it, tail down as if wracked with guilt. Another time, my son discovered Rusty nosing a brood of baby bunnies. He pulled Rusty away, but noted our dog was trying to gently pick up the babies—like a parent, not a predator.

I wondered if my dog would like his own pet. As an experiment, I bought Rusty a stuffed gray squirrel, figuring he would destroy it within a week.

I was wrong.

Rusty didn't wrestle the toy. He didn't gnaw out its plastic eyes or its threaded toes. He didn't pull out all its stuffing. Instead, he carried it in his mouth like a proud papa. He slept with it and occasionally placed it in our laps. We called his stuffed toy Squirrel.

It wasn't long before Rusty wanted to take Squirrel for a walk.

At first, I resisted, figuring Rusty would drop Squirrel like he does his sticks when a kid or another dog crosses his path.

I was wrong.

Not only did Rusty carry Squirrel the entire route, but he did so in a way that Squirrel's button eyes stared up at me.

It's ridiculous, but he was happy.

During the COVID-19 stay-at-home order, Rusty got more walks than usual, which meant Squirrel was getting more walks than usual. And since our whole neighborhood was home at all hours, our strange walking party had witnesses.

Early one workday morning, as I refilled my coffee, my husband muted his Webex meeting.

"Can you take the dog for a 'W'? He won't stop crying."

Rusty stared at me, Squirrel in his mouth, tail wagging. He knew what "W" meant.

Sigh.

I put down my coffee and took up the leash.

Most people were still indoors. Around the back loop, a man I had never met came outside with a small child. As I approached, he called out to me. "I think your dog caught something."

Keeping my required six feet of distance, I explained it was a toy and told him about Squirrel. The man burst out laughing. The toddler by his knee clapped and stomped his feet, clearly ready to breach social-distancing protocol to pet a dog.

I resumed my walk.

A voice called after me. "It feels good to smile. Your dog made me smile."

I looked at Rusty. Squirrel looked at me. The corners of my mouth twitched.

It was a ridiculous reason to smile, but when smiles are at a premium, the ridiculous will do.

— Nicole L.V. Mullis —

Smokey Meets Clara

After years of having a dog, you know him. You know the meaning of his snuffs and grunts and barks.
~Robert McCammon

Smokey, my half wolf, half longhaired German Shepherd, is a king-sized, powerful-looking pet. Smokey's muscular body is a luxurious black to light charcoal color. He stands three feet tall, and from the tip of his nose to the end of his long, flowing tail, he measures five feet. He weighs 120 pounds.

Smokey's powerfully built chest, inherited from his German Shepherd ancestry, is flecked with variegated shades of white. Medium-sized, dark black ears with tufted white centers stand straight up on his head. Smokey's elongated muzzle is splashed with white, and his burly legs end in extra-wide, grayish white paws. Piercing stares from his oval-shaped, dark brown eyes quickly send the message, "Watch out! I'm in charge!"

Why have Smokey in my life? Well, he was a gift. It was my husband's birthday, but I got the gift, Smokey. "Honey, dear," remarked my ever thoughtful, always protective husband, "Smokey's the prefect birthday gift for both of us... a natural alarm system."

Smokey protects our six acres like an expert and his inborn instincts have led to a natural alarm system of various types of howl-barks. For the fox and her kits, she emits a high-pitched, elongated howl. For marauding raccoons, it's three agitated, rapid howls, repeated twice. The buck and his harem of does receive a soft, low, long-lasting howl.

As starlings dive-bomb Smokey's food dish, his bark is a quick yip, yip, yip followed by three lone, mournful howls.

Human visitors are greeted with five long, loud howl-barks and three staccato howls repeated four times. I don't have to guess; I just listen and know who or what is setting foot on my homestead.

One evening last October, as my husband and I lounged on our front deck, we heard howling and barking like nothing we'd ever heard before. Something new was in Smokey's domain. His frantic, deep-throated howls made the hair on my arms stand at attention. As my husband and I raced to Smokey's rescue, the foul, eye-burning, nose-watering odor of skunk spray filled the air.

Unlucky Smokey spent the rest of the night and all the next day rolling in mounds of soft dirt, all four feet extended into the air, wriggling back and forth, scratching and clawing at his fur. The scent of skunk juice followed him everywhere.

Imagine my surprise when, the very next evening, I heard the same agitated howling and unhappy barking of the previous evening. Silently, my husband and I opened the front door and looked out. There, on the lawn, silhouetted in the moonlight, was the largest skunk we'd ever seen. She was busily eating from Smokey's food dish.

To our amazement, Smokey stopped howling, dropped to his belly, stretched his front legs out straight and rested his head on his paws. The alarm was quiet, and the intruder did not send out her smelly "I'm in charge" message. Why?

Clara (that's what I named the lady skunk) took up residence in the drainage culvert pipe that ran only a foot away from Smokey's food and water dishes. Each day, as Clara emerged from her culvert hideaway, Smokey gave a gentle wave of his tail, tossed his head back and sent a soft, almost quiet, welcoming howl into the air. Tail held high, Clara sauntered in front of Smokey, paused for a moment, looked up at Smokey, and then drank slowly from his silver water dish. Did Clara ask Smokey's permission to drink?

To make sure she got each piece of Smokey's food, Clara always tipped over his food dish and ate every crumb. Smokey never made a move to disturb Clara. He simply stretched out full length on the ground, placed his head on his paws, pointed his ears forward and watched as Clara rapidly finished her meal. Clara left no trace of a pungent order as she disappeared into her drainpipe home, as if she was leaving a simple "Thank you, Smokey, my friend." Could an animal-to-animal friendship go any deeper?

My husband and I watched in amazement as Smokey and Clara walked together across our homestead, took naps under the shade of the ponderosa pine, and drank as a twosome from the same water dish.

Then one day, when winter came knocking, Clara did not come out to eat any of her daily three meals. Each day for the next week, Smokey scratched and pawed the culvert pipe as an invitation for Clara to come and dine. She did not come. Was she hibernating?

Christmastime came and went. March rolled in warm and sunny. "Mercy me," laughed my husband. "Smokey spends a lot of time sniffing and scratching at the culvert pipe. Do you think he misses his unusually clever friend, Clara? Did she sneak out and leave?"

Early the next morning, Smokey woke us up with a new type of howl-barking—a series of six quick yips followed by three short, happy howls, repeated over and over again. A come-and-see-me message?

When my husband and I arrived at Smokey's side, Clara was eating quietly from Smokey's food dish. As three young kits circled around Smokey's feet, he lowered his head and howled softly. When Clara finished eating Smokey's food, she gently nudged her babies away from Smokey, raised her tail high in the air, and led her kits across the lawn and down the hillside. As Clara stepped into the dry creek bed, she paused for a moment, turned around, looked back at Smokey, and seemed to say a silent "Thank you and good-bye." Clara and her new family disappeared into the willow brush of the creek. Smokey let out three mournful, spine-chilling howls and lumbered off to his bed in the barn. The end to a tender friendship?

Smokey still sniffs the culvert pipe each day. Sometimes, he stretches out on top of it and howls quietly for a few minutes. Other times, he races from one end of the pipe to the other, stopping briefly to look into the dark end holes. Some nights, he lies by the culvert pipe, tilts his head back and lets out a long, regal howl that increases and decreases in volume up and down in a flowing, harmonious scale. Is it an "I remember you" friendship message sent into the darkness of night? Clara has not returned. Yet a courageous, loyal friendship lingers.

— Kathy Padgett —

Dances with Coyotes

Dance is the hidden language of the soul.
~Martha Graham

It was a late summer afternoon and time for my dog Nora and me to go for our usual walk before dinner. Temperatures were still warm during the day, but at night I could feel the first hints of the coming fall in northern Arizona.

Our house was in a secluded neighborhood surrounded by acres of beautiful Forest Service land. Though we lived only a ten-minute drive from town, it often felt as if we were out in the middle of nowhere.

Nora and I always started our day with a hike, and thanks to the riding stable down the road, we could choose from a number of pretty trails to explore. I made a point of varying our route each morning and treasured that time we spent together. Nora was the perfect trail dog. She would run ahead of me in joyous pursuit of new scents, and then circle back to check in.

My relationship with Nora hadn't always been so seamless and easy, though. Several years earlier, I'd started stopping by our local animal shelter, thinking about adopting a dog. For years, I'd been a successful pet sitter but sorely missed having that special bond with a dog of my own.

I wanted a dog I could walk and hike with off-leash, who responded to my verbal requests, and who wanted to be with me enough that she would never run away. I wanted to be able to exchange a look with her that both of us knew meant an upcoming car ride, long before I got out my keys. I wanted to be able to speak quietly to her and have her respond happily and willingly, and I wanted to give her as much freedom as was safely possible.

I'll never forget the day I first met Nora. I was in town running errands with no plans of stopping at the shelter to look at the dogs when a voice in my head said clearly, "Go to the shelter NOW!" It was so commandingly clear that I obeyed, and when I saw her in the run, pacing and obviously unhappy, I almost gasped. She looked almost exactly like my beloved Sheena, whom I had rescued from a busy street many years before. I stared at her for a long time and knew there was no way she would let me come in to visit her. She was far too agitated and upset.

Instead, I went into the run next to hers where there was a puppy and sat down with him. I wanted this beautiful, nervous dog to know that I was trustworthy. I glanced at her from time to time as I played with the puppy and started to make plans for my next visit. It took me more than a week to decide to adopt her because, even to my then untrained eye, I knew she had some fairly serious issues.

In the beginning, I made many mistakes in my relationship with Nora, but amazingly she forgave me and loved me wholeheartedly anyway. No matter whether I was gone for twenty minutes or two hours, she always greeted me with what I called her "whirly dance," an ecstatic bouncy circling accompanied by whines, and kisses.

As usual, Nora was off-leash on our walk that day, busily sniffing all the new scents by the side of the road. Suddenly, she dashed off toward an overgrown grassy area as she often did when she smelled a rabbit. In those days, she chased every cottontail she came across with tremendous gusto and determination. And although she was very fast, she never caught one. Looking back, I think it was more of a game for her, and I figured it gave her a good burst of aerobic exercise.

But this time, she didn't return as quickly as she normally did, and I wondered what was keeping her. Shading my eyes against the sun, I peered toward the field where she'd headed and strained to catch a glimpse of her.

The wheat-colored grass there was about two feet high, and Nora, who looked like a scaled-down golden German Shepherd, blended in. By now, a few minutes had passed, and I was beginning to consider going over there myself when I suddenly caught sight of something moving—and it was definitely larger than a rabbit.

I stood watching in amazement as Nora and a large coyote romped in the grass like puppies! I couldn't believe my eyes. Normally, Nora was very shy when meeting a new dog for the first time. Yet, there she was, completely relaxed, acting as though she'd known this coyote all her life.

All my protective instincts told me to run over there and chase that coyote away, but I forced myself to stop, listen and look again. As the seconds passed, I didn't hear any growling or other signs of aggression. Neither did I see any other coyotes lurking nearby.

Slowly, I relaxed, realizing that I was witnessing something rare. A shy dog and a wild coyote were simply enjoying each other's company.

Time seemed to stop as I watched the two of them leap, jump and wriggle in complete joy. I don't know how long I stood there transfixed, but I will remember it always.

Then, when the two finished playing, Nora came trotting back to me as she always did after one of her little adventures, looking quite content. I bent down and gave her a heartfelt hug and kiss, still stunned by what I'd just seen. I glanced back at the field, wondering if the coyote was still there, but it had disappeared.

As we continued home, I was filled with a deep sense of gratitude and peace. I'd been blessed that day with an incredible gift. Nora had come to me filled with fear, having been badly abused as a puppy, and it had taken about two years of focused, daily rehabilitative work to stabilize her enough so that I felt comfortable taking her out in public.

Yet, on that beautiful summer afternoon, she met a wild coyote for the first time and showed absolutely no fear. In fact, she'd had fun!

During the many wonderful years she lived with me, I gave Nora many endearing nicknames. But that day, as we walked home together, both of us grinning, I added a new one: Dances with Coyotes.

— Deborah Dobson —

Sweet Metamorphosis

Find what makes your heart sing and
create your own music.
~Mac Anderson

My dog Foxy has turned into a cat. He refuses to eat dog food of any kind, canned or kibble, he sleeps with a fifteen-year-old tomcat draped across his back, and he has taught himself how to meow. His backstory is complicated and strange, but considering the dog, it's not totally surprising.

In 2007 I rescued my best friend, a Pug/Jack Russell Terrier mix who was about three years old. I found him the week of the Fourth of July and named him Sparky. I scoured the neighborhood to see if anyone lost him, and ran a "found ad" in the local paper with no response. Some kids at my local park told me they'd seen a driver pull up and toss him out, then drive away.

That did it for me. I updated all his shots and got him a new collar and license.

He was an amazing friend. He loved cats and was very protective of me, his rescued cat family and our house, but still a total love-bucket to people he met on our walks and friends who came to visit.

In 2010, Sparky rescued a sidekick—a matted, rag-tag pup who had been severely abused, neglected and finally abandoned behind the locked gate of an abandoned house when his family was evicted. Sparky adopted him, and I named him Foxy because he looks like a black, furry fox.

Unfortunately, Foxy was brain damaged from the abuse he suffered as a pup with the rough kids in that family. It was not anything that would kill him or require special treatment, but he basically never grew up. He has remained "puppy-like" all of his life.

Sparky was always Foxy's guard, guide and mentor. Whatever Sparky did, Foxy did. Foxy developed Sparky's great love for cats and kittens and even went one step further. While Sparky was tolerant of all the cats, his heart belonged to the litter he had found in the bushes of our front driveway. Foxy loved them too, but also loves all cats, allowing them to snuggle into his long, thick fur on cold days.

One big difference between the two dogs was that Sparky loved to jump onto the couch and curl up with his rescue cat Ringo. Sparky and Ringo also slept on my bed with me every night. Foxy was and still is, terrified of furniture, probably from brutal experiences with his former owners. Nothing can cajole him to jump onto furniture or even jump up to be petted. If I try to entice him with treats, he falls over on his side and whimpers. I rub his furry belly and give him a goodie and then he runs around in circles in puppy heaven. The issue was solved with dog beds that Foxy loved but Sparky totally ignored, preferring my furniture and his cat.

In mid 2019, I noticed a small lump on Sparky's chest and took him to the vet. It was cancer. Sparky died in his sleep in the spring of 2020. As hard as this was for me, it was devastating for Foxy. His big brother, hero and mentor was suddenly gone. For Ringo the cat, his father was gone. Sparky had raised him from the day his little cat eyes opened. Both animals were devastated. The other eleven cats felt their pain and rallied around them for comfort. It was a very hard time for Foxy. He kept close to me for comfort for a long time and searched for his best friend for days.

Slowly, strange things started to happen. First it was the food. Foxy would not touch any dry dog food, but ate only cat kibble. I wound up putting the dog kibble outside for the raccoons so it would not go to waste. The canned dog food was not wasted because cats are not as picky and happily gobbled it all up along with their food. Foxy would, and still will, only eat canned cat food.

Then strange sounds started coming from the back yard. At first the neighbors and I thought a bobcat or some other wild creature had drifted down into our area because of the many recent forest fires. It was a very loud "Meow-r-oo-oow"—a huskier sound than any normal cat could make. We all kept an eye out for the beast and hoped for the best.

Then I caught him. I heard the yowl and rushed to the back door to see if I could spot the wild thing before it disappeared again. I peeked through the curtain, hoping not to scare it away by opening the door. But it wasn't some strange wild animal; it was Foxy. He was sitting on top of the doghouse with old Ringo lying next to him, practicing his best canine version of a meow. I think Ringo was tutoring him. Now all the neighbors know what the sound is and Foxy is proud to show off his "new language" to anyone on cue.

Every creature on earth has a way of coping with loss and heartbreak. With Sparky gone, my little thirteen-year-old Foxy has decided to become a giant cat and take over as leader of our feline tribe. He and Ringo are curled up next to my chair as I type this, and looking down at them snuggled together makes me smile.

—Joyce Laird—

Passing the Baton

The world would be a nicer place if everyone had the ability to love as unconditionally as a dog.
~M.K. Clinton

We hadn't thought much about getting another dog, but while looking at our aging Shepherd with her graying muzzle, the idea kept creeping into my mind. Bee had been with us for nine years, and her excellent behavior was something I hoped to pass on to the next dog. She knew the word "no" well and would stop on a dime if I used it. It had saved her from running out into traffic, approaching a raccoon, or chasing the cats that shared the property.

Since the disappearance of her latest feline friend, I noticed her moping more and more, as though she missed the gentle play and mischievous antics of the kitten she had adopted. My husband and I discussed it. Did we really want another dog? We had plenty of space but wondered if a puppy would be too much for our busy schedules.

I began surfing the net, checking out pure breeds and mixed breeds. I signed on to dog forums hoping that someone would know someone who knew someone who had the right puppies. And as I sat at my computer, Bee lay on her pillow by the door, watching me with soft, sad eyes.

One morning, I turned on my computer and began yet another search. A picture flashed across my screen of three black puppies for sale. The owner had listed ten pups only the night before, and they were being snatched up quickly. I read the description: three males left — father is Irish Wolfhound, mother is Mastiff/Labrador mix. We didn't care whether the dog was a purebred or a mix as long as it had the right personality. Something about these puppies tugged at my heart. We wanted a big dog but weren't sure something that big was a good idea. We wanted a dog that would be gentle with our grandkids and Bee. We wanted a dog that was smart and willing to learn. I e-mailed the picture to my husband and waited until he came home from work.

"Yeah, I think one of them might work."

Immediately, I sent a reply to the owner that we wanted a pup and paid the deposit. We made arrangements for our first visit so we could choose from the three pups that had not yet been spoken for. The puppies' mother greeted us at the door with a hearty bark and a wide grin. Her tail wagged as she sniffed and nuzzled our hands. Ten fat bundles of fur waddled around the enclosed indoor kennel, seven of them boasting colourful collars. We petted and held the final three, choosing the one who would come to our home in another month. On the way home, we decided to name him Jay.

Bee seemed to sense that something had changed. She sniffed us thoroughly that night when we returned. She whined as though she wanted a say in the decision. She perked up whenever one of us came into the house and seemed to wait for whatever was coming.

We picked up the puppy on a cool October evening and brought him home. A jolt went through Bee as she caught the first whiff of Jay. The two touched noses and then went bouncing off into the kennel together. I watched them carefully, waiting for any signs of aggression. Bee slipped into her doghouse. Jay joined her. They hunkered down together and stayed there until morning.

Jay grew rapidly and tried to keep up with Bee when we went on our autumn walks through the woods. He barked at the things she barked at. He ran along the trails she ran on. They wrestled in the long grass of the hayfield. He learned to lock down when he heard the word "no" — because she did. When she sat and received a treat for her obedience, he sat.

It wasn't long before he was doing all the things she did on command. As he grew, his speed increased on their runs through the field. He challenged Bee to run faster, and as she did, it was as though she was enjoying a second youth. They bounded through the snow, kicking up powdery clouds. They slept, ate and played together. Jay learned to be on his best behavior when our grandchildren arrived. Often, the kids would go into the kennel and play with both dogs or just sit and pet them.

By nine months of age, Jay was a whopping ninety pounds. Bee could no longer keep up with him. He would race in circles around her while she trotted at a contented pace.

Summer came again. Jay was approaching his first birthday, and Bee had just passed her tenth. We noticed that she didn't run with him as often but stayed by my side more and more. She didn't wrestle with him with the same enthusiasm of just a few months before. She stood and watched him eat, waiting until he was done before nibbling at her own meals instead of diving in along with him.

One morning, she refused to walk with us. She looked at the field and then turned to a warm spot on the cement patio to stretch out. I led Jay out to the field and let him race around until he was tired, and then we headed back to where Bee rested. She licked his face and joined him at the food dish. I noticed for the first time that she seemed weak and tired. I checked her over to make sure there were no injuries and saw that she was fine — just old. That night, a raccoon decided to make his bed in the tree beside their kennel. The uproar woke us, and I smiled as Bee returned to her ferocious self — snarling threats at the nighttime bandit. Jay danced around with her, unsure what the fuss was about.

The next morning, Bee was sound asleep on her bed and lifted her head long enough to watch Jay head to the field with me to burn off his youthful energy. The day after that, I found her curled up in a patch of sunlight by the kennel door. She had drifted away. Her job was done. She had prepared her successor for his task as the new family dog, and she had done it well.

I often think about Bee as I watch Jay snooze on her pillow in the house. How hard would it have been to train him if it weren't for her? And would we have had that final year with Bee, or would she have faded away earlier? Yes, Bee gave us a gift by training Jay, but Jay re-energized her and gave her one more joyful year of her own.

— Donna Fawcett —

Violet and Diesel Shelter in Place

If you are a host to your guest,
be a host to his dog also.
~Russian Proverb

When I walked through my dining room this morning, there was nine-pound Violet the Cat sprawled across the table in the sun. She had perfected her sprawl so that she could now touch all four placemats at one time — one with her head, one with her tail, one with her right front paw, and the last with her left back paw. I understood her feeling of accomplishment. She had been practicing this position for months.

Violet loves these placemats the way other cats love catnip-stuffed felt mice. Her morning ritual is to lie on one and suck the corner of another one for at least half an hour before anyone else in the house wakes up. At the same time, she does that thing only cats do — kneading bread with her paws in the air, and purring like she has sleep apnea with her eyes half-shut. Non-cat people find this disturbing. And no, I never set the table with Violet's placemats.

Violet is just over a year old. My husband and I adopted her from the SPCA when she was twelve weeks old and still small enough to hold in one hand. As soon as we saw her, we knew she was the one. She was solid gray and round, with a smiling face just like Iris, the cat we had shared our lives with for sixteen years.

On the other hand, I did not understand Diesel, my brother John's Bull Mastiff who would be arriving any minute. John, his wife Cheryl, and Diesel had been handed an emergency evacuation notice just two days earlier when one of the furious fires in California jumped a fire line and raced toward their house. The three of them would be staying with us until they got the "all clear" to return home.

The serious issues swirling around us were numbing. In addition to worrying about the immediate fire threat, Covid-19 and maintaining safe social distancing with houseguests, I was on edge about how Violet and Diesel would get along. Until a month earlier, she was technically still a kitten and she hadn't spent time with a dog before.

My concern only got worse when everyone arrived and I opened the door. Diesel had become a 120-pound small grizzly bear with the facial expression of Alfred Hitchcock. As we unloaded the car, Diesel wandered around the house making loud noises I'd only heard at farms until then. He did not seem to be in distress, but I was starting to be. I had no idea what all those sounds meant and it made me edgy. I was used to an occasional polite feline squeak. If Violet makes the slightest noise, I know exactly what's on her mind.

I looked up Bull Mastiff on my laptop for some help. Apparently snorting, snuffling, wheezing, grunting, loud snoring and flatulence are normal. I thought about the sounds coming from the kitchen and identified them as snorting, wheezing and grunting. I figured flatulence could come at any moment. Wikipedia added helpfully that I should follow Diesel around with a large drool towel.

That afternoon, John and Cheryl left to do some errands, so I took Diesel for a walk to let him sniff around the neighborhood. When we got back home, I played Frisbee with him in the yard to give Violet a chance to watch him through the window. Then I had to leave the house for an hour, so I put Diesel in his double-wide crate in the laundry room. The dog is so big that my brother made him a giant crate by splicing two large ones together. Diesel didn't seem to mind getting in and before long his nasal snuffle turned into a loud snore.

When I returned home, the house was quiet, to my great relief.

The whole time I was away, I had visions of one of them injuring the other one so badly it would require a rush to the emergency vet. I peeked in the laundry room and there was Violet, sitting on top of the washing machine, with her paws folded neatly underneath her. She was calmly staring across the room at our sleeping visitor.

While I was gone, Violet had dragged one of her placemats from the dining room table through the kitchen and into the laundry room where she left it for Diesel, right in front of his crate — a welcome gift to her canine guest.

Violet is a very good hostess.

— Suzanne Cushman —

Lone Ranger

Happiness is... the company of our four-legged friends.
~Author Unknown

A loud slurp stirred me from my sleep. What was that? A steady continued slurping noise made me sit up and look around my dimly lit bedroom. I reached around clumsily for the flashlight that I knew would be by my bedside. I shone it around my bedroom and was surprised to find the source of the noise was my beloved Pepper sitting atop my headboard.

Her large girth hung over both sides of my headboard. She had snuck up there to drink water from my cup. *Ew, Pepper* I thought. *I wonder how many times she's done that.*

Pepper was my tortie-colored British Shorthair. She usually slept right on top of my stomach or my dad's. Her cute face said it all, but her rolls of fat certainly added to her charm. However as large as she was, she would move like greased lightning when she heard us filling up her food bowl.

I had many cats as best friends but Pepper was one of a kind. In the economic failure of 2008 my family had to uproot from my childhood home in North Carolina and move to Texas. I held Pepper in my lap for the entire trip, because we were both afraid of this new chapter in our lives.

Once we arrived at our new home, we let Pepper do something new, and that was to explore outside. When we adopted her she had already been declawed and as a safety precaution we'd always kept her inside. She'd sit in the window and longingly stare outside. I felt so bad for her.

Being in rural North Carolina there were many dangers for a sweet kitty, including cougars, wolves, and black bears. When we moved to Texas though, it was into a secluded neighborhood where many other cats roamed freely. I watched Pepper sit in front of a screen door and stare outside, and I decided to take her outside and sit with her to keep an eye on things. I slid the door open and walked outside but she seemed reluctant to join me.

As I encouraged her, she slowly crept out. Once she got used to it, she loved it, acting like a puppy begging to be let out every day. We grew accustomed to letting Pepper out. She would wait by the door and cry to let us know she wanted back in.

Everything was going quite wonderfully until one day I heard a scuffle outside. As I swung open the door, I saw Pepper surrounded by three dogs. Crying out in shock, I took off after them, knowing I would have to fight them off. One was a friendly Australian Shepherd named Ranger who I knew from the neighborhood. The other two were Terriers that I had never seen before.

Pepper was being held by the nape of her neck by Ranger while the two Terriers were trying to attack her. As I neared them, I started yelling. That got Ranger's attention and he brought Pepper to me as the Terriers continued tearing at her.

After Ranger gently released Pepper into my hands, he turned his attention to the two Terriers and drove them out of our yard. Aside from a few cuts on her paws Pepper was completely fine.

When I went to Ranger's home to thank him and his owners, I was surprised to learn he lived with several cats. While he didn't play with them, he knew they needed his protection, and this was not the first time he had saved a cat in distress.

We continued to let Pepper out in the back yard after that, and she was surprisingly warm to Ranger when he visited. He still didn't want to play with a cat, though. But we praised him when he visited, and on Thanksgiving Day later that same year he was paid very handsomely in bones and scraps.

After that, Ranger became just as much our dog as his actual owners. One neighbor told us, "I tell you what. If Ranger ain't at home, he's over here. I can always count on that."

Our reply? "Ranger will always have a home here."

—John Ryder—

And Dog Makes Family

The Black Volkswagen

In times of joy, all of us wished we possessed
a tail we could wag.
~W.H. Auden

Floyd started to wag his tail when he saw the black Volkswagen approach us. He knew the drill; he'd seen it play out pretty much the same way every week. Some nights, Denny's bedsheets would remain untouched, and the next day we'd drive to the grocery store. We'd park in the same spot and wait. While I'd check my e-mails or browse the Web on my phone, Floyd would watch the cars drive in and out of the parking lot until the black Volkswagen parked next to us. Then, he'd see Denny emerge from the black car and watch him hug the man who drove it. After listening to our conversation, he'd get to lick Denny's face until we pulled into our driveway.

Floyd's tail thumped against the window faster and faster on that breezy March evening. He had no idea that our routine was about to change. After brief chitchat, I blurted out the phrase that had been playing on repeat inside my head, "I think it's in everyone's best interest if Denny stays with us for a while."

Al pursed his lips and asked, "How long do you think this virus will be around?" Many people had been asking me similar questions lately.

"It's hard to say. It might be months of social distancing, if not a year or longer until someone develops a vaccine," I responded. He stared at his shoes. He always stared at his feet when he didn't know what to say. I decided to break the awkward silence and continued, "I know it will be hard for you and Denny, but we need to practice proper social distancing."

"I agree," he said, "better safe than sorry." Then he gave Denny his last firm hug for the foreseeable future and told him that they would video call each other every day.

Denny and Floyd hugged and played as usual while we drove home. Yet, their cheerful sounds couldn't drown out my panicked thoughts. *I'm pushing forty. What if I get sick? What if my parents get sick? Won't Denny miss seeing his dad in person*? A calm voice chimed in, *Don't be silly. Kids are more resilient than we think. He'll be okay.* My logical side took the microphone next. *The virus doesn't care about custody schedules. It can infect and sicken anybody. You are doing the right thing.*

After I went to bed, I found a new worry: how to keep a ten-year-old boy active and busy now that he didn't have school or swim-team practices. I tossed and turned without a clear solution, but when I woke up in the morning, I knew what to do. I talked about my plan at breakfast. "I will take Denny and Floyd for a hike every morning," I declared.

"Every morning?" asked my husband, Jim, with one eyebrow raised.

"Every morning!" I repeated.

"Rain or shine? Even if it's cold?" asked Denny.

"Rain or shine, even if it's cold," I said. "Okay now, brush your teeth and put on your boots!"

Jim and Denny were skeptical that we'd hike every morning. Floyd, however, quickly adapted to the new routine; after a few days he waited at the door while we ate breakfast. Denny, on the other hand, used every excuse in the book to avoid our daily hikes. It took him more than a week to accept that this was happening every morning.

Finally, by the time we entered our third week, Denny was putting on Floyd's harness without even being asked. "I love our new life," he announced one morning while hiking.

"Do you?" I asked.

"Yes. I run around with Floyd instead of going to school."

"But you don't see your dad in person," I said. He sighed and kept walking, kicking pebbles. "Why don't you call him and ask if he would like to join us for a hike on a day he doesn't work?" I asked.

"Why haven't we thought about that before?" Denny cheered.

The next morning, we met Al at the parking area of a hiking trail that Denny picked. Al was neither fond of hiking nor dogs, but he loved his son and had even endured Boy Scout camp for Denny's sake. Now, here he was in his white Adidas sneakers and jeans.

"Those shoes will turn brown," Denny said. "We were on this trail the other day, and it was pretty muddy."

Al shrugged.

"Okay, then, follow me, Dad!" Denny said, and charged toward the path. The six-foot distance between Denny and Al didn't bother them. They chatted the entire hike and threw sticks for Floyd to catch. Floyd didn't fetch any sticks, but he ran after every wild turkey and squirrel. Al called him ridiculously cute. Floyd took no time warming up to the man he's seen many times behind a car window.

After that day, Al joined us on all his free days. Soon, he learned the names of some of the trails and noticed the changes in places where we hiked more than once. Hiking with Floyd became a way to socialize and bond for both families. Now and then, we walked as a larger group when Jim, Al's wife Tanya, and her son Vlad joined us. "I wish I had a dog like Floyd," said Vlad at the end of a hike.

"You're always welcome to join us until you can go back to college," I said.

"I'd love that," said Vlad with his beaming smile as he petted Floyd one last time.

After we got into our car, Floyd watched the black Volkswagen drive away until it was out of sight. Now he had a new reason to wag his tail when that car parked next to us. He knew the black Volkswagen carried friends, who were there to hike and play with him in the woods.

— Eser Yilmaz —

Rescuing Spot

Before you get a dog, you can't quite imagine what living with one might be like; afterward, you can't imagine living any other way.
~Caroline Knapp

We first set eyes on Spot on a blistering hot June afternoon in Texas. The black-and-white dog made her way to the family farm where my brother Bill and his bride-to-be were preparing for their outdoor wedding reception. She trotted behind them all day long and made herself at home in the small farmhouse. At the end of each day, they had to roll her out the front door before they left.

Their earnest attempts to find her owner or a new home proved fruitless, so they invited Spot to the party. Sporting a jaunty red bandana, she mingled calmly with the wedding guests.

Our three children were drawn immediately to Spot. While my husband Rich and I visited with friends and family during the social hour, they played with their new pal. My eyes returned repeatedly to the happy scene of children and a dog, a natural combination.

To date, ours had been a dog-free home. Erik, our youngest at age eleven, would get down on his knees at the dinner table, raise his arms above his head, and bow up and down. "Oh, please, oh Daddy! Please, oh Daddy! Please, may we get a dog?"

Even that failed to diminish Rich's resolve. And now I was sad as I watched the kids romp with Spot. Rich and I were perched on the front porch, enjoying plates of barbecue, beans and biscuits, when Rich said something that shocked me. "I could live with Spot. What do you think?"

Hardly believing my ears, I seized the moment before it vanished. "Yes!"

His next question was superfluous. "Shall we tell the kids?"

Erik threw his arms around his sister, Karen, jumping at the news. Carl, ever skeptical, eyed Rich warily.

"Daaaad...." He drew out the name, pausing. "How much wine have you had?"

Rich lifted his glass, grinning. "Just this one." Carl's eyes brightened. Dad really meant it.

Hugging the dog, the kids repeated over and over, "Spot, you're coming home with us!"

We returned to the farm the next day to collect our new pet. My brother's house in town had a dog kennel where she would stay until we brought her home. Rolling through the Texas countryside with hot air blasting through the open car windows, we sang to the radio at the top of our lungs, "Who let the dogs out? Woof, woof, woof, woof, woof." We didn't really care who let them out. Spot was coming into our lives for keeps.

The brilliant idea turned out to be easier to conceive than carry out. We had flown from Minnesota to Texas for the wedding, and quickly discovered that airlines refused to fly dogs in the heat of summer. Spot also required a vet visit and shots in the brief period remaining before she could travel. I watched the kids slump with disappointment.

But a promise was a promise. Just as adamantly as he rebuffed the appeals for a dog, Rich stood by his word.

"If I have to, I will rent a car to drive Spot home. All 1,200 miles."

Our niece was a devoted animal lover and volunteered for a local vet. At her urging, the vet opened early Monday morning to administer the required checkup and shots. He reckoned that Spot was two to three years old and took a stab at her breed: Bassamation, or so we dubbed her. Think Dalmatian with short, bowed legs and most of the spots concentrated in one large black puddle on her back. The Basset Hound contributed droopy ears, doleful eyes and gentle personality.

Still, the issue of transportation lingered ominously as we approached our departure date. The whole assembled family was rooting for us, but we seemed to be out of options. Rich started checking rental-car agencies.

Then my mom called. "I found a way to get Spot home!"

She had been out on a drive through the countryside with my sisters.

"I saw this sign for a dog breeder. It said, 'We ship our dogs anywhere in the country.'"

Demanding that they stop immediately, she hurried up to the gate to talk to the owners. Mom had a knack for telling a good tale — even if it meant embellishing a bit. She launched into the saga of our attempt to rescue Spot, which promptly struck the hearts of these dog people.

"Can you believe it? Right away they offered to help us ship Spot to Minnesota!"

Spot wasn't home free quite yet. The breeder had a special license to fly animals year-round, but there were stiff requirements to meet. She had to be on a flight that left before 7 a.m. It must be a non-stop flight going north. And the temperature had to be below seventy degrees at the time of departure.

It was a high bar to meet, but all the stars aligned to make it work. The day after we flew home, Spot's kennel inched down the conveyor belt toward us at the airport. She'd made it!

Spot wormed her way into our hearts and filled the empty niche in our family life. We laughed when she first experienced snow — licking the air and plunging her nose into the fluffy whiteness. In the sub-zero temperatures of our Minnesota winter, she tried to minimize paw contact with the icy ground. We called it a three-paw walk. When she was irritated with us for disciplining her for barking too much, she retaliated by eating the bathroom rug. Emergency surgery was required to remove the soggy pink mass of yarn from her stomach. She never got over her fear of thunderstorms, quivering under the bed until they passed — maybe a lingering effect of her homeless days in the open Texas countryside.

Despite all her quirks, the kids doted on Spot for her twelve remaining years. But as often happens, a stray will attach itself to the one person perceived to be its rescuer. For Spot, that was Rich.

Little did I know that he was the family member who needed her most. His own boyhood dog had lasted only a matter of weeks before his parents gave him back. All this time, he'd been waiting for Spot; he just didn't know it.

The two of them became inseparable.

When Spot began going downhill, it was Rich who carried her up and down the stairs. When she could no longer jump onto our bed, he put her bed beside it. On her last day, Rich held her in his lap as she drew her final breath. And he grieved for her the longest. He still carries her name tag in his pocket.

— Molly Brewer Hoeg —

Collared by Love

He stirred my soul in the most subtle way
and the story between us wrote itself.
~Nikki Rowe

My husband of fifteen years and I had separated, but we shared joint custody of two finches. I was standing in the local pet store in our Northern California town looking at bamboo nesting houses for them when a vibrant dog collar caught my eye.

Our two Shetland Sheepdogs had died two years before, and I longed for another canine companion. The finches were nice for noise and funny when they cheeped along to Lady Gaga, but the birds were not much to pet and didn't contribute anything to my exercise routine.

The collar that caught my eye was intricately patterned in a rainbow of hues and tightly loomed like an Oaxaca rug. Symbols representing mountains, sun, stars, and rain had been incorporated into the detail. It was handmade in Guatemala, the card clipped to the collar read. With its sturdy brass D-ring it was the ideal size for the German Shepherd, Husky, or Malamute I wished I had. What I did have was a job that put me on more than 100 airplanes over the past eleven months, a lifestyle that was neither dog-friendly nor sustainable.

I purchased the collar anyway, in anticipation of a different future.

Fast forward two years. I was thankful the high-stress job and I had parted ways. I now worked for myself and loved every minute of it. It was why I could pop up to Seattle to spend time with friends before flying to Japan to deliver sixteen paintings to my new distributor. On a surprisingly clear October day, I sat in a diner where a dozen people had pushed together four tables to celebrate a birthday. My best friend and former co-worker, thirty years my senior, sat at the far table. She grinned a little too knowingly as she placed me next to her only single son, across from two of his teenaged children.

Rick and I had met at a picnic when we were both married, and he was chasing his three kids around. (He didn't remember.) And then our paths crossed again in 2008: at his stepfather's memorial service, and during his mother's breast-cancer surgery and recovery. In October 2013, we bonded for three hours over greasy breakfast food and beamed so much at each other that his kids texted each other: "Never seen Dad smile so much." Hours later, Rick asked me out after realizing I'd only be in town for one more night.

The next month, I returned to Seattle and met Nacho, his Red Heeler Cattle Dog. Rick had warned me that Nacho could be wary of strangers. They had rescued him from a high-stress situation where Nacho had lived with six other dogs and a few cats cramped in a small house with a smaller yard.

During our introduction, Nacho greeted me at the back door of the house by baring his teeth and growling. If Rick hadn't been holding his choke collar, he might have lunged at me. I steadied my nerves and held my fist out to let him know it was okay to sniff; I came in peace. His nostrils flared a bit as he took in my scent and relaxed, but Rick still held onto him until he was sure the dog would do no harm.

Over the week of that first visit, which was during Thanksgiving, I played with Nacho outside several times a day. I chucked the orange-and-blue ball, and the dog ran to retrieve and return it, charging toward me so fast that I was sure he would knock me over. I respected the power of his build: barrel chest, short legs, and a head and body that could withstand cattle kicks. I chucked the ball for him over and over until he lay exhausted and panting, his extra-long tongue hanging out of his mouth. We still didn't completely trust each other but we were working on it.

Finally, on the day I was to return to California, Nacho bade me goodbye by slurping my left cheek. Rick, a witness to this kiss, said, "I hope he remembers you next time."

When I returned for Christmas, Nacho was tentative at first. He growled, then sniffed me, and then, instead of baring his teeth he gave me an exuberant kiss.

For Christmas that year, I spent the holidays with Rick and his kids. I brought gifts for everyone, including Nacho. I gave him organic grain-free treats, tennis balls, and a stuffed alligator. Nacho seemed thrilled with these offerings and wanted to use them right away, so we went outside to play.

Throughout the new year into spring, I worked alternately from my house in California and from Rick's house outside of Seattle. Rick, Mr. Tough Guy, admitted to tearing up every time we parted. I said it would make sense when my lease ended in the summer for me to move, since he couldn't easily relocate.

In May 2014, Rick gave me a birthday gift wrapped in paper covered in cartoon dogs to which he added even more dog stickers. He declared the rubber garden shoes were from him and Nacho. Later that night, during an elegant supper at an award-winning restaurant, he proposed. In the spirit of our relationship, he included in the proposal the effect I'd had on his life, his kids' lives, and the dog's life.

Later that summer, I moved to Seattle, bringing that colorful dog collar. Though Nacho's legs are much shorter than a Shepherd, Husky, or Malamute's, his neck circumference is about the same. Suddenly, I understood that I had bought the collar for him, this loyal, now very loving dog who came with an equally loving man. The first time I clicked the collar closed around Nacho's neck, he sat up a little taller. This collar is now the only one he will wear.

—Jill L. Ferguson—

The New Girl

A dog can show you more honest affection with a flick of his tail than a man can gather through a lifetime of handshakes.
~Gene Hill

Two weeks before Woodstock, my girlfriend Spirit sat in the lotus position on my couch and said, "I'm moving north with some friends to join the Morning Star Ranch commune." I admired her tie-dye dress and the flowers in her long, blond hair.

"I need to get into teaching," I said, "and out of my insurance inspector's job." Then I loosened my tie.

We had only met at college four months earlier, so we talked about changes in people's lives until my phone rang, and the employment-agency woman said, "A teaching job just opened up. Are you willing to relocate?"

"How propitious," I said. (I was an English major.)

I wrote down the information, hung up and said, "I'm moving to the Central Valley where I can learn more about the 3 Rs — reading, writing and relationships."

We parted amicably. I packed up and drove east from San Francisco. Spirit hitchhiked north with friends.

Miller's Landing, population 355, and its old country school with wooden floors, real chalk and real chalkboards, was a twenty-minute commute from my one-bedroom duplex in Modesto. My landlord lived next door and raised cats. I had my job, books and TV, but they didn't socialize, converse or call. Walks in the nearby walnut orchard only partially filled the void in my life.

One day, when I was on yard duty the boys and girls gathered by the fence. I anticipated a scuffle. Instead, they were lined up to feed a stray dog.

"She followed us to school," a girl said.

None of the children cared that the dog was a mosaic of mud and weeds. They liked feeding the animal a portion of their lunch in exchange for a "handshake" through the fence.

"She shows up every day," a boy told me.

On Friday, when I heard that the principal was calling the dog-catcher after school I said, "No, he's not."

Caveat emptor!

During my first teachers' meeting at Miller School, Mr. Beatty, the elderly sixth-grade teacher, had said, "I tell my students, if you smell a goat and can't find one, it's time to take a bath." Well, this dog smelled like a goat. I drove with my windows down and took her directly to the Groovy Groomer Dog Spa.

"What's her name?" the groomer asked.

"We just met," I said.

"Let's call her Girlfriend," the groomer said.

While I waited, I purchased a leash, flea collar, sleeping pad and dog food. The clerk donated a sample of cat food.

"Cat food?" I questioned. The clerk shrugged.

I walked past stations where well-groomed dogs waited for their owners. Then my eyes locked with the loving brown eyes of Girlfriend, the former smelly goat who was now a beautiful golden Border Collie. Her tail wagged slowly. I grabbed the paw she held out and whispered, "Hello, Girlfriend."

When we arrived at my duplex, Girlfriend refused to leave my car. I put her sleeping pad on the floor outside my bedroom, opened the back door, and returned to my car. I carried Girlfriend across the threshold and set her down on her pad. I patted her head and her pad. I picked her up. She trembled as I carried her outside and set her down on the lawn. She sniffed the air, sniffed the lawn and, when nature called, stood up and did her business. I patted her head and said, "Good girl." After I carried her inside and set her on her pad, I knew we had bonded because she wagged her tail.

Girlfriend was my topic of choice during lunch-hour conversations in the teachers' room. Like a proud parent, I talked about her tail wagging when I arrived home.

Strange to me was that she ignored her dog food but ate the cat-food samples. More baffling was when the neighbor set a bowl of cat food on his front porch and called, "Here, kitty, kitty!" Girlfriend walked to the front door. She got out once and was eating the neighbor's cat food until I retrieved her.

Mr. Beatty explained that my dog had lived in an alley near the school. When someone in the neighborhood called their cats, my dog knew where to find survival food.

Sunday, we strolled in shallow river water at a nearby park and heard, "Mom, that teacher saved his dog from the pound!"

Suddenly a boy appeared. Girlfriend sat down and stuck out her paw.

He shook her paw and said, "She looks different."

"She had a bath," I said.

Richie, a third grader at our school, had been fishing. His attractive young mother in shorts and tank top introduced herself. Bobbie Jo and I got acquainted while Richie and Girlfriend splashed in the river.

Spirit called the Saturday morning of the veterinarian appointment. I said, "Girlfriend's appointment with Dr. Edwards is now. No time to talk."

"You met someone? Where?"

"School," I said. "Babies are involved. Bye."

Just before Easter vacation, Girlfriend gave birth to three puppies in my kitchen in her cardboard box filled with shredded newspapers.

Easter Monday, Spirit opened the front door without knocking. I barely recognized her in regular clothing and short hair. Girlfriend barked ferociously.

"Where'd you get little Lassie?" Spirit said.

Girlfriend, ears laid back, sniffed Spirit, sat down and stuck out her paw. Spirit held the paw and said, "Hello, Girlfriend, who does your nails?"

My dog's tail thumped as she lay down and nursed her puppies.

While I heated food on the stove, Spirit praised my clean birthing box and said the people at her commune smelled like goats. Spirit picked up one puppy, and when Girlfriend returned from doing her business outside, she sniffed her puppy, licked it, wagged her tail and settled into the birthing box.

Normally, she barked if the landlord or mailman even came close to our front door, but that day she wagged her tail for a stranger, which confused me. Girlfriend had not wagged her tail for me since before her pups were born. I felt hurt by her change in loyalty. I mean, I brought her home and fed her. I never asked who had fathered her puppies.

"Females prefer the company of females when babies are involved," I told myself, but I didn't realize the depth of my jealousy until I barked, "Janet, why are you here?"

Janet was Spirit's given name.

My dog sat up. Embarrassed by the jealousy in my voice, I shut off the stove, walked outside and plopped on the bench. I was upset and couldn't pretend to be in any other state of mind. Girlfriend left Janet to care for the puppies, trotted outside, sat down, faced me and wagged her tail.

"What do *you* want?" I said gruffly.

Girlfriend put her paw on my knee.

"Aww, geez," I said, and went through a different kind of meltdown. I lifted her onto my lap, wrapped my arms around her and whispered, "Are you telling me to not be myself, to be someone nicer?"

As if in response to my question, Girlfriend turned her brown eyes on me and gave me a hard look that said, "If you have to ask the question, you already know the answer."

I suspected I was putting words into my dog's mouth, which may sound strange to the reader. It sounds strange to me. But, on some metaphysical level, Girlfriend and I must have been simpatico. Why else would she have listened so closely and responded so appropriately?

Girlfriend stared at me in one of those moments when I thought she was going to speak. Sadly, she didn't talk but did express her feelings for me—she licked my ear and got down.

Girlfriend then worked her mojo on Janet at the kitchen table. First, the handshake, then the lap climb, and then arms were wrapped around her and Janet said, "How'd you know I needed to hug somebody?"

My dog looked at her, as if to say, "No special talent. All of you humans need the same thing—more love."

As I watched from the doorway, I wiped away a tear because I knew in my heart that I was a better person than what I had shown the two females a few minutes ago.

Janet turned to me and said, "Do you want me to leave?"

"How about if we catch up first?"

I sat at my kitchen table with her.

"On what?" she said.

"The commune?" I said.

"And you'll tell me about the widow with the little boy?" Janet said.

"Sure."

"I dropped out of the commune," Janet said, "enrolled in the new college in Sonoma County and completed my credential work. I'm now a sub in San Francisco on vacation, same as you."

"The widow and I have connected," I said. "Her son fed my dog at the fence. During back-to-school night, he brought his mom to see the dog he used to feed. BobbieJo works at a hospital. Husband was killed in Vietnam. I work in a very small community where gossip quickly becomes fact, but so far no one knows about us, not even her son."

Janet drove away quietly.

I filled a bowl with warm cat food and set it near my dog, who wagged her tail.

—John J. Lesjack—

Loving Sammie

Fall in love with a dog, and in many ways you enter a new orbit, a universe that features not just new colors but new rituals, new rules, a new way of experiencing attachment.
~Caroline Knapp

My name is Sammie, and I was adopted by my parents in the hopes that a new addition to the family would rekindle their dying relationship. My sleek black coat and penetrating eyes belied the terror I felt as my new mom unhinged the kennel door at the shelter. There was something about my eyes, my mom said later. Looking into my eyes, she knew I was the one.

They discovered I was impeccably trained and they took me home. It was May in northern Colorado, and they were excited about taking me to the lake and on hikes.

The first time they realized I had incapacitating separation anxiety was when they left me in my mother's brand-new Toyota Corolla while they stopped at the store for a quick grocery run. My mom was making her savory red sauce to go with the gluten-free pasta they were having for dinner, and she needed an onion and a can of diced tomatoes. After paying the cashier, she left the store, excited to see me. However, as she approached the car, she heard me barking loudly. I was terrified. Mom opened the car door to find me panting and frantically ripping at the cloth bucket seats.

For the next month, my parents tried everything to manage my acute separation anxiety, which was the official diagnosis given by the vet. They put me in a large crate and walked around the block quickly, at the vet's suggestion, only to discover that I nearly dislocated my jaw trying to bite my way out. They also tried to enclose me in a small room, thinking that might reduce my anxiety, arriving home later to find that I had destroyed all the molding around the door trying to escape my confinement. I'd finally escaped by chewing a large hole in a window screen.

I felt sorry for them. They studied my behavior in a desperate attempt to find a pattern that would allow them to predict and manage my anxiety. Did it happen more during daylight? Nighttime? Hot days? Rain? They consulted vets, pet psychics, animal communicators, and canine behavioral specialists, and took any advice that was offered. There was no shortage of theories to explain my distressing behavior, and none of them worked.

My parents were both trained mental-health professionals. Surely, between them, they could figure out the solution to my problem. Finally, they did. From April to October of each year, they determined, I could not be left alone, ever. I was relieved.

Months later, my parents separated. After seven years, the relationship between them was finally over, and there was no question that I was to stay with my mom. She was my universe, and I was hers. Fortunately, my parents remained best friends and committed co-parents to me.

When October came, like clockwork, my anxiety ceased, and I was as normal as ever. I could be left alone and live an ordinary life until April, when I would begin to become terrified and destructive. That's when normal life for them would be cancelled for the next six months.

For the next five years, between April and October, my mother dropped me off at my dad's house every morning on her way to work and picked me up on her way home each night. They arranged their days according to my needs, making sure I was never alone. They found all the restaurants that had dog-friendly patios and befriended all the storekeepers whom I came to know and love over the years. From time to time, my parents would enlist friends to babysit me if necessary.

Some people thought my parents were crazy to rearrange their lives six months a year for a dog. "Give her up" or "Put her down" were their unhelpful and unsolicited suggestions. But they loved me. The October to April Sammie was obedient, loving, sweet, and never in need of a leash. The April to October Sammie required patience, unconditional love, commitment and teamwork. I taught my parents how to become true friends after years of fighting and heartbreak. They worked together, collaborated, and shared a mutual love of me that transcended everything, including the new relationships they both found with other people. Their lovers quickly learned that from April to October I was a full-time job, part of the package that they could choose to take or leave. Most of the time, their new lovers got onboard and became part of the "village" of caregivers required to support my life and special needs.

I passed away at the age of ten, after being in their lives for only five years. My ashes remain on my mother's mantel to this day, ten years after my death. To some, I was a nuisance, a dog who required an intolerable amount of care. To my parents, I was an angel who taught them what parents who have children with special needs know: When someone you love needs you, no matter how hard or inconvenient, you do what has to be done, knowing that in the end, you would do it all over again if it meant having just one more day with your beloved.

— Ellen Abell —

Finding Joy

Life is funny... we never know what's in store for us
and time brings on what is meant to be.
~April Mae Monterrosa

"He followed me home." Chuck half-smiled and then shrugged, as if he had nothing to do with the big brown blob at his feet. "I thought we could call him Zeke."

Zeke, a mixed-breed mutt, waited patiently as Chuck explained his dilemma. He looked up and, for a moment, his eyes locked with mine. He whined and stepped toward me, his tail wagging, but I was too filled with my own misery to understand. We had bought this house, and then I'd lost my job a month later. Add to that the fact that Chuck and I argued over everything lately, and two of our boys were going through divorces. The last thing I needed in my life was a dog.

Besides, a rabid dog had chased me as a young girl. Chuck knew that most living creatures terrified me, particularly dogs. Even though I had put up with a variety of animals while our three sons grew up, I was not an animal lover.

Zeke was here to stay though, so we settled into a routine. I got another job, and when I came home, Zeke bounded up the stairs to greet me. I would take him out and then feed him. Occasionally, I'd pat him on the head. But I did little else to encourage him. Still, he would act as though I was his best friend, following me around the house and reveling in the time I spent taking him out to do his business.

Before I knew it, I looked forward to seeing him each day. I let him be with me in the house even when Chuck wasn't there, and I found myself taking longer walks with him. Chuck fenced a corner of the yard for Zeke and put a doggie door in the end of our screened-in porch so he could come and go when he needed shelter.

The next time Chuck's work shift took him away at night, I let Zeke stay in the bedroom with me, even though I was still a little afraid of a fifty-pound dog. I fell asleep right away. Sometime in the night, I woke up, and Zeke was lying at the foot of our bed, cuddled against my legs and feet. That became his favorite sleeping place. I found I was much more tolerant of Zeke than I had been of our previous pets. I could give Zeke his medicine, putting my hand into his mouth without fear. Soon, we were posing on picnic tables for family pictures and playing ball and Frisbee with grandkids. We would go to the lake camping for the weekend, and Zeke was eager to go, too. He claimed his spot on the front of our pontoon boat and loved swimming, whether with the grandkids or the ducks.

One day, a mother duck and her babies were swimming near our campsite. Zeke jumped into the water to chase them, despite my trying to call him back. Several people stopped at the commotion and watched as Zeke swam closer to the young ducklings. I held my breath. When he reached the babies, he didn't give them a glance. He swam right past them, and the mother flew off when she saw her babies were no longer in danger. In a few minutes, he tired of the game and swam back to shore. Everyone who watched was astonished, but it dawned on me that he never meant to harm them. It was just the chase he liked.

Zeke was so much a part of the family that hardly anything went on that didn't include him. He not only filled a void in my life but helped me to move past the heartbreak of losing my job, dealing with the pain my children were experiencing, and feeling sorry for myself. I found joy in my life again and a new capacity to care about things other than myself. I became not only tolerant of animals but found I was more tolerant of people.

Chuck and I rebuilt our relationship, and after thirty-six years of marriage, we renewed our wedding vows. Zeke had become so much a part of our lives that as we greeted everyone following the ceremony, our youngest grandchild looked up and asked, "Where's Zeke?" I laughed as hard as everyone else.

One year later, I came home from work to find that Zeke had gotten out of his protected area of the yard. We searched the neighborhood and could not find him. Later that night, as I sat on the sofa and looked out my living-room window into the cold winter night, I pictured him trying to find me. I kept hoping he would scratch on the door, begging me to let him in and forgive him.

I knew Zeke was gone, even though I wouldn't hear it officially until the next morning. I could tell by the hole in my heart. Neighbors said a big black dog was roaming our street, and we guessed that Zeke had gone out to play. A car hit him as he crossed a busy road not far from our house. We had made his life better, as everyone reminded us over the next few weeks and months, but we still felt responsible for him and the loss was shattering.

As I dealt with Zeke's death, however, I found peace when I realized that he had come into my life for a reason. I no longer feared animals; instead, I made an effort to understand and protect them. Instead of killing spiders now, I gently encourage them to return to the yard. I feed the birds. Now I share my home with two dogs, one a stray I saved from near death. But more importantly, I share a closer bond with my husband, children, grandchildren and friends.

He had been my best friend, a loving, sharing, giving part of our family. Even now, years later, Zeke's spirit lives on in our family. Our current pets, Sunny and Cody, don't know it, but they have a pretty good life because of Zeke. These days, I picture him riding on a heavenly lake somewhere feeling the wind in his face, happy that he grew up with us and taught me the joy of sharing life with a dog.

— Patricia Hope —

All Ours

The bond that links your true family is not one of blood,
but of respect and joy in each other's life.
~Richard Bach

When my husband Ron and I met, he had two boys from a previous marriage, and I had one. We tried to correlate schedules, personalities, parenting practices, and belongings from two homes, but it was a challenge. I guess any newly blended family has the struggle to move from "yours and mine" to "ours." We were hopeful a puppy would create a shared excitement, a new family member for all of us.

We were at the town pound meeting an adorable Husky. "There's a week-long waiting period. His family may be out there. After that, if you want him, he's yours," the caretaker said.

After several days, there was no call about the puppy, so we went back to the facility. The somber man greeted us. "I'm sorry, but you're a few days late."

My heart sank for us, but I was happy the puppy had found his family.

"The Husky—well, he got out and ran into the road. He was hit by a car."

My heart pounded. "What? Oh, the poor thing."

"He's still alive. He must have a broken leg. He wouldn't let me near him. Not sure where he is now. He doesn't look good. I don't think he'll make it."

My head spun, and my heart ached. I couldn't absorb any more of the conversation. As our tires rolled across the snow-covered driveway, tears fell down my cheeks. "The poor thing is just dragging himself around? It's so cold out. So, now what? He just suffers until he dies?"

My husband patted my knee. "I'll tell you what. I know you have to work tomorrow, but I'll see if my mom can help. We'll go back and search for the dog. We'll take him to the vet and have him put to sleep so at least he doesn't freeze to death or suffer anymore."

I wasn't sure that eased my sadness. I knew I didn't want the little guy to suffer. It was a long, sleepless night, and the day dragged with sadness. When my phone rang, I wasn't sure I wanted to answer it.

"They listed the puppy as 'Pup' since he doesn't have a name." Ron sighed.

Pup? My heart sank as if weighted down with an anchor. Such a short, sad life for this puppy without a name. No one claimed him while he was in holding. He was only four months old. I wondered if he ever had the chance to feel loved. Now, in the last few minutes of his life, he was surrounded by strangers.

"The vet told me that it's a good thing we found him when we did. He probably would have died within a day; his one back leg has gangrene setting in the wound. The other back leg is shattered, and his hip is dislocated. His tail is also broken. Other than that, the vet said he's a healthy, four-month-old puppy."

I wasn't sure I heard him right. "Healthy? Really? With all those injuries, they can save him?"

"Sounds like it. Are we claiming him and paying for his surgery, or are we having him put down?"

I chuckled. "How well do you know me?"

"Right. I'm right there with you. Surgery it is."

The vet told Ron, "If we amputate his back leg to the hip, remove a portion of his tail and treat his other wound, he should recover nicely. It'll be a bit of a recovery. He'll need to keep calm and only take sedate, calm walks for a while."

What a sight Pup made with his amputated leg, bandaged tail and Elizabethan collar. We named him Rocky because of the typical

Husky, dark raccoon band around his eyes. Thanks to the veterinarian, the day after his amputation surgery, Rocky walked out of the clinic on his own and into our hearts.

Rocky's recovery took time. There were a few additional minor surgeries to remove the rest of his tail. The kids, my husband and I, and even my in-laws changed bandages and took him on his quiet walks several times a day. Once he was able to be a normal puppy, Rocky loved to run on our twenty acres with our senior dog, Rigs.

A year after we brought Rocky home, Rigs passed away, and I believe Rocky grieved as much as we did. Separation anxiety never looked so destructive. We gated Rocky in the kitchen while we were gone. When we got home, we'd find the gate knocked down, and Rocky would be sitting amongst the ruins of a tattered pillow, chewed videodisc, shoes, or anything else in his path.

In an attempt to help Rocky with his separation anxiety and destructive tendencies, I left the television set playing while we were gone to keep him company. I called home and talked to him over the answering machine. Nothing seemed to help. We bought him bones, toys and stuffed animals, but Rocky preferred our pillows, blankets and furniture.

Even with Rocky's grief manifesting as a chewing disorder, he was always such a joy to be with. Instead of our blended family running to individual activities, we found ourselves rushing home to be with Rocky. The puppy didn't care what kind of day we had or what baggage we carried from the past; he cared about today. Celebrate every day, he taught us. Life can change in a heartbeat or with the squeal of tires. We did nothing special—a family walk, playing outside, and the daily cleaning up after Rocky. The difference now was that we were doing the activities together. He was "our dog" and we all pitched in.

But we needed to find a cure for Rocky's anxiety. "He needs a pal to keep him company," Ron said.

I thought a puppy was the last thing we needed. Ron surprised us with a fur ball named Tucker. Now, Rocky had a buddy to match his energy and keep him company. Tucker helped cure Rocky's chewing disorder. From day one, the two of them were inseparable.

As a family, we started to camp. I would ask Rocky, "Are you ready to go camping?"

Although he only has three legs, he can spin in a tight circle and leap into the truck. He is always ready to go for a hike or swim. He follows Tucker over, around or under anything. We wanted to try canoeing, but with Rocky's child-like enthusiasm, we were certain he'd tip us over, and we'd all end up in the water.

Rocky changed our lives. "Our" stray is a healer. He moved us from a blended family to a family. We worked and played together. In dog words, we became a pack.

He also showed us how to heal our broken parts, just as he did. He was a model of resilience. It's a classic tale of who rescued whom?

—Victoria Roder—

Settling In

I have found that when you are deeply troubled,
there are things you get from the silent,
devoted companionship of a dog that
you can get from no other source.
~Doris Day

It was adoption day. The pet store was working with the Lexington Humane Society to find good homes for abandoned dogs and cats. After endless pleas from my sons, Mark (age seven) and Luke (age six), we decided to stop in. We had been talking about getting a dog for a while.

I didn't know it at the time but adopting a homeless dog would really make me feel better. I was struggling with homesickness and a little bit of depression. We'd moved from Ohio to Kentucky because of my husband's career, and I was having trouble adjusting. Ohio had been my home for forty years, and I missed my parents, friends, and the familiarity of home.

Inside the pet store, there were rows of cages filled with warm, furry animals with big, curious eyes. People were milling about trying to figure out which one would make a good pet for them.

I spotted ours immediately: a cute, little Jack Russell who trembled as she watched people walk by. I read her story on the side of the cage: two-year-old female Jack Russell named Princess, dropped off by owner. A lump rose in my throat. "How could someone just drop her off?" I asked my husband.

"Bad times, job loss, divorce?" my husband said. "Maybe they were moving and couldn't take her. I'm sure they brought her here because they wanted the best for her."

I knew he was right; it wasn't my place to judge. They took the time to take her to a shelter where she'd be safe.

She had black fur around her eyes, which reminded me of a panda. Her speckled paw glided down the inside front of her cage, and it felt like she was saying, "Someone take me home." My motherly instincts kicked in, and I knew we had to help her. I could tell she was having a rough time. The workers were dedicated animal lovers doing their best to care for her, but the noise from customers and other barking dogs seemed to be wearing on her.

I peered into her cage. She blinked at me, her ears folding back. "You okay, girl?" I asked softly. She pushed her nose toward the cage, sniffed, and then lowered her head. Shaking uncontrollably, she gave a soft whine.

"She's cute," Mark said.

"Can we hold her?" Luke asked.

"Let's look at all the dogs first, and then we'll make a decision," my husband answered.

I looked at Princess. "Don't be scared," I told her.

We walked down the aisles. There were Lab puppies, mixed breeds, and a beautiful Irish Setter, all deserving a loving home.

I looked back at Princess, who was still shaking in her cage, unsure of her surroundings. I could relate. I wondered if Princess felt that way when she'd been brought to the animal shelter, surrounded by people she didn't know. Is that why she was shaking so hard? It made me want her even more.

"What do you think?" my husband asked.

I bit my bottom lip and turned toward Princess's cage. "I can't get that one out of my mind." Or my heart. I was relieved to see my boys agreed.

I asked the worker about her. She smiled and unlocked her cage. "This girl's a little skittish, but once you get to know her, she has a very warm temperament." She looked at Mark and Luke. "She's great with children, too. Did I mention she's already potty-trained?"

"A bonus," I said.

Princess let the lady put a collar and leash on her. We walked her down the aisle. My boys took turns petting her. We spent time with her, but she still seemed scared.

"It's okay, little girl," I said.

Later, the worker asked what we'd decided.

"What do you think?" I asked my family.

The boys couldn't contain their excitement and shrieked, "We want her!" And my husband agreed. The worker put Princess back and hung a note above her cage that read "Pending Adoption." While I filled out the paperwork, my husband and the boys picked out a bed, leash, and dog supplies.

After the adoption was completed and she had her first checkup, Princess rode home between the boys in the back seat. She laid her front paws on the back of my seat so she could see out. We decided to change her name from Princess to Lilly. But it really didn't matter because we treat her like a princess anyway.

She barely ate and didn't bark the first few days, but gradually she relaxed and settled into her new home. In a strange way, it made me feel better knowing that I had a friend who was adjusting to her new surroundings, too.

One morning, I woke up feeling terrible with a sore throat, sneezing and fighting a case of homesickness. Feeling sick and blue, I went to see a doctor. He called in a prescription for my head cold and sinus infection. After it was filled and I picked up a few items, I came home, took my meds, and plopped into bed.

I was about to doze off when I felt Lilly jump on the bed. Her cute face was staring at me, her tail wagging, I couldn't help but reach out to her. She settled in next to me, her small, furry body against mine, and I covered her with the blanket. It felt good to have a friend next to me.

I felt awful the entire day, but she stayed with me, only leaving my side when I took her out to potty. I petted her and talked to her, and she helped keep my mind off my illness. Finally, after two days, I felt a lot better, and my sinus infection was clearing. We had fully bonded by then.

A few months after adopting Lilly, I realized I wasn't as homesick either. Taking care of her helped keep my mind off it. I still missed my parents and friends, but I started adjusting better to my surroundings. I made some wonderful friends and enjoyed going places in Kentucky like the horse park and the beautiful walking trails. When I felt lonely, Lilly was right there by my side. She also seemed more relaxed.

Nowadays, we go for walks and play fetch. She loves to chase the sweeper and her squeaky toys. It's nice to see how happy she is. She has a very good appetite and loves her doggie treats. Her best friend is our other rescue dog, Zoey. The whole family loves her, but she and I are especially close. I think it was because we were both adjusting to our new home back in the beginning.

When my son Luke turned seven, we had a birthday party. While I was frosting the cupcakes, I looked down, and Lilly was settled on the floor next to me. She was taking in everything: the sounds of children laughing, the smell of food and two of my new friends sitting at the kitchen table. She looked around and then up at me and wagged her tail. I thought it was her way of saying, "I'm finally home." And you know what? She was right. We were *both* home.

— Terri Knight —

A Puppy Named Joy

When you walk in purpose, you collide with destiny.
~Ralph Buchanan

Retirement is an amazing gift. For me, it's been the time to carry out the dreams I've stored in my heart. At seventy-one, my body doesn't have the energy it used to, but my brain hasn't accepted this reality. So, I keep dreaming.

After all, my belief in following my dreams has helped me create a new life from the ashes of the past. When my beloved husband Ernie died, I was open to new love and found it in a wonderful relationship with my new husband, Fred. When I faced unwanted, early retirement because my teaching position was cut, I went back to school to become a chaplain. Soon I had a meaningful life running grief support groups and visiting the lonely.

So, when a friend told me about the desperate need for therapy dogs for nursing homes and hospice centers, I was sure this was my newest calling. I began reading about therapy dogs. Fred and I already owned two dogs. They are loyal pets, but the Schnoodle has an unnerving bark and is not fond of strangers, and our elderly Standard Poodle has an old dog's aches and pains and isn't up for a new mission. I read that a Maltese was the ideal therapy dog for the sick and elderly, but that Maltese puppies are notoriously hard to house train, but I ignored that part. After all, I'd trained nine puppies during my adult life.

It wasn't easy to find the perfect dog, but the search was fun. I spent every evening studying Craigslist and showing the pictures to

Fred. He'd comment, then say, "Are sure you're up to this, Lou?"

I was sure.

When I shared my dream with the dear woman who grooms our dogs and runs the kennel we use, she said, "Three dogs are a lot more work than two. Are you sure?"

I WAS SURE!

My dream was filled with love, prayers, and good intentions.

We had to drive over three hours to meet her, but we finally found a darling puppy who smothered us with kisses. Of course, the kisses sealed the deal. I named her "Joy" for the joy she would bring to others.

When we arrived home late that night, we had everything prepared for our new arrival. We introduced her to the other dogs, ate, played, and prepared for bed. I'd crate trained every puppy I'd ever owned, and I had a cozy crate ready for her. I covered it with a sheet, slipped little Joy into her new bed, and confidently shut the bedroom door. I expected that she would whine for a bit, then go to sleep.

That didn't happen. Our sweet little ball of fur let out a scream unlike any I've ever heard! Then, our other two dogs began to bark and howl. After a few minutes that felt like hours, Fred said "This won't work. We're going to wake the neighbors."

Thus began our routine of Joy-filled nights. We left the crate in the other bedroom and placed the puppy's little dog bed next to ours. Joy curled up sweetly and went to sleep. Two hours later she cried. When I took her outside, the other two dogs decided they wanted to go, too. After habitually sleeping ten to twelve hours a night, the two older dogs now wanted to go outside every time the puppy did.

After Joy went out, she looked for someone or something to play with. This went on all night. The next night we tried the crate again, and again we gave up.

During the day, house training little Joy kept me more than busy. I took her out consistently, and she adored it. She danced around on her tiny legs, smelled the flowers, tasted the grass, and played with the neighbors. She lived up to her name. Because of her happy nature, I met all of the children in the neighborhood. Kids of all ages, even previously sullen teenagers, loved to sit on the grass and play with her.

Joy often peed and pooped outside, but she felt no guilt whatsoever at doing it again when I brought her back into the house.

One of Joy's favorite games was tormenting our gentle Poodle, Daisy. The old dog would fall asleep and Joy would then grab Daisy's big, bushy tail and sink her sharp puppy teeth into Daisy's skin and bone. First, Daisy would growl, then she would swat at our six-pound darling, and then with great exasperation, she'd put her paw on Joy to try and control her.

Little Joy was definitely not bringing happiness into Daisy's life. It soon became evident that we had to keep the big dog and the tiny dog separate, but this was almost impossible because both of the dogs wanted to be by Fred and me, and Daisy had slept by Fred's side all her life.

I was a light sleeper, and I wasn't getting any sleep at all. Day after day, our dog circus continued. Since I continued with my determination to train Joy to be a therapy dog, Fred suggested that we temporarily sleep in separate bedrooms. I would take the day shift, Fred would take the night shift, and hopefully I would get some sleep. It didn't work.

Instead, I found myself more and more sleep deprived. Day after day, I found myself canceling my chaplaincy appointments. I'd gone thirty-two days without sleep, and I couldn't function. My friends advised getting rid of the puppy. I was heartbroken and felt like a failure.

Joy needed a younger family, and she needed to be the only dog in the family. Early one morning, while I cried softly and prayed silently, my dear Fred wrote a beautiful ad and put our precious puppy on Craigslist. Much to my surprise, the phone rang almost immediately. A young mother and her five-year-old son, Ryan, were soon at our door.

Ryan sat on the floor while our rambunctious puppy sat calmly in his lap. Tears streamed down my face as I helped the young mom load Joy and her possessions into their car. But… my tears were happy tears.

Little Ryan is a special needs child, and Joy is now his constant companion. Ryan's mom sends pictures of them running in their fenced-in yard, playing with toy cars, and the sweetest picture of all, Joy in the arms of her young master lying exhausted in a lawn chair, both of them sound asleep.

My dream came true. It just didn't go the way I expected.

Joy was born to be a therapy dog. Fred and I were simply God's conduits to get her where she was meant to be.

— Lou Zywicki Prudhomme —

Grieving & Recovery

Just Be There

Just being there for someone can sometimes bring hope when all seems hopeless.
~Dave G. Llewelyn

Before we were married, my husband Chris surprised me with a picture of a four-week-old English Bulldog puppy and informed me that she was ours. We had been talking about getting a puppy for several months, but I never thought it was the right time. We had picked out this puppy together, but I hadn't been brave enough to call the breeder and put down the deposit. Chris took matters into his own hands. Little did he or I know at the time what a gift he was giving me.

Ruka turned out to be one wild little girl. From the moment she marched her round little belly into our home, she was stronger in will than I ever could have imagined. If she didn't get what she wanted, she'd tell us by means of puppy whimpers and barks. If she didn't want to do something, she wouldn't. There was no negotiation.

She was also persistent. For years, we tried to keep her off our bed, but every night she'd come and check to see if we changed our minds, just in case. Despite her stubbornness, she was also full of exuberance and mischief. She harboured an admirable zest for life, befriending anyone who wasn't afraid of a long tongue and lots of slobber. She was in our wedding photos, accompanied us on weekend getaways, and had us laughing and crying at the same time.

Our phone conversations with family and friends included how

Ruka was doing, and we joked about what someone would think if they stole our phones and saw how many dog pictures and videos we had. She truly became part of our family.

Four years after Ruka entered our lives, and just three weeks before our second wedding anniversary, Chris died from cancer at the age of thirty.

Not only was my husband ripped from me, but I felt as though my future had been as well. Gone were our dreams of a family together, of travel, of sitting together on the front porch as an elderly couple. The days were gray; I couldn't sleep; I couldn't eat; the pain of heartbreak was inconceivable. I felt like I was living in a horrific nightmare, but one that I couldn't wake up from. The silence in our home was deafening, but Ruka's endearing snuffles were always present.

The first night I spent at home without my husband, Ruka was up and on the bed in a flash, promising to stay close for as long as I needed. She was a very heavy sleeper, yet when I'd cry, she'd wake up and sit next to me. She'd lean into me as if she was hugging me the only way she could. If I was crying especially hard, all fifty pounds of her would walk clumsily onto my lap and sit or lie down and stay there until I started petting her and was able to calm down.

In the mornings, if I slept too late, she would jump off the bed and stand back, just far enough so I could see her eyes peering over the top of the mattress. If I didn't get up, she'd bark gently at me. She didn't care if I only moved to the couch; she just knew it was time to get out of the bed. If I was late in feeding her, she'd come find me, stare at me intently, and lead me to her dish. She knew what she needed and what I needed to do.

She'd bring me toys and invite me to play. If I didn't want to, she understood and would take her coveted stuffed pig into the corner and suck on it like a nursing puppy, something that always made me laugh. I was fatigued by the platitudes I'd heard and by questions that others would ask me about my plans for a new life. Any new widow will tell you that no words make the pain go away, and thoughts of an unknown future, without the one you were planning to spend the rest of your life with, can be scary. Ruka spoke no words but reminded me silently that she was there with me.

Despite her intent on caring for me during my grief, I knew she was grieving, too. She'd wander through our home, moving slowly from room to room and waiting for a few moments in each. This was something she never did when my husband was still here. The only way I could explain this behavior was that she was looking for him. I don't know what broke my heart more — when she started doing it, or when she stopped.

Ruka and I would often go for walks through the nearby forest and down to the river. We'd go to the spot that she and I and my husband enjoyed during the summers. I would replay our last day there and think about how, at the time, I never would have imagined it would be our last… ever.

Ruka would gaze out into the water with me and watch the branches as the snow would gently sprinkle down from them. I tried to believe that those random signs of movement in an otherwise still forest were signs that my husband was in some way, and in some form, walking alongside us. I liked to think that when Ruka stopped and stared at those flickers of life, that maybe she could see him, as some say dogs have the ability to do.

As life moved forward, Ruka moved forward with me. She was always there to greet me happily when I came home from work. She welcomed a new puppy into our home by eagerly shoving her face into the puppy's crate, as only Ruka could. Until the day she too left this earth, Ruka continued to make me laugh and cry. Through the intense, raw period of my grief, Ruka never spoke a word, but I will be forever grateful to her for her love, companionship and undying support.

Though I have lived through this pain, I still find it challenging to articulate just what one needs in times of grief. In answering this, I look to Ruka and all that she did for me. When someone you love is grieving, continue to love them. Let them know the sun has risen again, take them for walks, ask them to play but don't be offended if they say no. Try to make them laugh, remind them to eat, stay close. But, most importantly, just be there.

— Kathryn Kazoleas —

That Stupid Little Puppy

When you feel lousy, puppy therapy is indicated.
~Sara Paretsky

When my girls were seven and ten, they set out on a mission to convince my husband and me that our family needed a dog. They promised to groom it, feed it, and walk it daily. My husband, wise soul that he is, told them, "If you're serious, you need to prove it to us."

And so… the "Dog Project" was born.

The girls would need to research what type of dog would fit our family's needs and how much it would cost—not only to buy the dog, but all the costs for that dog's first year. Then they would need to walk a neighbour's dog, every day, for a period of six months, rain, snow, or shine.

I should mention that neither one of us thought there was a chance in… well, you know what, that they'd be able to follow through with this plan.

Surprise, surprise, they did.

They walked ten different dogs in the neighbourhood. Every single day for more than six months. With a little help from their human family members, these dogs gave our girls gifts, invited them over for dinner, and welcomed them ecstatically each time they showed up for a walk.

Apparently, the entire neighbourhood was pulling for our girls to get their dream dog.

***

My parents had moved in with us when my oldest was a baby. They had a lovely, two-bedroom suite with nine-foot ceilings in our basement. Because they lived with us, they were constant fixtures in our girls' lives. The death of my beloved father, near the end of the Dog Project, rocked all our worlds.

My mother, who relied on my dad for everything, was devastated. She'd been unsuccessfully fighting clinical depression for her entire life. Dad's death tipped her over into the depths of her worst bout ever. She had no interest in anything — food, books, her favourite TV shows, or even her grandchildren.

Dad's death also hit our girls hard. He was such a positive force in their lives. Not a day in their lives had passed without one of his famous hugs.

My older daughter developed stomachaches when she left the house, which would disappear mysteriously as soon as she returned home. My younger daughter lost her hundred-watt smile and sent balloons to heaven with little notes for her grandpa.

And me? I missed him every moment of every day. He was my hero.

My husband and I thought long and hard about the girls' Dog Project and decided a new puppy might be just what our family needed. Our girls had proven to us how responsible they could be, and they were in desperate need of an outlet for their love — something to care for, hug, and share their deepest concerns with, something to bring joy back into their lives. Not that a dog can replace a person, but there is plenty of research about how owning a dog has positive effects on mental health. And a new puppy to take care of might be just what Mom needed to pull her from her depression. A nurse by profession, she had always thrived best when she felt needed.

And so, Madeline Abigail Arthur, a ten-week-old golden-haired Cockapoo, a living, breathing incarnation of Lady from *Lady and the*

Tramp, came to live with us. We like to say she chose us. When we went to the breeder to pick out a puppy, Madeline was the only one who waddled over and climbed into our laps. The girls were overjoyed. Within two weeks, they'd taught her to sit and lie down.

When my older daughter had one of her stomachaches, she'd curl up on her bed and talk things over with the dog. When my younger daughter released a balloon to heaven, she took Madeline with her to watch.

The new puppy was adorable, but she was also a lot of work, as puppies often are — crying in the middle of the night, chewing everything in sight, and peeing on the floor. When she was excited, when she was happy, when she was hungry, when she was sad... she peed.

The plan was for Mom to keep an eye on the puppy while my husband and I were at work and the girls were in school. She reluctantly agreed.

We'd come home from work and hear things like: "Your stupid little puppy peed on the floor again." Or, "I fed your stupid little puppy." And, "Your stupid little puppy had to go outside TEN times today!" And, sometimes, when she was really annoyed, we'd hear, "That damned, stupid little puppy of yours chewed up my slippers."

Later this changed to, "Your stupid little puppy likes marrow bones." And, "I taught your stupid little puppy to stay." Even, "Your stupid little puppy likes her ears scratched."

We tried not to smile at Mom's attempts to seem annoyed by the puppy.

After a month, we noticed that our stupid little puppy was spending an awful lot of time downstairs, even when we were home. The girls would head downstairs after school to hang out with Madeline and their gram. It was a win-win situation in my book.

One day, I went down to find Madeline to take her for a walk and found my mom sitting at the kitchen table having a full-on conversation with said stupid little puppy.

Eventually, Mom started calling her "Maddie," which we all loved so much it became her name. Soon, they were inseparable.

Maddie followed Mom around the yard when she headed back

out to putter in the garden after weeks of sitting in her chair all day. After the girls were in bed, Maddie went back down to Mom's. When Mom started watching her favourite TV shows again, Maddie curled up at her feet.

And, although Mom will deny this vehemently, I know the two of them shared Mom's lunch on more than one occasion.

That little dog brought a spring to my mom's step and a smile to her face. She gave Mom a reason for getting up every morning and to keep moving.

Maddie licked away my girls' tears when they missed their grandpa (she always seemed to know when they were sad) and brought smiles to their faces.

And me? I had a new furry daughter to love. How could that not be a good thing?

All and all, it was a match made in heaven.

Between you and me, although of course I can't be certain, I'm pretty sure it was my dad who encouraged Maddie to walk over to us on that very first meeting.

What I can tell you for certain is that this stupid little puppy made *all* our lives better, and in her own sweet way, she helped us cope with the loss of my wonderful father.

— Leslie Wibberley —

Animal Therapy

You know, a dog can snap you out of any kind of bad mood that you're in faster than you can think of.
~Jill Abramson

On a Saturday morning, I phoned the fertility clinic to let them know we were stopping treatment. The receptionist was there seven days a week because ovulation waits for no man (or woman). Our most recent treatment had failed, and we couldn't handle the financial or emotional strain anymore.

The depression that followed shouldn't have surprised me, but it did. It enveloped me, knocking the wind out of me and making way for a new challenge: crippling anxiety. I became fearful of everything. If I had a twinge, I was sure I had cancer that would render us unable to adopt a child. I started having tingling and twitching in my arms and legs, and I couldn't sleep at night. As the women in my life conceived and gave birth to beautiful, healthy babies, I would sit on our front porch steps each night, crying and waiting for my husband to come home.

A friend came up with the idea of my husband and me volunteering at a no-kill animal shelter. At first, I didn't think it would be a good idea. It would cut into my moping and obsessing time on the weekends. But it was something we could do together, and our little family of two rescue dogs and two rescue cats was indeed our greatest source of joy.

The no-kill shelter sat out in the country. It was a beautiful drive from our little house to the sprawling shelter. Row after row of pens were filled with all types of dogs: quiet ones, senior ones, sick ones, adorable ones, and the ones who were so ugly they were cute!

We went through training, and an idea was presented to us. We could take a couple of dogs and cats each weekend to a local pet store to try to find them homes! This was such an exciting idea for me. Little did I know this new opportunity would provide me with something I'd been missing: a purpose.

The first weekend, my husband and I loaded up portable crates into my beat-up old Jeep. It was hard work. The crates were heavy and prone to finger pinching. The animals we loaded were nervous and unsettled. There were stinky accidents that needed urgent attention. But there were sloppy kisses, nuzzles, and sweet tail wags to reward us.

It was wonderful to have my muscles, fingers, and heart ache for such a purpose. Finding a home for these animals was the ultimate goal, but even the simple interactions with the children in the store were so good for them. They would go from cowering and shaking to "smiling" in the way that dogs do. Taking them back to the shelter was hard, but it also felt like the culmination of a great adventure for them.

Each month, we tried to carve out a few hours of time with the shelter animals. I can still remember riding out to the shelter with my legs and arms buzzing with anxiety. And by the time we were riding home, my legs and arms were buzzing with exhaustion. The hard work was good for my body and soul.

Eventually, our lives changed — we adopted our first child — and we had to stop volunteering at the shelter. Someone commented to me that I must feel good about helping those rescue dogs find new homes. The truth was, those dogs rescued me.

— Kelly A. Smith —

My Caregivers

A dog is the only thing on earth that loves you more than he loves himself.
~Josh Billings

This past December, two days shy of Christmas, death took my friend Maddie. She was thirteen. The weather was wet and gray, and it would stay that way for some time. In the vet's office, I sat holding her, kissing her, and feeling her heartbeat until it beat no more. It's odd that so many things, like driving to work in traffic, can take forever, yet death isn't one of them. Death is nothing but straight-ahead green lights.

In a cool drizzle, I walked to the car, opened the door, and waited. Then reality hit with cruel force. No little red dog would be brushing past me to take the front seat.

I drove along the river, seeing the same things I've passed these last thirty years. At one time, my wife and I found this drive comforting, with the beauty of the softly flowing water and the sight of geese forming squadrons in the air.

I realize I've seen it maybe one too many times. After all, this was the route Genie and I took to her oncologist to hopefully hear good news, only to hear bad. It was the route we took when we rushed to the emergency room in increasingly frequent trips because cancer does nothing with subtlety or restraint. It was the route to the radiologist, where, in one last-ditch effort to kill cancer, Genie would be lit up like a Christmas tree, just without the beauty of an actual tree. But it all failed.

This was also the route we took to hospice — the longest and quietest drive I've ever made.

Then — just ahead — one more familiar destination. The absence in the front passenger seat grew even more profound. That flat spot on the river's edge was where I'd held Genie's memorial service. It was there that people spoke in kind and reverent tones. As they spoke, I watched one hardheaded and determined Maddie prowl and sniff. She was calling on ancient canine cunning to find a way to change the reason we were there. A forty-five-pound dog might be able to cause a 1,200-pound stampeding steer to change direction, but not even a Border Collie can have death agree to a do-over.

Now here I was with another death. When I arrived home, I went to Maddie's bed and plopped into it. I needed to smell her. The feeling was primal.

I scrolled through memories.

I remembered Genie being wheeled into the hospice facility. A trim and tidy administrator with pens in every pocket started asking Genie a series of questions about her life. There wasn't a whiff of irony in all this. Even the dying need to fill out forms, it seems. I wanted to help, but another person pulled me in another direction.

The questions for Genie seemed routine, so I tried to do what I could on my end to speed things up. Wait, why in the world was I trying to speed things up?

Something caught my attention. Genie had said, "Maddie! M-A-D-D-I-E."

A follow-up question was asked.

To this, Genie responded, "No. She's not our daughter. Maddie's our dog. A Border Collie. Sharper than a tack. She'll take care of him. Hell, she already is." I could tell how proud Genie was, and when she smiled, I couldn't help but break into my wry grin, even if I was in a house of death. But I recognized that Genie was doing what came natural to her — making a bad situation better.

Both Genie and I smiled, but the administrator remained baffled.

I stepped closer. "Excuse me, is there an issue?"

The administrator took me aside. In a quiet voice, she said, "We're concerned about your welfare because this… well, hospice can be trying, and most people aren't prepared for what… um, comes. I was asking your wife if you had anyone — friend, family — you want us to call to, um, help you… you know… afterward."

I laughed, but not at what the administrator said, but because of what Genie's response had been. Genie had heard, understood, and given an honest answer. Not for the first time, but maybe the last, I fell in love with the way my wife's mind operated.

To the administrator, but in a voice loud enough for Genie to hear, I said, "I'm set. Maddie will take care of me. Do you need me to sign something?"

Hospice personnel are right to pursue such things. They know a dying person can get hung up on leaving their loved ones, especially their spouse, especially if their spouse doesn't have someone to lean on afterward. A dying person has more than enough on their mind. That's why hospice personnel are adamant that the surviving friends and family not only say their goodbyes but also openly attest they'll be okay. That gives the dying person the peace of mind to make the next, and final, step.

What we said to the administrator was our declaration that Genie and I were on the same page. We'd said our goodbyes, and though we'd miss one another, Genie knew I'd be in good hands, which meant Genie could step into the warming light as soon as she wanted.

When Genie died, Maddie did as we expected. She stepped even closer to my side, and her eyes stayed on me.

When Genie was first told her cancer had metastasized, I started having horrible nightmares. That was also when we adopted Maddie. Even though she was young and slim, she was as fiercely protective as any dog we'd ever had. One night, Maddie found me tossing and turning. Recognizing I was in distress, she found a way into my dreams. As I slept, I saw her running across a shadowy dreamscape. Her sharp eyes were locked onto mine and brought me comfort. But she wasn't done. Somehow, she lifted me by the back of my collar and yanked me from the dream.

Genie wasn't surprised when I told her about it. In fact, she said, "David, why do you think she's here? Things have reasons. Someone — God? — knew you were going to need help. You have no one else. So they sent you this little dog."

For the next few years, the nightmares stayed at a distance. But when Genie died, they thundered back. Even at her age and with arthritis eating away at her joints, Maddie remembered her way into my dreams. She dealt with one, then another, then all the rest, until the nightmares stayed away for good.

Then Maddie died.

As I lay in her bed, smelling her, thinking of her, I heard two sets of paws heading my way.

A few years ago, in something that can only be called kismet, I'd taken Maddie to pick up bird seed. They were having a pet-adoption event, and a number of cages had been set up outside with dogs of various ages and sizes. Maddie, being a know-it-all Border Collie, didn't like other dogs. In all her years, she'd never met a dog — even other herding dogs — she thought was her equal.

But on this day, something peculiar, maybe magical, happened. Maddie froze in front of a cage holding two look-alike puppies. They were dark-coated Australian Shepherd mixes, herding dogs similar to Border Collies. One of our first dogs had been an Australian Shepherd.

"Hey, kindred spirits," I said to Maddie. "They're like you. Well, maybe not as pretty, but who is, right?"

Maddie snorted a reply.

I started into the store… but Maddie refused to budge. Her eyes were taking in the nearly identical puppies, assessing them, weighing them, considering them. Then I saw something in her eyes I'd seen in her eyes when she was looking at me: She'd locked on them.

I realized that if I didn't act, she would. So that day, Remy and Baux came home with us. They grew fast, but Maddie was the one who worked with them, not me. I was still a wreck, beat and tired from losing Genie. Amazingly, Maddie not only enjoyed being the mother, but she was good at it. That's something I never thought I'd say, but Genie had always said that Maddie would make a great momma.

The afternoon I lost Maddie, Remy and Baux got into the bed with me and pressed close. Like Maddie, they found a way into my head and heart. That day, they became my new caregivers.

— David Weiskircher —

A Gift I Never Knew I Needed

We call them animals, and so they are, for they cannot tell us how they feel, but they do not suffer less because they have no words.
~Anna Sewell

I walked into my home, broken and distraught. My thirty-four-year-old son, Stuart, had died suddenly, and I was in a fog of disbelief. My husband took me in his arms and led me to the nearest chair. As I wept, Custis, Stuart's dog, came and hopped up as if to hug me. He wrapped himself around me in a loving, knowing embrace.

Confused at first, I wondered, *Why is Custis here?* Then, I realized that our home was his home now. Stuart was gone. Honestly, my next thought was, *I can't deal with this dog right now!*

Little did I know how desperately we needed each other.

Custis, a big black Goldendoodle, had previously made snacks out of my rugs and other household items. I had declared our house a "Custis-free zone!! But here he was, soothing me in my greatest time of need.

If anyone had told me that a dog could grieve or even offer true comfort to a grieving heart, I think I would have rolled my eyes — until the day I witnessed it.

Any time I cried, Custis was there in a flash. He jumped up and wrapped his front legs around my shoulders in a giant hug. If I was standing, he sidled up next to me until I stopped crying.

He could sense when I needed him most. I could be in another room and, as if on high alert, he'd come running at the first sound of a sniffle.

This dog I had all but banned from my home knew what I needed and when I needed it. When he was near, it felt like a gift. I couldn't hug my son, but I could snuggle with the dog he loved so much. It felt good to have Custis near.

Looking into Custis's eyes was like looking into eternity. I searched for the end, but they just went on forever. They were full of love, and somehow they were full of what I can only describe as understanding.

At times, his demeanor was comforting; other times, heavy with pain. He was grieving. He had lost Stuart, too, and he missed him. He missed his home and familiar surroundings. His world had changed in a moment, just as ours had. As brave and supportive as he was, this beautiful, self-appointed comforter of mine was also depressed. His eyes would take on a sad, broken look, and he'd plop down on the hardwood floor with a mournful sigh. It broke my heart to see him so sad. Yet, even then, he would care for me if he sensed I needed him.

One day, I brought in a rug that had been in Stuart's house, and Custis ran to it immediately and folded himself into it as if it was saving his life. He smelled Stuart and his former home on that rug. Witnessing his grief, so raw and real, was heart-wrenching. Taken aback by his reaction, I broke down because Custis and I felt the same thing—profound loss. We missed our person, and we wanted any little piece of him we could get.

Custis became a significant part of my healing. Burying my tear-stained face into his fur and letting my heart spill out all over him allowed me to grieve freely. I could tell it all to him and cry all over him in a slobbery mess, and he never judged me or left me alone in my sorrow.

He drew near anytime I needed him. Often, he'd lumber over to me with those downcast eyes, and I'd see mine reflected in his. I'd tell him that I knew he was hurting too, and we could sit together awhile. We made quite the team — him, a giant ball of fur with soulful eyes that looked deeply into my own, and me, a broken human in need of compassion.

Custis was the gift I would never have known to ask for during a time I could never have seen coming. Selfless, loving, and tenderhearted, he offered comfort in the most unexpected ways. Our mutual love of Stuart stitched our hearts together and, to this day, brings a bit of peace when we both need it most.

— Faith Griffin Sims —

Loving Lenny

Until one has loved an animal,
a part of one's soul remains unawakened.
~Anatole France

It was a bright, cold Saturday morning in February. I had popped out of bed early and thrown on a pair of old jeans and a comfy sweatshirt, excited that this much-anticipated day had finally arrived. After six full days of this animal lover's pleading and begging on Facebook for someone to adopt a sweet, lonely Pit Bull mix that had found his way to our local animal shelter, my prayer had finally been answered. Little "Lenny" (the name I promptly bestowed upon him after observing his gentle-giant ways that mirrored his namesake in the classic *Of Mice and Men*) was going home! And who had adopted him? Me!

After seeing that there was no public interest in saving this sweet boy from his ever-looming demise date, my big-hearted husband finally gave in. Lenny was coming home to join our family. Lenny would be pet number five.

The only problem we faced was timing. The shelter (which was unfortunately not a no-kill shelter) had scheduled sweet Lenny to be put to sleep on Friday. But because of my husband's and my out-of-town work schedules, neither of us could pick up our sweet boy before closing time on Friday. So, the shelter graciously agreed to extend his date to Saturday—with our promise that we'd definitely show up by the time they closed at noon. No problem! I rose with the sun, my happy heart pounding out of my chest. Our baby was coming home!

And then I walked into the living room, and everything changed.

My precious calico kitty, Patches, lay on her little pet bed, struggling for air.

"Something is wrong."

At first, the words came out in a whisper, but as I realized the seriousness of the situation, they gained strength.

"Something is wrong!"

I called out to my husband, "Richard! Something is wrong with Patches!"

My husband came into the room and said, "Let's get her to the vet. Hurry."

I began scrambling for my shoes and a large towel to wrap my sweet cat in. We rushed to the car and started the thirty-minute drive to town. I held my fluffy girl like a baby in the passenger seat. We made it to the emergency vet, and while my husband ran to the counter to explain what was happening, my beautiful cat's gentle, sweet soul left her body as she lay in my arms in the waiting room.

My girl was gone, just like that. I heard voices swirling around me, offering help — burial services, cremation — but all I could do was look at the lifeless eyes lying in my aching arms. My sweet girl had seen me through so much over the past few years. She had watched my children grow with me. She saw my marriage fall apart. She saw me fall in love again and welcomed this amazing man into our world. She had been my constant through all the changes swirling around me.

And now she was gone.

I looked into my husband's empathetic eyes and saw the pain I was feeling reflecting back at me. Gently, he took my arm and led me to the car. I wouldn't let Patches go. I held onto her lifeless body and couldn't bring myself to put her down.

"Honey, we have to get to the shelter."

My husband's sobering words pulled me out of my stupor, and I glanced at the clock: 11 a.m. In the rush of the morning's tragic events, time had slipped away from me. We lost my baby that morning, but we still had work to do. We didn't have time to take my sweet Patches home, bury her and come back to get Lenny. We had to go straight to the shelter, or we'd be too late.

We pulled into the parking lot of the shelter, and my strong, stable husband finally convinced me to turn my kitty over to him. He took her from my arms gently, covered her lifeless body with the towel, and placed her in a box. We had no choice but to lay her sweet body in the trunk until we could get her home to her proper burial. After we got her in place, my husband took my hand and walked me into the shelter. There, we found our Lenny.

And he was terrified.

My eyes locked onto his, and I saw his fear of the unknown. I saw the uncertainty and questions that I was feeling, too. Could I do this? Could I switch gears so suddenly? From the heartbreaking pain of loss straight into the joy of a new adoption?

No, I couldn't. And my sweet Lenny didn't expect me to.

Dragging our terrified new pet to our car, my husband placed him in the back seat. And, in a last-minute mindless decision, I climbed back there with him. We both cried all the way home. Both of us were scared. Both of us were leaving what was familiar to us and embarking on a journey where nothing would ever be the same. Both of us were shaking, sad, and weak.

We needed each other more than ever.

Now, four years later, we've adjusted. My sweet Lenny helped me through one of the hardest days of my life. And I think I helped him through his, too. We snuggled on the couch on that cold Saturday back in February until our pain began to subside. We held onto each other until we realized that our broken hearts had just enough room for each other. My gentle giant coaxed me back to happiness and taught me to open my heart to another furry soul. And I taught him that some people won't ever leave you.

They just won't.

We're a team now, sweet Lenny and me. We didn't have the happiest of starts, but we've promised each other that we'll have a happy ending. While I saved him, he saved me.

Someone told me once that they believed my precious Patches

chose to leave that day on purpose. She knew that this would be the day that I would be able to accept her departure. I don't know about all that, but I do know this: A big, furry ball of gentleness and love immediately filled the spot that she left behind. Was that divine intervention? I don't know.

But I certainly know who's a good boy: my Lenny, that's who.

—Melissa Edmondson—

Daphne's Gift

An animal's eyes have the power to speak
a great language.
~Martin Buber

"Get your ball." My voice cracked as I held back tears. Sensing my intense pain, our fluffy Australian Shepherd retrieved her favorite toy and bounced back to me to sit at my feet. She didn't understand the phone call I had just had with my husband. I had told him that my dearest friend of forty-five years had finally succumbed to the cancer that had wreaked havoc on her body for the past three years. She couldn't comprehend my sudden manic cleaning as I tried to keep my mind busy and think about anything other than the great sadness filling me. No, my sweet Daphne knew nothing of this, yet she understood that her girl needed her.

She offered her slimy, hair-covered ball to me. I could not help but take it and smile. It was a gift from the heart. She would not share it with just anyone.

"Come on, furbot," I said, making my way slowly toward the bedroom. "Come sit with me."

At my side, Daphne's tongue drooped out the side of her mouth as she smiled. She was a truly happy dog. I climbed into bed and propped two overstuffed pillows behind me. My day was over. I hadn't the energy or will to do or think about anything else.

With a running leap, Daphne landed safely on the foot of the bed. It always amused me how she circled seven or eight times before settling in. This time was different, though. Without hesitation, my lovable seventy-pound pooch approached me. She nestled in close to my side, placing her chin on my upper leg. Her nose buried under my hand so that I was forced to pet her. She looked up at me with sad eyes, and I wondered if maybe I hadn't given her enough credit.

Her warmth calmed me, and her affection comforted me. I offered her the ball, her prized toy, but she did not take it. My fingers repeatedly traced the furry contours of her head as a steady stream of tears fell from my eyes.

It was a couple of hours before my husband was able to return home from work. Daphne stretched and leaned into me, not offering to move from her spot as he entered the room. My husband smiled. Our dog was energetic, but her girl's heart was breaking. She had a job to do — one that she was perfectly designed for. She could not be distracted by a favorite ball.

I cannot begin to put into words what Daphne's simple show of affection did for me that day. I was broken, yet my dog's kindness created a soothing calm within me. We would get through this. *I* would get through this.

And she would be by my side as long as it took.

— Leanne Watkins —

The Dog Who Needed Me

There is nothing truer in this world
than the love of a good dog.
~Mira Grant

July 4th is typically a holiday for most people, but last year I felt more like crying than celebrating. The day started out with our typical morning routine. One of my caregivers helped me out of bed and into my wheelchair. We got me dressed for the day. The next stop was the kitchen where I was preparing breakfast, but the meal wasn't for me. Leah, my eleven-year-old service dog, had suffered a stroke two months earlier. Dr. Tom, my vet, told me that it was anybody's guess if she was going to get better or worse. I bowed my head in prayer for my strength and her health several times per day, trying to prepare myself for any outcome.

She hadn't been eating well for a while, so I got some chicken and rice out of the fridge. It was her favorite. Ever since her stroke, I had told myself that I was going to put every ounce of effort I could into getting her better, so I mixed the chicken and rice with some of her kibble.

A minute or so later, I saw her out of the corner of my eye. Something was off, so I went to check on her. "Hey sweet pea, are you okay?" Her typical response to that question was to wag her tail or put her head under my hand so I would pet her. She did neither.

Instead, she rolled over and had a seizure. I asked my caregiver to get everything soft off my bed so we could surround Leah while the seizures continued. I forced down the panic as I tried to call Dr. Tom, forgetting that the office was closed because of the holiday. Eventually, I remembered that I had the cell-phone number of one of the staff members who worked there. I found out that Dr. Tom was out of town, but his partner was on call for the clinic. A quick conversation resulted in her telling me that she would be at my house within the hour.

The waiting was torture. The seizures were almost continuous. Watching Leah, this creature I loved with everything in me, made me feel as helpless as being stranded on the floor without my wheelchair. The only thing I knew in those moments was that I wanted my voice to be louder than whatever was going on in her head.

"I love you, Leah, to the moon and back again a billion times. If my love could make you well, you would live forever." I shouted the words as loud as I could. It became clear that the end was near. My voice kept cracking. "You couldn't have done a better job for me than you have. I could not have asked any more of you. If this gets to be too much, sweet pea, I want you to run as fast as you possibly can to heaven. For the first time since we have been together, think of your needs before you think of mine."

The vet came and assessed the situation. We couldn't get Leah to stand up. We made the decision to let her go, and it was done in about ten minutes. It's not lost on me that she chose to leave on Independence Day. In our time together, she helped me in so many ways so that I would not need to rely on other people. I believe she chose that day to leave this earth as a symbol to me that she thought I was strong enough to handle her passing.

In the weeks that followed, I don't know that I would have agreed with her.

The weight of my grief was palpable, like a boulder on my heart that wouldn't budge. I found out that, at the dog school I go to, the waiting list for another service dog was two years long, and the fees were incredibly high.

My house felt empty. The energy was drastically different, and I didn't like it at all. I called Dr. Tom since he had seen many people go through this experience, and I asked his advice.

"Lorraine, have you ever thought of getting a dog as a pet?"

"Well, it would have to be the right dog."

"Send me a list of your criteria."

Ultimately, Dr. Tom suggested that I get a Cavalier King Charles Spaniel. The breed is significantly smaller than the Labs that had been my service dogs, and Dr. Tom thought I might benefit from being able to cuddle a dog on my lap. As soon as I saw some pictures, I was totally smitten.

Within a week, I was on a Facebook page for people who loved this breed, sharing the story of Leah and me and what we had been through. I said I was interested in getting a Cavalier King Charles Spaniel and was hoping to find a breeder relatively close to me. I fully expected the process to take at least six months.

That same night, I got a response from a breeder who was five hours away. She said she had puppies and was touched by my story. She offered me a male at a greatly reduced price. Then she sent me his picture, and I knew this adorable guy was going to be my next dog. He had patches of copper color over both of his eyes. They reminded me of the patches that some people used to put on torn jeans. Therefore, I named him Levi. His name also honored Leah a bit.

There were moments before I got him when I began to have doubts. Would I forget Leah too soon if I got another dog so quickly? Was I betraying her memory? Those were hard questions, but every time I closed my eyes and thought of Leah, something told me she wanted me to move forward.

When Levi came home about two weeks later, he was a bouncy five-pound ball of fluff. For the first few days, he was confused and scared. He had been taken away from the only family he had ever known, and it was obvious that he was disoriented.

He spent a lot of time being cradled in my arms. I told him how much fun we were going to have together and how we would become a family over time. I showered him with attention and affection. My life became a flurry of activity. I had never potty-trained a puppy before, and it was quite an experience for both of us. But we also played, and he loved to be held. His antics made me laugh several times per day. Training and loving Levi kept my mind occupied, so I didn't have much time to think about how much I missed Leah.

Who knew that the answer to grieving a dog who had given me so much independence was to get a dog that needed *me* so much?

— Lorraine Cannistra —

A Snowy Rescue

Blessed is the person who has earned the love of an old dog.
~Sydney Jeanne Seward

Mike tragically left this world in March 2018. The loss of our beloved son left my husband Rick and me with shattered hearts. The world and everything in it changed forever. Never again would we hear Mike's kind and sweet voice or see his radiant smile.

Struggling, Rick and I spent countless hours together and with our close family. We all sat on the sofa, talking and wondering. *How are we ever going to move on with our lives? What are we supposed to do now? Will we ever stop crying?* I wanted to wrap myself in a blanket, curl up on the couch, and watch Netflix... forever. It felt like all hope was gone.

Several months later, during one of those couch conversations, Rick looked over at me and said, "Maybe we should get that dog now."

Little did he know that, between my crying jags, I had been searching online for a dog. It had to be hypo-allergenic so that he or she wouldn't irritate my allergies. House-trained so that we (as people in our third act of life) wouldn't be getting up in the middle of the night. And it needed to be older and smaller, so that he or she would require less exercise.

It turns out there are countless large-breed, senior dogs who need to be rescued. German Shepherd/Labrador mixes and mutts of all kinds are waiting for their new owners to come calling. But, unfortunately for me, these dogs all represented bushels of allergens. It became crystal-clear that what I was looking for would be harder to find, much like searching for a needle in a haystack.

But then, a fifteen-year-old Shih Tzu named Beau caught my eye. His photo stared back at me from the Heaven Can Wait website. His tiny underbite was adorable. His coat was a bit shabby, and he looked as if his fuzzy ears had been chewed on. He was hypo-allergenic, house-trained and a senior. He was perfect!

But alas, sweet little Beau had already been spoken for. He was awaiting adoption. Sighing loudly through the phone, Kim, the saintly owner of Heaven Can Wait, couldn't help but detect my disappointment. She went on to mention that a ten-pound female Maltese had just been surrendered. My ears perked up! "Snowy is used to quiet," she said. "The dog has come from a single female senior's home. She's not used to noise, she's not used to children, and she's not used to men." Not used to men? Well, considering I had a man, this was going to be interesting!

After some back-and-forth e-mails, photos and texts, Kim thought Snowy, Rick and I could be a good fit. We drove to a rural area south of town, home to Heaven Can Wait. Behind the wire mesh fence, we saw Beau, tracking and sniffing his way around the perimeter of the enclosure, apparently waiting for his adoptive family to pick him up. Trailing along behind him was a slight, shiny-haired white dog with beautiful dark eyes and an unusual curlicue tail. "Rick!" I said (as if he'd know the answer). "Is that her?"

It was. I was so excited. She looked more like a puppy than a senior. She was absolutely adorable.

So, after some extensive doggy dental work, Kim gave us the green light to pick up Snowy for a ten-day trial period. "I know she'll bond with you," said Kim. Wheeling around and pointing her index finger in the direction of my husband, she said, "But let's see how she takes to him."

At home, Snowy the Maltese followed me everywhere, and I mean everywhere! When I went to the bathroom, she stood outside the door until I reappeared. When I went to do my work, she trudged down the basement stairs and slept at my feet under the desk. When I was in the kitchen cooking, she was always underfoot. Each night, she slept with Rick and me on our king-sized bed, seemingly careful to sleep only on my side of the bed.

Truth be told, Snowy wasn't afraid of Rick, not at all. She wasn't wary of him nor was she suspicious. But it was obvious that she preferred the company of a female and wasn't sure exactly what to make of him. Determined to win her over, Rick doted on Snowy night and day. He fed her, stroked her glistening fur and held her close. He spoke gently to her. Soon, Snowy began to trot to the front door to greet Rick when he came home. She seemed to smile at him and wag her tiny, crooked tail. Day by day, he was winning her over.

Ten days passed in the blink of an eye.

We signed some paperwork, and then Snowy was ours for good. In just ten short days, that little dog with the deep black-brown eyes, sunny disposition and comically twisted tail had brought us immense joy. She was love. Her mere presence soothed our fragmented souls. Her sweet nature began to mend our broken hearts. She filled our spirits with newfound hope.

Snowy is twelve years old now. She has Cushing's disease, her shiny hair is thinning, and she needs medication. Both her eyesight and her hearing are waning. But none of that matters. She is sweet, soulful and perfect in every way. We will take wonderful care of her until her last day. This little dog came into our lives when we both needed her most. Snowy is our magical, miraculous blessing.

— Kim Hanson —

The Little Bed in the Corner

Thank you... for gracing my life with your lovely presence,
for adding sweet measure of your soul
to my existence.
~Richard Matheson

A nose at the window, a wagging tail,
The warm welcome home, after such a tough day.
A nice long walk, through field and stream,
His little legs twitch away, as I watch him dream.

We grew old together, we shared our best years,
Through many a worry, he licked off my tears.
Companions we were, good friends and soul mates,
But alas we get old at different rates.

He could walk no more, it was the end of the line,
From his bed he looked up, and I knew it was time.

The usual spark was no longer there,
He stayed in his bed; it just wasn't fair.
My heart was broken, as I held my old friend,
And I saw his last chapter draw to an end.

At the end of the garden, I laid him to rest,
Wrapped in his blanket, the one he loved best.
I added his ball with his collar and lead,
I left his bed in the corner, it had planted a seed.

The weeks turned to months, and the emptiness grew,
I saw a poster on a wall, it was then that I knew.
I called the number at the bottom of the page,
I didn't want to be lonely at my age.

A discarded puppy at the rescue centre,
A nose pushed through the bars, I just had to have her.
I don't know how, but her eyes said to me,
"Please take me home, please pick me."

As she waits in the window, just like you-know-who,
I've a feeling I'm being watched, by not one but two.
As I looked at those eyes, so full of mischief,
My heart's filled with happiness, hope and belief.

It's as if he's been telling her just what to do,
"We're both here now, and we'll look after you."
Now there's love in this house, and it's so much warmer,
As her legs twitch away, in the little bed in the corner.

—John Astley—

Meet Our Contributors

Ellen Abell has a doctorate in counseling psychology and is the chair of the psychology department at Prescott College in Arizona, where she lives with her fourteen-year-old Chi/Terrier mix, Tessa. E-mail her at eabell@prescott.edu.

Teresa Ambord is a full-time editor/author for a global business publisher. That's how she pays the bills, but for fun she writes stories about her family and pets. She lives in the rural northeastern corner of California with her posse of small pets. They inspire her writing and decorate her life.

John Astley has worked in mental health for more than twenty years. He lives with his wife Estelle and their little dog Mitch in the northwest of England. He writes an occasional poem as a relaxing hobby.

Laurie Batzel is an author of romantic fiction who lives in northeastern Pennsylvania with her husband, four children and two dogs. Her debut novel, *With My Soul*, was published by Anaiah Press in 2019. When not writing or reading, she is pursuing her lifelong dream of perfecting her chocolate chip cookie recipe.

Raising the light quotient of humanity one story at a time, **Kristine Benevento** is married with two sons and one cat named Moonlight Graham. She received her B.A., with honors, in emergency services management. She is writing her first novel, a series of children's stories, and writes on medium.com. E-mail her at kristine.benevento@gmail.com.

Robert E. Boertien holds a B.S. from Washington State University and an M.S. from the University of Portland. He is retired and lives with his wife in the foothills of the Cascade Mountains. He enjoys volunteer work, hiking, reading, and writing.

Tamra Anne Bolles received her journalism degree from the University of Georgia, and a Master of Education from Georgia State University. She is currently a teacher living in northwest Georgia. Tamra enjoys traveling, kayaking and bike riding at a favorite beach in South Carolina where other dog lovers gather.

Barbara Bolton-Brown, a UCLA graduate, taught in Punahou, HI and Rancho Santa Fe, CA. She has been published in anthologies and is the author of two novels, one about teens growing up on a military base and the other about the unlikely relationship of a mother-in-law and daughter-in-law. Barbara lives on five acres with her family of fourteen.

L. M. Bruno had a writer-father and artist-mother; she was doomed to be creative! She writes short stories about her Italian heritage and growing up in the 60s. She's written scripts for indie films, plays, many poems, and is writing her autobiography (in case she becomes famous some day). She's currently working on creating a vlog website.

Jill Burns lives in the mountains of West Virginia with her wonderful family. She's a retired piano teacher and performer. She enjoys writing, music, gardening, nature, and spending time with her grandchildren.

Jack Byron received his degree in illustration and has published art criticism in addition to writing for the *Chicken Soup for the Soul* series. Always encouraging others to write, he believes that the best stories are written first in our daily lives before ever being committed to paper. Follow him on Twitter @jackbyron13.

Lorraine Cannistra's first book, *More the Same than Different: What I Wish People Knew About Respecting and Including People with Disabilities*, is available online. She loves cooking, writing, wheelchair ballroom dancing, laughing out loud, and her new puppy, Levi. Learn more at lorrainecannistra.com.

Eva Carter is a freelance writer with a financial background in the telecommunications industry. She enjoys photography and writing. She and her husband Larry live in Dallas, TX.

Kandace Chapple is a freelance writer and editor. Her essays have appeared in *Writer's Digest*, *Literary Mama*, *Motherwell*, the *Chicken Soup* *for the Soul* series and more. She loves to mountain bike on northern Michigan trails, hike with her (bad) dog, Cookie, and spend time with her husband and two sons.

Nancy Collins grew up in Knoxville, TN and graduated from the University of Tennessee with a degree in political science before becoming an international flight attendant and re-locating to London, England. She now resides in the Great Smoky Mountains with her lazy cat, Mosaic. E-mail her at mymaddox2004@yahoo.com.

Christie Schmitt Coombs has a degree in journalism from the University of Arizona. She pursued a career in writing and PR in the Boston area and runs a nonprofit in memory of her husband. Mom of three, Christie enjoys traveling. Her favorite trips have been to Antarctica, Copenhagen, and a writing retreat in Montana.

Gwen Cooper received her B.A. in English and secondary education in 2007 and completed the University of Denver Publishing Institute in 2009. In her free time, she enjoys krav maga, traveling, and backpacking with her husband and Bloodhounds in the beautiful Rocky Mountains. Follow her on Twitter @Gwen_Cooper10.

Suzanne Cushman lives in Carmel-by-the-Sea, CA with her husband Noel and cats Violet and Buddy. She earned her Bachelor of Arts in English at the University of Utah and Master of Arts in journalism at Pepperdine University.

Heather Debord is a writer and full-time zookeeper. When not spending time hiking with her husband and three children, she likes to curl up with her dog and a good book.

Elizabeth Delisi received a B.A. in creative writing from St. Leo University. She's been married to her high school sweetheart for forty-two years and has three children, three grandchildren, a dog and a bird. She writes paranormal romances and mysteries and teaches writing online. Elizabeth enjoys reading, knitting, and watching old movies.

Deborah Dobson has been a dog lover since childhood, where she grew up in a small coastal Connecticut town with an energetic Beagle/Terrier mix. As a result of her lessons with Nora, Deborah has taught dog behavior and is currently writing a memoir about their amazing journey together.

James Michael Dorsey has published three books about his travels. He has written for the BBC, United Airlines, *Christian Science Monitor*, Lonely Planet, *Los Angeles Times*, *The Best Travel Writing Volume 11*, *The Best Travel Writing Volume 12* and *Geographic Expeditions*.

Melissa Edmondson lives in Creston, NC with her husband Richard. She is the mother of four amazing adult children and fills her home with rescue pets—currently four cats and three dogs, one of which is her sweet Lenny from the story in this book. She would like to dedicate this story to the memory of her friend, Kevin.

Mindi Susman Ellis is a writer, artist, adventurer, and owner of a marketing and communications business. She is a frequent contributor to the *Chicken Soup for the Soul* series. Mindi enjoys just about anything outdoors, water activities, hiking, biking, yoga, and travel.

Joanna Elphick is a lawyer, lecturer and true crime freelance writer who loves nothing more than investigating crime scenes with her trusty dog Bertie by her side.

Janie Emaus is an author/blogger. Her debut picture book, *Latkes for Santa Claus*, was published in 2020. She is also the author of the young adult novel, *Mercury in Retro Love*. Her essays and short stories have appeared in numerous anthologies and websites. Learn more at www.janieemaus.com.

Andrea Farrier is a wife, mom, teacher, writer, and tireless crusader for the preservation of the Oxford comma. When she's not helping out at church or home schooling her children, she's often found reading nonfiction books or walking her needy one-eyed Basset Hound.

Donna Fawcett is a retired creative writing teacher at Fanshawe College in London. She has written several novels under the pen name Donna Dawson, four of which have won awards through The Word Guild Awards. In addition, she has written for magazines and newspapers.

Jill L. Ferguson is an award-winning writer and the author of thirteen books. She is the founder of Women's Wellness Weekends and Creating the Freelance Career. She is sad to report that Nacho, her beloved Heeler, died in August 2020, but he has since sent her Coconut, another Red Heeler, to live with and love.

Nancy Fine's award-winning writing flows from God's love, people, critters and creation. She and her gone-to-heaven husband, Matt, have three married sons and eight grand kiddos. Nancy and canine partner Jake love living in the more-cows-than-folks country of eastern Oregon.

Rosalind Forster has a Master of Social Work from McGill University, Montreal. She is a clinical social worker and psychotherapist. Rosalind enjoys writing, hiking, reading, playing with her grandchildren, unraveling mysteries and encountering serendipitous events.

Peggy Frezon is contributing editor of *All Creatures* magazine. Her newest book is titled *Mini Horse, Mighty Hope* (with Debbie Garcia-Bengochea, Revell 2021). Her work appears regularly in *Guideposts*, *All God's Creatures: Daily Devotions for Animal Lovers*, and *Strength and Grace*. She and her husband rescue senior Golden Retrievers.

Yvonne Evie Green received her Bachelor of Arts degree from the University of Oklahoma. She taught grades 1-11 in outdoor environmental education for thirty-seven years. She also taught zoology classes at the Topeka Zoo for twenty years. Her creative writing is inspired by her three children, four grandchildren, and love for animals.

Kim Hanson loves to write, design quilt patterns and take beautiful photographs. She works daily in her home-based studio. Nature, Snowy and her two grandchildren are her greatest source of inspiration.

Marcia Harris taught children for forty years, then raised guide dogs. She is a mom, author, edu-tainer (her word for educator and magical entertainer combined), historical re-enactor, and community volunteer, who lives by the motto, "aspire to inspire before you expire!" Learn more at www.magicalmarcia.com.

Jill Haymaker is an attorney and full-time writer of contemporary romance novels set in her beautiful home state of Colorado. If you love cowboys, you'll love her books. When not writing, she loves long walks with her toy Australian Shepherd, Merlin, and all outdoor activities. E-mail her at jillhaymaker@aol.com.

Molly Brewer Hoeg, from Minnesota, is a regular contributor to regional and national magazines, favoring stories of memoir and being active outdoors. She spends a month each year bicycle touring with her husband and is writing a book about her life on a bike. You can follow her adventures on her blog SuperiorFootprints.org.

Patricia Hope has won awards in poetry, fiction and nonfiction. Her work has appeared in *Tiny Seed Literary Journal*, *Liquid Imagination*, *American Diversity Report*, *The Avocet*, *Weekly Avocet*, *Plum Tree Tavern*, *Muscadine Lines*, *Southern Writers*, as well as *Mature Living*, *The Writer*, *Blue Ridge Country*, and many newspapers and anthologies.

Bonita Jewel moved to India when she was sixteen and called it home for twelve years. After returning to California with her husband and three children, she received an MFA in creative writing. A freelance writer and editor, Bonita loves finding ways to weave words into beauty.

Kim Johnson is a southern girl who has always loved to write. From doodling on the back of napkins to the bottom of receipts, her creative juices are always flowing. She derives the inspiration for her stories from life's little ironies and the antics of her family — especially her young grandsons.

Steven Johnston earned his GED, along with his diploma in catering and gourmet cooking, while in prison. Steven desires to advocate for prisoners to be able to take home their trained dog after being released. His hobbies are gardening, walking in the rain, and playing in the snow with dogs. He hopes to someday make special food or treats for dogs.

Kathryn Kazoleas is from Alberta, Canada where she lives with her dog Koa and her cat Keeva. Kathryn currently works as a registered nurse, but in her spare time she can be found playing ball with Koa, enjoying the outdoors, reading and writing. E-mail her at k.kazoleaswriter@gmail.com.

Jennifer Kennedy is a senior writer for *StoryTerrace* and lives in the Philadelphia suburbs with her husband Travis, sons Kyle and Tyler, and lovable black and white rescue dogs, Barkley and Maggie. This is her fourth story published in the *Chicken Soup for the Soul* series. E-mail her at jenniferkennedypr@gmail.com.

Terri L. Knight has a degree in psychology, teaches elementary students, and writes. She has several pieces published in literary magazines, books and newspapers, and has won several writing contests. When she is not writing or working, she takes care of her family, two rescue dogs and a cat.

Nancy Julien Kopp lives and writes in the Flint Hills of Kansas and enjoys traveling with her husband. She started writing in her fifties and cannot seem to stop. She has had twenty-three stories published in the *Chicken Soup for the Soul* series, other anthologies, magazines, newspapers, and ezines. Nancy's blog has tips and encouragement for writers.

Joyce Laird has made her living as a freelance writer/journalist since 1984. She has also published many human-interest essays and short fiction stories. Her artwork, photography and a house full of fur-babies round out her busy life, along with three great-grandsons.

Kitty Larousse writes WWII and military romantic suspense stories. She is known to her family as "The Vampire," but she prefers "Queen of the Night," or just Kitty. Always aspiring to become a secret agent, Kitty hasn't been able to stick with one alias since she was four, so she may change her name and hair color when the mood strikes.

John J. Lesjack lives in California. In his dreams, "Girlfriend" runs in from a field of wildflowers, stands, touches his chest with her paws, shows him her eyes (she was blind in one eye), then returns to the wildflowers. E-mail him at jlesjack@gmail.com.

Charlotte Lewis is a retired accountant living in southwest Washington State. She has degrees in elementary education and accounting. She taught third grade prior to becoming an accountant. Charlotte has four children, nine grandchildren, five great-grandchildren, and two great-great grandchildren. She has self-published several novels.

Ilana Long loves to share her life stories in the *Chicken Soup for the Soul* series. She is a parent of twin teens, a teacher, an adventure traveler, a long-distance swimmer, and sometimes a stand-up comic. Ilana is the author of *Ziggy's Big Idea*.

Joyce Styron Madsen has done corporate and medical research and written children's books and articles. She is an avid animal advocate, rescue dog mom, Humane Society volunteer, and handler for Lila Comfort Dog. She usually writes surrounded by her three former puppy mill dogs. E-mail her at joycestyron@sbcglobal.net.

Sandra Martin loves to write about universal life experiences. Her children provided enough drama and humor for a newspaper column.

More recently, she fulfilled her life-long dream: producing a documentary collection. Sandra also loves traveling and writing about her many adventures. Learn more at www.facebook.com/sandramartinproductions.

Timothy Martin is the author of *Fast Pitch* (Cedar Grove Books), *Rez Rock* (Damnation Books), *There's Nothing Funny About Running* (Marathon Publishers), and *Summer With Dad* (Eternal Press). Tim is a contributing author to more than two dozen *Chicken Soup for the Soul* books. E-mail him at tmartin@sitestar.net.

Catherine V. Moise lives in rural Ontario where she is in awe of the trees and the secrets they whisper. Working with, and raising children, inspired her regular contributions to a parenting column. Her work has been published in *Today's Grandparent*. She is Grammie to seven inspirational grandchildren.

Sonia A. Moore has a Bachelor's in Information Sciences. She enjoys writing and loves art. Sonia has three sons and grandchildren. There is a great love for animals, and she has several adopted rescue pets, including Gracie. Sonia lives very close to Pittsburgh, a unique and interesting city.

Writer, humorist and photographer **Ann Morrow** is a frequent contributor to the *Chicken Soup for the Soul* series. (This book contains her seventh contribution.) She resides in the Black Hills of South Dakota with her three dogs and two cats. Learn more about Ann's memoir, middle-grade novel and collection of humor essays at AnnMorrow.net.

Nicole L.V. Mullis loves storytelling, whether for the stage, on the page, or over lattes. She is a produced playwright, a *Battle Creek Enquirer* columnist, a mosaic storyteller, and the author of *A Teacher Named Faith*. She lives with her family in Michigan, where she is currently earning her MFA.

Nell Musolf lives with her husband and her husband's dog in Minnesota. Another dog, Bailey, has joined the family and yet another dog, Courage, visits regularly. The family also has two cats who have decided to make the family room in the basement their new home.

C. L. Nehmer is the author of *The Alchemy of Planes: Amelia Earhart's Life in Verse*. Her work has appeared in *Southern Poetry Review*, *Pedestal Magazine*, *Southword*, and other journals and anthologies. She enjoys reading history, sampling cookbooks, and walking her two rambunctious hound dogs. Visit her at www.clnehmer.com.

Kathy Padgett is a retired elementary school teacher, mother of two, grandmother of four and great grandmother of two. She is a frequent contributor to *Good Old Days* magazine. She enjoys writing, quilting, crafts and watching sunsets over Bull Shoals Lake in the Ozarks of Arkansas.

Michelle Padula received her Bachelor of Arts from Eastern Illinois University in 1991. She volunteered at a Catholic Guesthouse in Port Au Prince, Haiti from July 1991 to July 1992. She has one adult daughter who currently serves in the U.S. Navy. Michelle is an avid hobby photographer and animal lover.

Amy Rovtar Payne lives on a hobby farm with her husband and an assortment of animals. She holds a degree in education and is a certified horseback riding instructor. Amy enjoys competing in agility with her rescue dogs, working with her American mustang horses, and showing Rhinelander rabbits.

Lee E. Pollock has had many different careers during his short seventy-one years of life. He has been a salesman, owned and operated a hardware store, and ended his work career as a pastor, to name a few. He is now retired and spends his time writing and ministering. Follow him at www.facebook.com/Author-Lee-E-Pollock.

Lou Zywicki Prudhomme earned a B.A. and two M.A.s from the University of Minnesota, Duluth. She is the mother of four children and taught high school English for more than thirty years. She and her husband Fred are enjoying retirement at their homes in Cocoa, FL and Duluth, MN. They agree that a home is not complete without at least two dogs.

Tina Rafowitz specializes in creative nonfiction, from stories about her neurotic Shih-Poo, Gibson, to travel adventures and her new cookbook, *Tina's Table*. She was recently published in *Wanderlust Journal* and *Moment* magazine. E-mail her at trafowitz@gmail.com or reach her on Twitter @tinabina50.

Tonya Ranum is a graphic designer, writer, and flunky for Hank, the family's Vizsla. She enjoys jigsaw puzzles, playing darts, and cheering on the Iowa Hawkeyes. Tonya is married to Brian and is mother of two daughters; all of whom continuously provide inspiration for her blog which can be found at complicatedblessingsoab.com.

Jill Ann Robinson graduated with a Master of Arts from Northern Illinois University in 2001. She spent her career as a pediatric speech-language pathologist in the Chicagoland area. Her favorite people are her husband of seventeen years and two boys. She writes to get the extra ideas out of her head and find some quiet time.

Diane Dowsing Robison is a writer/producer living in Los Angeles with her incredible husband, where a son, daughter, and five grandchildren have taken their blessings over-the-top. She's produced live events, was publisher/editor-in-chief of an industry magazine, co-wrote *A Martian Wouldn't Say That* and is producing a film in Europe.

Victoria Roder is the published author of the children's books *What If a Zebra Has Triangles* and *Sled Dog Tales*. She has also published the adult books *Bolt Action* and *D.I.C.K.s: Dames Investigation Crimes and Killers*. Victoria lives in central Wisconsin, enjoying camping and hiking with her husband and dogs. Learn more at www.victoriaroder.com.

Marianne Rogoff is a professor and author of the Pushcart-nominated story collection *Love Is Blind in One Eye*, the memoir *Silvie's Life*, and many travel stories, short fiction, essays, and book reviews. During breaks from teaching, she leads Writers Studio Trips for Writers. Learn more at marianne@mariannerogoff.com.

Amelie J. Rose is a freelance writer from Merseyside, UK. She makes most of her living as a copywriter but is the published author of a number of short stories and poems. She has a B.A. (with honors) in English Literature and is currently working on a novel and a musical play.

Holly Rutchik, M.A., is the inspirational and humor columnist behind "Minivan Matriarch," a slice-of-(real)-life column on the messiness of motherhood, and the book recommendation column "OverBOOKed." Holly uses her trademark self-deprecating humor and relatability to encourage others. E-mail her at hollyrutchik@gmail.com or visit her at hollyrutchik.com.

John Ryder graduated from his local college in 2013 with an

Associate of Science degree. He loves to travel and desires to see much more of the planet in all its natural beauty. He currently is working on his first novel after being inspired by his favorite author Micheal Crichton.

Besides writing/designing/self-publishing a humor book and a poetry book titled *Poems for People Who Don't Read Poems*, **Joe Sainz** has also written numerous pieces, including a short piece in the *Don't Sweat the Small Stuff* series and one in *Writer's Digest*. He has also written short stories, educational articles and three novels.

Kathryn Santichen grew up in western Pennsylvania. She studied broadcasting at Point Park University in Pittsburgh. Kathryn works in media and enjoys traveling, crafting and exploring parks near her Brooklyn apartment with her dog Cooper. Follow his antics on Instagram @cooper_pierogi.

Loretta D. Schoen grew up in Brazil and Italy and now resides in sunny Florida. She loves traveling and spending time with her grandsons. Having spent a lifetime surviving medical adversity she has written a book, *Surviving Medical Mayhem: Laughing When It Hurts*. Learn more at www.LorettaSchoen.com.

Crystal Schwanke is a freelance writer, blogger, and author. She lives in the Atlanta metro area with her husband, daughter, and dog. Crystal enjoys trying new coffees from around the world, working out, dabbling in art, and journaling.

Laurel L. Shannon lives and works in rural Ohio with her multiple "donated" cats and Australian Terrier rescue, Trixie. She likes to think she's in charge, but the animals know better.

Maureen Simons writes short stories and narrative nonfiction. Her story "Remains" was the finalist for the 2019 Lascaux Prize for short fiction; she has also been published in *PANK* literary magazine and the *Palo Alto Weekly*. She and her husband live in Sea Ranch, CA close to their daughter Claire, a gifted teacher.

Faith Griffin Sims has been married for more than forty-one years. She is a mom of six and a grandmother of seventeen. After losing her oldest child to suicide, she leaned into her faith and found the hope she desperately needed to carry on and live a full life. Devoted and loyal, she is a believer in second chances.

Kelly A. Smith has been writing stories since she was a little girl. After earning bachelor's and master's degrees in English, she became a teacher. Kelly lives in Missouri with her husband and three sons and tries to instill a love for reading and writing in her students. This is her third contribution to the *Chicken Soup for the Soul* series.

Respecting all life threads through author **Tanya Sousa's** life; her writing includes the award-winning picture book, *Life Is a Bowl of Cherry Pits*. Her novel, *The Starling God*, was on the 2015 shortlist for the Green Earth Book Award. She also writes for magazines and anthologies. Find her on Goodreads and Facebook.

Diane Stark is a wife and mother to five human kids and two canine ones. She is a frequent contributor to the *Chicken Soup for the Soul* series. She loves to write about the important things in life: her family and her faith. E-mail her at dianestark19@yahoo.com.

Ronica Stromberg writes fiction and nonfiction for books, magazines, and the National Science Foundation program she manages. Her children's books include *The Time-for-bed Angel*, *The Glass Inheritance*, *A Shadow in the Dark*, and *Living It Up to Live It Down*. Her stories appear in more than twenty anthologies.

Sharon Struth believes you're never too old to pursue a dream. She's the author of the popular *Sweet Life* series set in Europe and the *Blue Moon Lake* series. When not writing, she and her husband explore the scenic towns of Connecticut, travel the world, and spend time with their precious pets and two grown daughters.

Lynn Sunday is a writer and animal activist who lives in a coastal community near San Francisco with her son and rescue dog, Allie. This is Lynn's seventeenth story to appear in the *Chicken Soup for the Soul* series. E-mail her at sunday11@aol.com.

Phil Taylor is a retired corporate banker. He, his wife and their fur-friend spend most of their time at their cabin in the mountains. Phil enjoys hiking, mountain biking, cross country skiing, paddling, reading and writing.

A.L. Tompkins is a writer from Ontario, Canada. She holds a Bachelor of Science, with honors, in Biology, and is usually found working surrounded by animals. When not writing, she is usually found trying to read anything she can get her hands on.

Before **Elise Warner** became drawn to writing, she sang, acted and stage managed in musicals on Broadway and across the nation. She loves travel, gelato and animals and now pens history and travel articles for magazines. She wrote a cozy mystery published by Carina Press and is working on a novel.

Leanne Watkins lives in central Ohio with her husband of twenty years and three daughters. In her spare time, she enjoys writing young-adult fiction, drawing and painting, and collecting antique buttons.

When his wife died of breast cancer, **Mr. David Weiskircher** was thrown into a torrential storm. But he had a unique group by his side: herding dogs. They not only helped him endure the storm, they showed him where the sun was. His books, including *Flying Geese and the Hope of Dogs* and *A Thin Place*, are available online.

Leslie Wibberley lives in a suburb of Vancouver, British Columbia with her amazing family and an overly enthusiastic Cocker Spaniel. She writes across a wide range of genres, age groups, and narrative styles. Her award-winning work is published in multiple literary journals and anthologies. E-mail her at lawibberley@gmail.com.

Kelli A. Wilkins was raised in upstate New York where she began writing short stories and taking creative writing classes. She has published romance novels, short horror fiction, online writing courses, and several nonfiction books. Kelli is a pet care advocate who strives to make the world a better place for all animals.

Barbara Woods enjoys the company of her children and grandchildren, as well as her work with Special Ed students within her local school district. With a B.A. in communication, she teaches communication skills to others and continues to write. Learn more at www.redbirdcommunication.com.

D.M. Woolston grew up in the hot sands of the wild west of Nevada. Aside from a career in software development, he enjoys a good run after consuming a nice, dark brew—beer or coffee. And still youthful in appearance, he bears only a slight resemblance to a Chocolate Labrador wearing a tight-fitting jogging suit.

Eser Yilmaz is a science writer and holds a Ph.D. in neurobiology. She lives with her son, husband, dog, and cat in Western Pennsylvania.

D. B. Zane is a teacher, mother of three, and of course always has her trusty dog by her side every morning. She enjoys reading, writing, and knitting.

Karen Zimmerman has been the editor for the Central Indiana Writers' Association since 2017. She is a published poet and writer, with her work appearing in poetry journals, anthologies, newsletters, and websites. Karen dabbles in art, crafts, and photography. She enjoys spending time with her family and two cuddly dogs.

Meet Amy Newmark

Amy Newmark is the bestselling author, editor-in-chief, and publisher of the *Chicken Soup for the Soul* book series. Since 2008, she has published 182 new books, most of them national bestsellers in the U.S. and Canada, more than doubling the number of Chicken Soup for the Soul titles in print today. She is also the author of *Simply Happy*, a crash course in Chicken Soup for the Soul advice and wisdom that is filled with easy-to-implement, practical tips for enjoying a better life.

Amy is credited with revitalizing the Chicken Soup for the Soul brand, which has been a publishing industry phenomenon since the first book came out in 1993. By compiling inspirational and aspirational true stories curated from ordinary people who have had extraordinary experiences, Amy has kept the twenty-eight-year-old Chicken Soup for the Soul brand fresh and relevant.

Amy graduated *magna cum laude* from Harvard University where she majored in Portuguese and minored in French. She then embarked on a three-decade career as a Wall Street analyst, a hedge fund manager, and a corporate executive in the technology field. She is a Chartered Financial Analyst.

Her return to literary pursuits was inevitable, as her honors thesis in college involved traveling throughout Brazil's impoverished northeast region, collecting stories from regular people. She is delighted to have come full circle in her writing career — from collecting stories "from the people" in Brazil as a twenty-year-old to, three decades later, collecting stories "from the people" for Chicken Soup for the Soul.

When Amy and her husband Bill, the CEO of Chicken Soup for the Soul, are not working, they are visiting their four grown children and their grandchildren.

Follow Amy on Twitter @amynewmark. Listen to her free podcast — Chicken Soup for the Soul with Amy Newmark — on Apple Podcasts, Google Play, the Podcasts app on iPhone, or by using your favorite podcast app on other devices.

Thank You

We owe huge thanks to all our contributors and fans. We received thousands of submissions for this popular topic, and we spent months reading all of them. Our Senior Editor, Barbara LoMonaco, and our editors Elaine Kimbler, Crescent LoMonaco, Laura Dean and Susan Heim read all of them and narrowed down the selection for Associate Publisher D'ette Corona and Publisher and Editor-in-Chief Amy Newmark.

Susan Heim did the first round of editing, D'ette chose the perfect quotations to put at the beginning of each story, and Amy edited the stories and shaped the final manuscript.

As we finished our work, D'ette Corona continued to be Amy's right-hand woman in working with all our wonderful writers. Barbara LoMonaco and Mary Fisher, along with Elaine Kimbler, jumped in at the end to proof, proof, proof. And yes, there will always be typos anyway, so feel free to let us know about them at webmaster@chickensoupforthesoul.com, and we will correct them in future printings.

The whole publishing team deserves a hand, including our Senior Director of Marketing Maureen Peltier, our Vice President of Production Victor Cataldo, and our graphic designer Daniel Zaccari, who turned our manuscript into this beautiful, entertaining book.

About American Humane

American Humane is the country's first national humane organization, founded in 1877 and committed to ensuring the safety, welfare, and wellbeing of all animals. For more than 140 years, American Humane has been first to serve in promoting the welfare and safety of animals and strengthening the bond between animals and people. American Humane's initiatives are designed to help whenever and wherever animals are in need of rescue, shelter, protection, or security.

With remarkably effective programs and the highest efficiency ratio of any national humane group for the stewardship of donor dollars, the nonprofit has earned Charity Navigator's top "4-Star" rating, has been named a "Top-Rated Charity" by CharityWatch and a "Best Charity" by Consumer Reports, and achieved the prestigious "Gold Level" charity designation from GuideStar.

American Humane is first to serve animals around the world, striving to ensure their safety, welfare and humane treatment—from rescuing animals in disasters to ensuring that animals are humanely treated. One of its best-known programs is the "No Animals Were Harmed®" animals-in-entertainment certification, which appears during the end credits of films and TV shows, and today monitors some 1,000 productions yearly with an outstanding safety record.

American Humane's farm animal welfare program helps ensure

the humane treatment of nearly a billion farm animals, the largest animal welfare program of its kind. And recently, the historic nonprofit launched the American Humane Conservation program, an innovative initiative helping ensure the humane treatment of animals around the globe in zoos and aquariums.

Continuing its longstanding efforts to strengthen the healing power of the human-animal bond, American Humane pairs veterans struggling to cope with the invisible wounds of war with highly-trained service dogs, and spearheaded a groundbreaking clinical trial that provided for the first time scientific substantiation for the effectiveness of animal-assisted therapy (AAT) for children with cancer and their families.

To learn more about American Humane, visit americanhumane.org and follow them on Facebook, Instagram, and Twitter.

AMERICAN★HUMANE
FIRST TO SERVE®

Editor's Note: Chicken Soup for the Soul and American Humane have created *Humane Heroes*, a FREE new series of e-books and companion curricula for elementary, middle and high schoolers. Through 36 inspirational stories of animal rescue, rehabilitation, and humane conservation being performed at the world's leading zoological institutions, and 18 easy-to-follow lesson plans, *Humane Heroes* provides highly engaging free reading materials that also encourage young people to appreciate and protect Earth's disappearing species. To download the free e-books and learn about the program, please visit www.chickensoup.com/ah.

Sharing Happiness, Inspiration, and Hope

Real people sharing real stories, every day, all over the world. In 2007, *USA Today* named *Chicken Soup for the Soul* one of the five most memorable books in the last quarter-century. With over 100 million books sold to date in the U.S. and Canada alone, more than 250 titles in print, and translations into nearly fifty languages, "chicken soup for the soul®" is one of the world's best-known phrases.

Today, twenty-eight years after we first began sharing happiness, inspiration and hope through our books, we continue to delight our readers with new titles, but have also evolved beyond the bookshelves with super premium pet food, television shows, a podcast, video journalism from aplus.com, licensed products, and free movies and TV shows on our Popcornflix and Crackle apps. We are busy "changing the world one story at a time®." Thanks for reading!

Share with Us

We all have had Chicken Soup for the Soul moments in our lives. If you would like to share your story or poem with millions of people around the world, go to chickensoup.com and click on Submit Your Story. You may be able to help another reader and become a published author at the same time. Some of our past contributors have launched writing and speaking careers from the publication of their stories in our books!

We only accept story submissions via our website. They are no longer accepted via mail or fax. Visit our website, www.chickensoup.com, and click on Submit Your Story for our writing guidelines and a list of topics we are working on.

To contact us regarding other matters, please send us an e-mail through webmaster@chickensoupforthesoul.com, or fax or write us at:

Chicken Soup for the Soul
P.O. Box 700
Cos Cob, CT 06807-0700
Fax: 203-861-7194

One more note from your friends at Chicken Soup for the Soul: Occasionally, we receive an unsolicited book manuscript from one of our readers, and we would like to respectfully inform you that we do not accept unsolicited manuscripts, and we must discard the ones that appear.

Paperback: 978-1-61159-067-8
eBook: 978-1-61159-302-0

More tales of miraculous, mischievous,

Paperback: 978-1-61159-988-6
eBook: 978-1-61159-288-7

magical canine companions

Chicken Soup
for the Soul